REPRESSION O

Conflicts over Land and Religion in Vietnam's Central Highlands

Human Rights Watch
New York • Washington • London • Brussels

Copyright © April 2002 by Human Rights Watch.
All rights reserved.
Printed in the United States of America

ISBN: 1-56432-272-6
Library of Congress Control Number: 2002104126

Cover photo: Copyright © 2001 Human Rights Watch
Jarai women watching police and soldiers who have entered Plei Lao village, Gia Lai province on March 10, 2001 to break up an all-night prayer meeting. In the confrontation that followed, security forces killed one villager and then burned down the village church.

Cover design by Rafael Jiménez

Addresses for Human Rights Watch
350 Fifth Avenue, 34th Floor, New York, NY 10118-3299
Tel: (212) 290-4700, Fax: (212) 736-1300, E-mail: hrwnyc@hrw.org

1630 Connecticut Avenue, N.W., Suite 500, Washington, DC 20009
Tel: (202) 612-4321, Fax: (202) 612-4333, E-mail: hrwdc@hrw.org

33 Islington High Street, N1 9LH London, UK
Tel: (171) 713-1995, Fax: (171) 713-1800, E-mail: hrwatchuk@gn.apc.org

15 Rue Van Campenhout, 1000 Brussels, Belgium
Tel: (2) 732-2009, Fax: (2) 732-0471, E-mail: hrwatcheu@skynet.be

Web Site Address: http://www.hrw.org

Listserv address: To subscribe to the Human Rights Watch news e-mail list, send a blank e-mail message to subscribe@igc.topica.com.

Human Rights Watch is dedicated to
protecting the human rights of people around the world.

We stand with victims and activists to prevent
discrimination, to uphold political freedom, to protect people from inhumane
conduct in wartime, and to bring offenders to justice.

We investigate and expose
human rights violations and hold abusers accountable.

We challenge governments and those who hold power to end abusive practices
and respect international human rights law.

We enlist the public and the international
community to support the cause of human rights for all.

HUMAN RIGHTS WATCH

Human Rights Watch conducts regular, systematic investigations of human rights abuses in some seventy countries around the world. Our reputation for timely, reliable disclosures has made us an essential source of information for those concerned with human rights. We address the human rights practices of governments of all political stripes, of all geopolitical alignments, and of all ethnic and religious persuasions. Human Rights Watch defends freedom of thought and expression, due process and equal protection of the law, and a vigorous civil society; we document and denounce murders, disappearances, torture, arbitrary imprisonment, discrimination, and other abuses of internationally recognized human rights. Our goal is to hold governments accountable if they transgress the rights of their people.

Human Rights Watch began in 1978 with the founding of its Europe and Central Asia division (then known as Helsinki Watch). Today, it also includes divisions covering Africa, the Americas, Asia, and the Middle East. In addition, it includes three thematic divisions on arms, children's rights, and women's rights. It maintains offices in New York, Washington, Los Angeles, London, Brussels, Moscow, Tashkent, Tblisi, and Bangkok. Human Rights Watch is an independent, nongovernmental organization, supported by contributions from private individuals and foundations worldwide. It accepts no government funds, directly or indirectly.

The staff includes Kenneth Roth, executive director; Michele Alexander, development director; Reed Brody, advocacy director; Carroll Bogert, communications director; John T. Green, operations director, Barbara Guglielmo, finance director; Lotte Leicht, Brussels office director; Michael McClintock, deputy program director; Patrick Minges, publications director; Maria Pignataro Nielsen, human resources director; Malcolm Smart, program director; Wilder Tayler, legal and policy director; and Joanna Weschler, United Nations representative. Jonathan Fanton is the chair of the board. Robert L. Bernstein is the founding chair.

The regional directors of Human Rights Watch are Peter Takirambudde, Africa; José Miguel Vivanco, Americas; Sidney Jones, Asia; Elizabeth Andersen, Europe and Central Asia; and Hanny Megally, Middle East and North Africa. The thematic division directors are Joost R. Hiltermann, arms; Lois Whitman, children's; and LaShawn R. Jefferson, women's.

The members of the board of directors are Jonathan Fanton, Chair; Robert L. Bernstein, Founding Chair, Lisa Anderson, David M. Brown, William Carmichael, Dorothy Cullman, Gina Despres, Irene Diamond, Fiona Druckenmiller, Edith Everett, Michael Gellert, Vartan Gregorian, Alice H. Henkin, James F. Hoge, Jr., Stephen L. Kass, Marina Pinto Kaufman, Wendy Keys, Bruce J. Klatsky, Joanne Leedom - Ackerman, Josh Mailman, Joel Motley, Samuel K. Murumba, Jane Olson, Peter Osnos, Kathleen Peratis, Catherine Powell, Bruce Rabb, Sigrid Rausing, Orville Schell, Sid Sheinberg, Gary G. Sick, Malcolm Smith, Domna Stanton, John Studzinski, Maureen White, Maya Wiley. Emeritus Board: Roland Algrant, Adrian DeWind, and Malcolm Smith.

ACKNOWLEDGMENTS

This report is based on research conducted by Human Rights Watch from February 2001 through February 2002. The report was edited by Sidney Jones, director of the Asia Division, Joe Saunders, deputy director of the Asia division, and Malcolm Smart, program director. Additional comments were provided by Jim Ross, senior legal advisor, and Rachael Reilly, refugee policy advisor.

More than one hundred highlanders who were witnesses to the turmoil in the Central Highlands of Vietnam in 2001 were interviewed for this report. Human Rights Watch would like to express its gratitude to all those individuals who spoke with us—sometimes under conditions of great duress or personal risk. For their own protection, they cannot be named here. In addition we thank numerous others who prefer to remain anonymous who contributed to this report in many ways, assisting with translation, information on the history of the Central Highlands, documentation, and logistical arrangements in the field.

Table of Contents

Map of the Central Highlands

I. Summary and Recommendations 1

II. Introduction 8
    An Independent Homeland 9
    The Government Response 10
    Rhetoric and Reality 11

III. A History of Resistance to Central Government Control 13
    Customary Lands 15
    The Dega People—An Oral History 16
    Promises of Autonomy: The French 17
    Promises of Autonomy: Hanoi 19
    The 1958 Bajaraka Movement 20
    The Second Indochina War: 1960-1975 21
    The FULRO Rebellions: 1964-1965 23
    Easing of Tensions in the mid-1960s 24
    The Highlands After 1975 25

IV. Government Policies Toward Ethnic Minorities 28
    "Mutual Respect, Participation, and Equal Rights" 29
    Fixed Fields, Fixed Settlements 31
    Regreening the Barren Hills 33

V. Population Explosion: The Impact of Migration 35
    Organized Migration 35
    Spontaneous Migration 36
    The Coffee Connection 38
    Soaring Population: The Example of Dak Lak 39

VI. The 1990s: Escalation in Land Conflicts 42
    Lack of Land Security 43
    State Confiscation of Land 45
    "A Plea for Help" 47
    Lack of Government Action 48
    No Response after Five Years: The Conflict in D Village 49
    Intersection of Land Conflicts and Religious Persecution 50
    Escalating Tensions over Land 52
    "One Day We Will be the Ones in Charge" 54

VII. Repression of Ethnic Minority Protestants.. 56
   Christianity in the Highlands 59
   Government Statistics: Protestantism in the Central Highlands (1975-2000) 60
   The House Church Movement 61
   Party Directives to Suppress Minority Christians................................ 64
   Pressure on House Churches 67
   Arbitrary Fines and Forced Labor 69

VIII. Ethnic Discrimination 71
   Poverty... 72
   Education... 75
   Pressure to Limit Family Size... 77

IX. The Movement for Land Rights and Religious Freedom 82
   The Run-up to the Protests 82
   Government Surveillance 84
   The January 2001 Crackdown 86
   The February 2001 Demonstrations 86
      February 2: Pleiku.. 87
      February 3: Buon Ma Thuot 89
      Clashes Between Police and Protesters....................................... 91
      February 5-6: Ea H'leo 92
      February 14: Kontum.. 93
      Coerced or Willing Participants?... 94

X. Government Response: The Initial Reaction 96
   The Immediate Response: Arrests and Police Sweeps 96
   Surveillance and Interrogations 100
   Police Torture 102
   Targeting of Christians 103

XI. Increasing the Pressure 105
   Travel Restrictions and Increased Surveillance.................................. 106
   Restrictions on Diplomatic and Media Access 108
   Intensified Repression of Christians 111
   The Trials.. 115

XII. Interpreting the Unrest 120
   Acknowledgment of Grievances... 120
   Hearts and Minds.. 122
   The June 2001 Party Advisory.. 123

XIII. Refugee Flight to Cambodia 127
   The Tripartite Talks 134
   Flight to Cambodia: Arrest, Mistreatment and Forced Return 138

XIV. Tightening Controls 144
   The Christmas Crackdown 145
   The One-Year Anniversary 147

XV. CASE STUDY: The Church Burning and Killing by Security Forces in Plei Lao 150
   The Church at Plei Lao 151
   The Prayer Meetings 152
   The Shooting 152
   The Church Burning 154
   The Arrests 155
   The Aftermath 157
   The Government's Response 160

XVI. CASE STUDY: The Goat's Blood Oath Ceremonies in Ea H'leo 163
   Crude—and Cruel—Rituals 163
   Humiliation 164

XVII. CASE STUDY: Arrest and Torture of Highlanders Deported from Cambodia 166
   Buon Ea Sup: Why People Fled 167
   Torture and Detention 168

Selected Bibliography 171

Appendix A: The Land Conflict in D Village: First Complaint, 1995 174

Appendix B: The Land Conflict in D Village: Second Complaint, 2000 176

Appendix C: The Interrogation of a Protestant Church Leader, Dak Lak, July 2001 179

Appendix D: Complaint from Buon Don District Villagers to Bureau of Religious Affairs 182

Appendix E: Employment Discrimination Against Minority Christians 183

Appendix F: Citizen Petition: "A Report on the Cruel Action Against the Tribal People in the Highlands" 185

Appendix G: "Official Pledge" Read During the Goat's Blood Ceremonies . 190

Appendix H: March 26, 2001 Deportations, Document 1 192

Appendix I: March 26, 2001 Deportations, Document 2 194

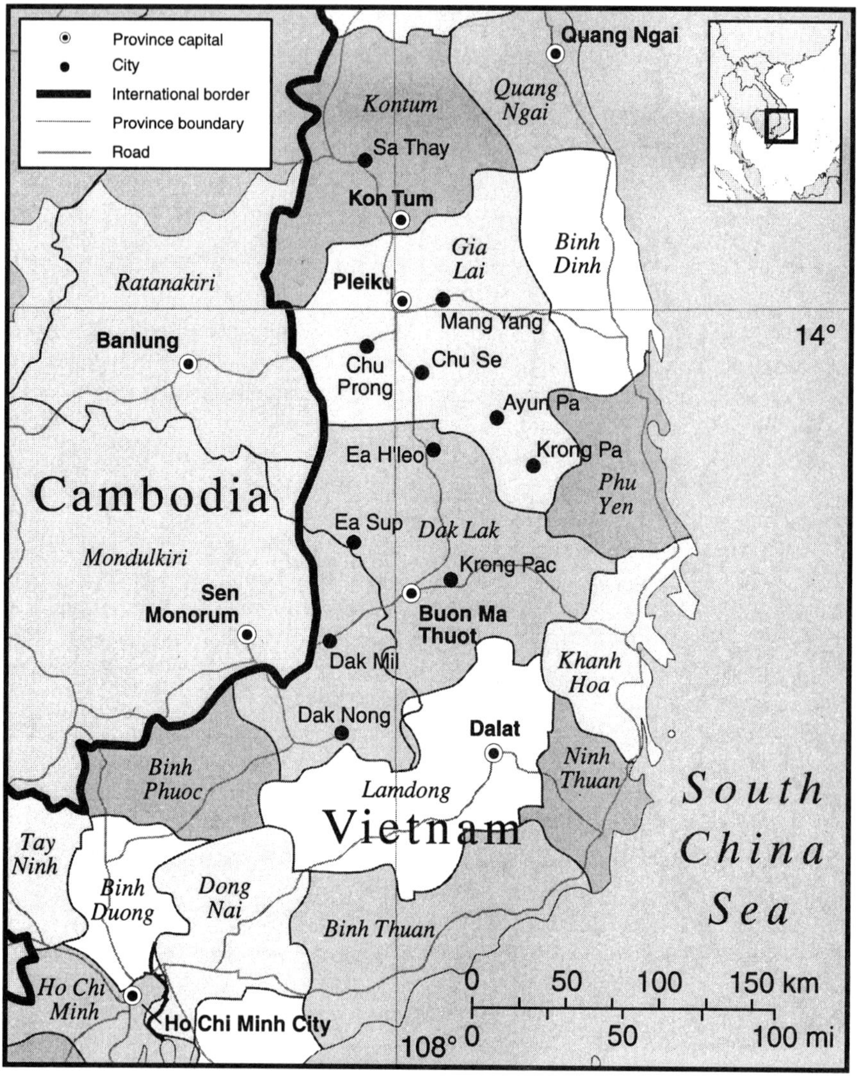

Province capital
City
International border
Province boundary
Road
Quang Ngai
Quang Ngai
Kontum
Sa Thay
Kon Tum
Gia Lai
Binh Dinh
Ratanakiri
Pleiku
Mang Yang
14°
Banlung
Chu Prong
Chu Se
Ayun Pa
Ea H'leo
Krong Pa
Phu Yen
Cambodia
Ea Sup
Dak Lak
Mondulkiri
Krong Pac
Sen Monorum
Buon Ma Thuot
Dak Mil
Khanh Hoa
Dak Nong
Dalat
Binh Phuoc
Ninh Thuan
Lamdong
South China Sea
Vietnam
Tay Ninh
Binh Duong
Dong Nai
Binh Thuan
Ho Chi Minh
Ho Chi Minh City
0 50 100 150 km
0 50 100 mi
108°

I. SUMMARY AND RECOMMENDATIONS

Since God gave birth to the world we ethnic minorities have always been in the same place. Since antiquity, our ancestors have always told us that this is our land. The Vietnamese never lived here. What we learned from our grandparents is that Vietnam started invading our land in 1930 ... Especially since 1975, the Montagnards and the Vietnamese have not been happy together...The life of Vietnamese and Montagnards together is like dogs biting each other; never easy.
—Mnong man from Dak Lak province, Vietnam

In February 2001 mass protests took place in Vietnam that were among the largest since the reunification of Vietnam in 1975. Several thousand members of indigenous minorities from the country's Central Highlands—often collectively known as Montagnards—held a series of peaceful demonstrations calling for independence, return of ancestral lands, and religious freedom.

Vietnamese authorities, who had long been closely monitoring political developments in the region, responded aggressively. Announcing that they had "battle plans" ready, authorities brought in thousands of police and soldiers to disperse the protesters. In the weeks and months following the demonstrations, authorities arrested hundreds of highlanders, sometimes using torture to elicit confessions and public statements of remorse by protest organizers. Local religious and political leaders were sentenced to prison terms ranging up to twelve years.

A number of key historical, demographic and political factors contributed to a climate of intense frustration that had been building for years: longstanding hopes of independence among the highlanders; the steadily increasing presence of ethnic Vietnamese in what used to be almost exclusively the home of minority highlanders, and resulting disputes over land; the recent upsurge in adherence to Protestant evangelical Christianity among minority highlanders; and the Vietnamese government's stance that the highlanders' desire to differentiate themselves politically and religiously from the majority population represented a threat to national unity.

That perception of a threat to national unity has been fueled by the link between some advocates of independence in the highlands and former members of a pro-United States (U.S.) Montagnard resistance army that effectively died out in 1992. That army was known as FULRO (Front Unifié de Lutte des Race Opprimées, or the United Struggle Front for the Oppressed Races). Former FULRO members, led by U.S.-based Jarai-American Kok Ksor, have been among those accused by the Vietnamese Communist Party of organizing the

February 2001 demonstrations. Although it appears that groups based in the United States may have encouraged Montagnard protests in the Central Highlands, there is no evidence that they advocated violence. With or without external support, the Central Highlands was a powder keg ready to explode by the end of the 1990s.

The February 2001 eruption in the Central Highlands represented the convergence of multiple grievances among the highlanders: religious repression, ethnic persecution, among the highest poverty and illiteracy rates in Vietnam, and most importantly, the struggle over increasingly scarce land. Government-organized resettlement schemes as well as spontaneous migration had quadrupled the population density of ethnic Vietnamese and other migrants in parts of the highlands since 1975, creating intense pressure on land and natural resources. Lacking official land use certificates, the highlanders were increasingly squeezed off their land. At the same time, the economic base of the highlands, centered on coffee production, was dealt a strong blow by the global plummet in coffee prices over the two years preceding the outbreak of unrest.

In this report, Human Rights Watch analyzes the antecedents to the February 2001 demonstrations, the protests themselves, and their aftermath. It finds that the government violated fundamental human rights in the course of suppressing the protests, and that those violations were continuing as of February 2002. Major violations included:

- Arbitrary arrest, detention or interrogation of hundreds of highlanders suspected of participating in, or helping to organize, the February 2001 demonstrations.
- Police torture of people in detention or during interrogation, including beating, kicking, and shocking with electric batons.
- Violations of the right to freedom of religion including destruction and closure of ethnic minority Protestant churches, and official pressure on Christians to abandon their religion under threat of legal action or imprisonment.
- Excessive use of force by security forces during a confrontation with ethnic Jarai villagers in Plei Lao, Gia Lai on March 10.
- Bans on public gatherings in violation of the right to freedom of assembly.
- Restrictions on travel. In some areas authorities were requiring written permission to be secured in advance of any temporary absence from the village, making it difficult for farmers to go to work in their fields.
- Arrest and mistreatment of highlanders who fled to Cambodia and were then forcibly returned to Vietnam.

Summary and Recommendations

The report is based on research conducted between February 2001 and February 2002. That research involved detailed interviews with more than one hundred eyewitnesses to the events in the Central Highlands before and after February 2001, documents obtained from sources in Gia Lai and Dak Lak, press accounts from Vietnamese state media and foreign wire services, and interviews with Montagnard refugees in Cambodia and the U.S., as well as diplomats, researchers, and nongovernmental organization (NGO) officials based in Vietnam. The scope of this report is limited by the fact that access to the Central Highlands is tightly restricted by the government of Vietnam, making it difficult for independent observers such as human rights monitors and journalists to verify data on conditions in the Central Highlands.

In its research, Human Rights Watch encountered a widespread perception among highlanders that Vietnamese government agencies discriminate against them in education, health, and provision of other social services. Official confiscation of their land without adequate compensation or prior notice is another key grievance of the highlanders. Because the Vietnamese Communist Party prohibits open expression of political dissent, however, there have been few outlets for the resulting discontent.

There is an international component to the turmoil as well. As of March 2002, more than 1,000 highlanders who fled the Vietnamese government crackdown remained in political limbo across the border in Cambodia. While plans were drawn up in January 2002 by the U.N. High Commissioner for Refugees (UNHCR), together with the Cambodian and Vietnamese governments to start a program of repatriation of refugees back to Vietnam, it was clear that until the situation in the Central Highlands improved, ethnic minority people from that region would continue to flee across the border to Cambodia, and many of those already in refugee camps would resist repatriation.

Recommendations

To the Government of the Socialist Republic of Vietnam
- Unconditionally release all persons in the Central Highlands who are being held for the peaceful expression of their political or religious beliefs—including Protestant Church leaders, land rights activists, and supporters of the highlander independence movement. Publish in a central register the names of all highlanders held in pre-trial detention in police stations or prisons, as well as any charges against them, and make public the names of those who have been convicted and sentenced.

- Ensure that all persons charged in connection with the protests in the Central Highlands receive trials that meet the standards set forth in Article 14 of the International Covenant on Civil and Political Rights (ICCPR) to which Vietnam is a party. The trials should be public, and those accused should have access to legal counsel of their choosing and the free assistance of an interpreter, as mandated by both the ICCPR and Vietnam's Constitution.
- End the arbitrary detention of highlanders who have returned from Cambodia to Vietnam either voluntarily or against their will.
- Respect the fundamental rights to freedom of expression, association, and assembly, and amend provisions of Vietnam's Criminal Code that restrict such rights, particularly the provisions on national security. Permit the right to hold and express political opinions that run counter to state policy, including peaceful advocacy of autonomy and independence. The ban in some parts of the Central Highlands on gatherings of more than four people should be ended.
- Repeal the 1997 Administrative Detention Directive 31/CP, which authorizes detention without trial for up to two years for individuals deemed to have violated national security laws.
- Cease the repression of ethnic minority Protestants, including bans on religious gatherings and other meetings, pressure to renounce one's faith, mandatory participation in non-Christian rituals, destruction of churches by local authorities and security officials, and abusive police surveillance of religious leaders. Uphold Article 27 of the ICCPR, which stipulates that "ethnic…minorities…shall not be denied the right, in community with other members of their group, to enjoy their own culture [and] to profess and practice their own religion."
- Invite the U.N. Working Group on Arbitrary Detention, which visited Vietnam in 1994, and the U.N. Special Rapporteur on Religious Intolerance, who visited Vietnam in 1998, for follow-up visits, with unrestricted access to the Central Highlands.
- Remove restrictions on access to the Central Highlands by the U.N. High Commissioner for Refugees (UNHCR), journalists, diplomats, and other independent observers.
- Improve implementation of Vietnam's 1993 Land Law, especially articles stipulating that prior to state appropriation of land, the land user shall be notified of the reasons why the land is to be recovered, the timeframe, the plan for transfer, and the methods of compensation. Provincial and district officials should be directed to promptly

investigate and resolve complaints by highlanders about discriminatory and uncompensated confiscation of land.
- Streamline the process of land allocation and issuing of land use certificates for highlander families in order to guarantee that they are able on a non-discriminatory basis to apply for and obtain certificates that can establish long-term land usage rights. To help ensure land security for highlanders, launch participatory land use planning and land allocation programs in all four provinces of the Central Highlands.
- Support development programs for independent NGOs working in the Central Highlands.
- Take steps to end all forms of discrimination against indigenous minorities of the Central Highlands, including discrimination in education and employment, and by developing channels for dialogue and participatory decision-making processes involving Montagnard leaders and local communities.

To the Government of the Kingdom of Cambodia
- Continue to offer temporary asylum and protection to Montagnard refugees and asylum seekers from Vietnam, in accordance with Cambodia's obligations as a party to the 1951 Refugee Convention.
- Provide protection to Montagnard refugees inside Cambodia and upon arrival at the border. Pushbacks of Montagnards highlanders at the border violate the fundamental principle of non-refoulement—the obligation of states parties to the Refugee Convention, and as a matter of international customary law, not to return any person to a country where his or her life or freedom may be threatened on account of race, religion, nationality, political opinion, or membership in a particular social group.
- Ensure that officials at all administrative levels are instructed to provide protection to refugees from the Central Highlands, and that those instructions are implemented.

To the U.N. High Commissioner for Refugees (UNHCR)
- Suspend repatriation until conditions are appropriate for voluntary repatriation, and refugees can return in safety and dignity and with assurances that their human rights will be fully respected. In particular, more detailed information should be available to UNHCR and the refugees about the human rights situation in the Central Highlands, and UNHCR should be able to station monitors in the region. UNHCR should insist that its staff be able to conduct home visits throughout the

Central Highlands without Vietnamese government monitoring or interference before, during, and after any repatriation.
- Suspend the screening-out or rejection of asylum seekers in Cambodia until more detailed information is available about the situation in the Central Highlands.
- Obtain assurances from the Cambodian government that individual refugees will not be returned to a place where their lives or freedom is under threat.
- Continue to insist that Cambodia uphold its obligations as a party to the 1951 Refugee Convention and make public and private interventions with the Cambodian government if and when Cambodian security officials expel refugees from Cambodia—either once they are within the territory of Cambodia or at the border—in violation of non-refoulement obligations.
- Obtain assurances in writing from the Cambodian and Vietnamese governments that any repatriation program for refugees is on a voluntary basis and in accordance with international standards, and that the right of individuals to continue to seek asylum in Cambodia is respected.
- For those highlanders for whom repatriation is not an option, UNHCR should continue to protect their right to seek and enjoy asylum in Cambodia, and to seek a durable solution to their plight, including the possibility of third-country resettlement.

To the International Community
- During bilateral discussions with Vietnam, senior government officials, especially those from member nations of the Association of Southeast Asian Nations (ASEAN), should express concern about ongoing rights violations in the Central Highlands of Vietnam.
- Urge the Vietnamese government to adopt the recommendations made in Part A, above.
- Encourage Vietnam to achieve greater transparency and accountability in its justice and penal systems and press for the establishment of an independent and impartial judiciary. Press for access to trials by international observers and independent monitors.
- Provide technical assistance for legal reform with particular attention to the criminal justice system.
- Fund development programs for independent NGOs in the Central Highlands, particularly programs that ensure full participation of ethnic minorities.

- Urge the Cambodian government to continue to uphold its obligations under the 1951 Refugee Convention and make public and private interventions with the Cambodian government if and when Cambodian security officials forcibly return refugees from Cambodia.

II. INTRODUCTION

This report provides the most detailed account to date of unrest that erupted in the Central Highlands of Vietnam in early 2001 and offers a rare glimpse into Vietnamese political repression.

In February 2001, several thousand members of indigenous minorities, often known as Montagnards, held a series of demonstrations calling for independence, return of ancestral land, and religious freedom.

This report, based on eyewitness testimony, case studies, public and internal Vietnamese government documents, and petitions from villagers in the Central Highlands that are published here for the first time, includes both detailed background information on the grievances that gave rise to the protests, and an analysis of the human rights violations that took place in response to them.

Those violations range from government infringement of religious freedom to torture by police. It is important, however, to understand three factors that help explain the sequence of events, although they do not justify the Vietnamese government's response.

The first is the degree to which highlanders have steadily lost land through the migration of hundreds of thousands of lowland Vietnamese, or *Kinh*, to the region. Some of the settlers came on their own initiative, but many came through state-sponsored transmigration programs that had both economic development and national security goals. Highlanders' resentment over the loss of land was compounded by the fact that they found themselves losing out to the migrants in education, employment, and other economic opportunities.

The second factor is the intertwining of politics and religion in the Central Highlands. In the early 1990s, many Montagnards became attracted to a particular type of Christianity practiced in the highlands called *Tin Lanh Dega*, or "Dega Protestantism," which brings together aspirations for independence, cultural pride and evangelism.[1] For Dega Protestants, prayer and worship services provide space for Montagnard expression not controlled by government authorities. Sometimes this expression involves praying for an independent homeland, or participating in political discussions, often conducted by the same individuals who lead the religious gatherings.

---

[1] Dega (sometimes spelled *Degar*), is derived from the Ede-language phrase *Anak Ede Gar*, which means "sons of the mountains." Politicized highlanders increasingly have adopted the word to refer collectively to the different indigenous ethnic groups who live in the Central Highlands. Not all highlanders are Christians, and not all highland Christians follow Dega Christianity; it is estimated that at least 250,000 highlanders, or one-quarter of the total ethnic minority population in the Central Highlands, are Christians, with Dega Christians a subset of that.

An independent homeland had been one of the goals of the Montagnard resistance army known as FULRO (Front Unifié de Lutte des Race Opprimées, or the United Struggle Front for the Oppressed Races), which fought on the side of the United States and South Vietnam during the 1960-1975 war. Though its numbers steadily dwindled and any real fighting capacity evaporated after the North Vietnamese victory in 1975, FULRO survived as a guerilla organization into the early 1990s. Many Montagnards converted to Christianity in the early 1990s when they abandoned armed struggle.[2]

The third factor is the size and nature of the demonstrations in February 2001. Thousands of people converged on town centers in Pleiku, Buon Ma Thuot, and Kontum, a potential public order concern even if the demonstrations had been entirely peaceful. Some of the arrests that followed, however, were linked to alleged acts of violence. The government would have been justified in arresting and charging with appropriate criminal offenses any demonstrators responsible for vandalism of public buildings, for example, as the police claimed, or who had used rocks in slingshots against individuals or police cars, regardless of the provocation.

The heaviest sentences meted out, however, were against organizers of the protests for the crime of "undermining national security," ostensibly because of the demands of the leaders of the protests for an independent state. Human Rights Watch takes no position on requests by any group for an independent state, but it supports the right of all individuals, including those advocating autonomy or independence, to express their political views peacefully without fear of arrest or other forms of reprisal.

An Independent Homeland

When the U.S.-based Montagnard Foundation, Inc. (MFI), led by Jarai-American Kok Ksor, launched a renewed effort to build support for an independent "Dega" homeland in 2000, it found an extremely receptive audience. While many MFI members, and highlanders in general, are former FULRO supporters, there is no indication that there was any armed component to MFI's efforts and, to Human Right Watch's knowledge, MFI has never advocated the use of violence as a means of achieving independence.

According to documents obtained by Human Rights Watch and interviews conducted with MFI members, the political platform propagated by a handful of MFI organizers in the Central Highlands in 2000 and 2001 was threefold: independence, non-violence, and redress of longstanding grievances. MFI sought the return through peaceful struggle of "their country," currently under

---

[2] While Christianity first became popular in the highlands in the 1950s, its practice waned during the first decade after Vietnam's reunification in 1975.

Vietnamese control, with Kok Ksor as the leader. They also sought attention to land issues, the lack of religious freedom, ethnic discrimination, pressure to join family planning programs, and lack of educational opportunities.

The Government Response

Vietnamese authorities had reasons to foresee an explosive situation developing in the Central Highlands: demands for independence from remnants of the FULRO movement; the growing popularity of evangelical Christianity; and escalating highlander grievances. The ruling Vietnamese Communist Party has reacted harshly when religion and politics have been mixed, particularly if the religion appears to be drawing a large mass following, and is one whose adherents include former resistance supporters.

Vietnam's Penal Code lists numerous "crimes against national security," some of which blatantly violate international human rights law. Article 87, "Undermining the unity policy," criminalizes "sowing divisions" between the people and the government or the military, between religious and non-religious people, and between religious followers and the government. Offenders are to be sentenced to between two and fifteen years of imprisonment. This criminalization of dissent contradicts the basic right to free expression found in the International Covenant on Civil and Political Rights, acceded to by Vietnam in 1982.

While the Vietnamese authorities in some instances may have been justified in using force during the February 2001 demonstrations, the force employed appears to have been disproportionate to the threat posed by the protesters. In the days and weeks following the demonstrations, moreover, the authorities committed clear-cut violations of fundamental rights, including torture; destruction of church buildings; and intimidation and harassment of members of evangelical Protestant congregations.

Many, if not most, of the people who attended the February 2001 demonstrations were villagers who appeared to have little knowledge of MFI aims but responded positively to MFI's call for demonstrations out of their own frustration with what they saw as unfair land-grabbing by the state, discrimination, and religious repression. Interviews with some of these participants suggested that they saw MFI's advocacy of independence as equivalent to "getting our land back" in both the immediate sense of recovering family homesteads and land lost in recent decades to government plantations, and the more historical sense of recovering an area, if not a nation, that had belonged to their ancestors.

Movements for autonomy or independence can pose legitimate national security concerns, but it is incumbent upon the state to demonstrate that any particular expression of ethnic nationalism or support for independence poses a genuine security risk. Article 19 of the International Covenant on Civil and Political Rights allows for restrictions on the right to freedom of expression only as is necessary for the protection of national security and public order and as provided by law. National security restrictions are considered permissible only in serious cases of political or military threat to the entire nation. The Human Rights Committee, the international body that monitors compliance with the Covenant, has been reluctant to permit restrictions on free expression, particularly in the absence of detailed justifications by the state. The 1995 Johannesburg Principles on National Security, Freedom of Expression and Access to Information, an authoritative but non-binding declaration of principles based on international human rights standards, evolving state practice, and the general principles of law, provide that apart from legitimate state secrets, "expression may be punished as a threat to national security only if a government can demonstrate that: a) the expression is intended to incite imminent violence; b) it is likely to incite such violence; and c) there is a direct and immediate connection between the expression and the likelihood or occurrence of such violence."

Rhetoric and Reality

There is a gulf between rhetoric and reality in Vietnamese government policies in the Central Highlands. On the one hand, Vietnam's Politburo leaders express pride in the party's policies toward ethnic minorities and in constitutional provisions guaranteeing minorities the right to use their own languages, and to preserve and promote local identity and traditions. On the other hand, government policies are based largely on perceptions of highlanders as nomadic, in need of development and stability, and ultimately untrustworthy in the political sense because of their longstanding desire for independence and the affiliation of some of them with the U.S. war effort. Despite the rhetoric, the Vietnamese government has not been able to create real benefits for ethnic minorities, and in fact, continues to implement repressive policies.

At the Ninth Vietnamese Communist Party Congress in April 2001, Nông Dúc Manh, an ethnic Tay, was elected general secretary of the VCP, becoming the first member of an ethnic minority ever named to the nation's most powerful position. While this development was groundbreaking, there has been no let up in the government's repressive policies toward ethnic minorities in the Central Highlands. In a speech in Buon Ma Thuot in September 2001, the new general secretary emphasized that Vietnam is a "country with many ethnic groups living together in unity."[3] That same month, fourteen Montagnard leaders who had reportedly organized the February 2001 protests were sentenced to prison terms of up to twelve years on charges of disrupting security.

In the course of researching this report, Human Rights Watch came into possession of more than ninety pages of previously unavailable government documents and citizen petitions, most of them from 2001 and early 2002. These documents, together with previously released confidential government directives from 1999, show that the Vietnamese government has launched a national campaign to monitor independent Christian groups in the highlands and shut down minority churches and other groups deemed to be "inspiring divisions among the various nationalities" or fueling anti-government sentiment.

The documents, while including some government acknowledgment of policy failures in the highlands, also show that the government perceives growing resistance among the Montagnards to be part of a broader conspiracy by outside agitators and a handful of "evil minded" local leaders and political "reactionaries" who allegedly are trying to use democracy, land, and religion to stir up trouble.

This report also found that the government's crackdown on fundamental freedoms in the Central Highlands in the year following the protests made a difficult situation worse. This in turn incited additional highlanders to flee the country to Cambodia—even some of those who did not participate in the demonstrations. If the government does not address underlying highlander grievances and find a way to replace confrontation with dialogue, even more serious unrest in the Central Highlands and further flows of refugees can be expected in the future.

---

[3] BBC Monitoring Service, Voice of Vietnam Radio, Hanoi, in Vietnamese, "Vietnam party chief asserts "key role" of Highlands chiefs to strengthen unity," September 11, 2001.

III. A HISTORY OF RESISTANCE TO CENTRAL GOVERNMENT CONTROL

My people suffered terribly under the Vietnamese communist regime. They came and took our land, and made it theirs. They try to erase our language and force us to speak Vietnamese. They have taken our fertile land and forced us to the bad land. They say they have come to build progress for my people, but they have come to kill, arrest, and oppress my people.
—FULRO commander before surrendering to U.N. forces in Cambodia, in a 1992 interview with the *Phnom Penh Post*

The twentieth century in the Central Highlands was a period of increasing migration of ethnic Vietnamese, or *Kinh*, into highland areas. The political situation in the region today has been decisively shaped by that demographic trend.

Today, the population of the Central Highlands provinces of Dak Lak, Gia Lai, Lam Dong and Kontum, is approximately four million, of whom approximately one-quarter are indigenous highlanders.[4] Among the highlanders, between 229,000 to 400,000 are thought to follow evangelical Protestantism.

Indigenous minority groups in both the central and northern highlands are often generically referred to as Montagnards, a French term meaning "mountain dwellers."[5] The indigenous minorities of the Central Highlands comprise more

---

[4] The Central Highlands, which border Cambodia and Laos, are bracketed on the west by the plains of eastern Cambodia, on the north by the Annamite mountain range, and on the south and east by the Mekong Delta and Vietnam's coastal lowlands. See map.

[5] In the Republic of Vietnam (better known as South Vietnam) from 1955-1975, highlanders were officially referred to as *dông bào thuong* (highland compatriots); since 1975 there has been no specific term to refer to the indigenous minorities of the Central Highlands, who are commonly referred to by the same label as Vietnam's other minority groups (of which there are officially fifty-four) as *dân tôc thiêu sô,* or "ethnic minorities," in distinction to the "Kinh," or ethnic Vietnamese majority. Less officially they are referred to as *nguoi thuong,* or uplanders. In an effort to move away from the pejorative Vietnamese term for highlanders, *moi,* or savage, the French adopted the word *Montagnard*, which means mountain dweller. The use of the word *Montagnard* to refer to present-day indigenous communities has been criticized by some academics, who charge that it is a French colonial term and one taken over by U.S. Special Forces during the American War, who often called those highlanders who were militarily allied with the U.S. and not the Viet Minh, "Yards." Despite this—or perhaps because of their former affiliation with U.S. forces—some highlanders in Vietnam and the U.S. refer to themselves as Montagnards. The term "Dega" (also spelled Degar) has also increasingly been embraced as a collective term for Central Highland ethnic minorities, with both negative and positive connotations. For the purposes of this report Human Rights Watch uses the English-language terms "highlander," or "indigenous minorities" as well as the

than half a dozen different ethnic groups, primarily from two language families: the Jarai (320,000), Ede (or Rhade, 258,000), Bahnar (181,000), Stieng (66,000), Koho (122,000), and Mnong (Bnong, or Pnong, 89,000).[6] Many of the politicized highlanders in the Central Highlands and refugees from there in the U.S. today increasingly refer to themselves as *Dega*. For them, Dega is a term not only of cultural pride but one that connotes the particular type of evangelical Christianity they practice and the name of the independent homeland they seek. The term "Dega" is also used by Vietnamese governmental authorities in a derogatory sense, as a synonym for rebels.

Most highlanders are farmers who traditionally practiced a form of shifting cultivation called rotational swiddening, in which new fields are cleared, cultivated for several years and then allowed to lie fallow for ten to twenty years before being brought back into cultivation.[7] As a general rule under the traditional farming systems, for each hectare of farmland currently under cultivation, another five (for relatively rich soils) to fifteen hectares must be kept fallow and held in reserve.[8] Despite appearances, these forest fallows are not vacant wasteland available for others to use, but an integral part of the swidden farming system, with former fallows put back into cultivation after their fertility has been restored. While pejoratively referred to as "slash and burn" agriculture, shifting cultivation can be a sustainable farming system in areas with relatively low population densities.[9]

The influx of settlers to the Central Highlands has increasingly fueled conflict and competition over scarce farmland, making traditional agricultural

---

more commonly used term, Montagnard. See UNHCR Centre for Documentation and Research, "Vietnam: Indigenous Minority Groups in the Central Highlands," Writenet Paper No. 05/2001, January 2002, p.7; available on the Internet at http://www.unhcr.ch/cgi-bin/texis/vtx/rsd?search=coi&source=WRITENET

[6] The Jarai and Ede are Austronesian (Malayo-Polynesian) speakers and the Bahnar, Mnong, Stieng and Koho are Mon Khmer, belonging to the Austro-Asiatic language family. Population figures are from the U.N. Development Program's Vietnam website, http://www.undp.org.vn/projects/vie96010/cemma/vie96010/populations.htm

[7] A. Terry Rambo et al, eds., *The Challenges of Highland Development in Vietnam*, East West Center, Center for Natural Resources and Environmental Studies, Center for Southeast Asia Studies, October 1995, p. xvii.

[8] A. Terry Rambo et al, eds., *The Challenges of Highland Development in Vietnam*, East West Center, Center for Natural Resources and Environmental Studies, Center for Southeast Asia Studies, October 1995, p. xvii. Sara Colm, "Land Rights: The Challenge for Ratanakiri's Indigenous Communities," *Watershed: People's Forum on Ecology*, Vol. 3, No. 1, Bangkok: Terra, July 1997.

[9] The population density of the Central Highlands is currently estimated at forty-seven people per square kilometer, while the threshold for sustainable shifting cultivation is often put at thirty people per square kilometer. "Country comparisons on Highland Peoples development issues—Vietnam," Highland Peoples Programme Management Team, UNDP Bangkok, March 1997.

practices more difficult. With less land to farm, fallowing periods are shorter, which means fallowed plots are put back into cultivation before the soil has become fertile again. As customary forms of agriculture become virtually impossible, highlanders find it much more difficult to make a living. Turning to cash crops such as coffee can supplement family income even on small plots of a hectare or less. This can be risky, however, because of market factors (the global plummet in coffee sales had a drastic effect) and because many highlanders lack official title to their land, making it liable to confiscation by the state or companies. In other cases, highlanders who have gained land use certificates to small plots of land end up selling their land because they lack the capital and labor to work it profitably.[10]

Customary Lands

Often referred to as nomads, very few highlanders are in fact even quasi-nomadic. While they may rotate their swidden plots every three to five years within prescribed village boundaries, the settlements themselves rarely move unless forced to do so by warfare, disease, or political developments. Instead most highlanders have traditionally lived in fixed village sites, rotating their swidden plots within an area that is often clearly defined by village elders.[11]

The customary lands of the indigenous minorities included paddy rice fields, swidden plots, graveyards, and house sites. Traditionally these lands were considered family property and inherited through the female line.[12] Families held customary user rights to their swidden plots whether they were being farmed or fallowed. Collective village lands included streams, grazing pastures, and drinking water sources. Special care was taken to preserve nearby forests upon which the indigenous populations depended for collection of "non-timber" products such as rattan, bamboo, mushrooms, bamboo shoots, and medicinal herbs.[13] Village boundaries were recognized and allocated by village elders, guardians of the villages' collective memory.[14]

---

[10] Oscar Salemink, "Customary Law, Land Rights and Internal Migration," *Vietnam Social Sciences*, February, 2000.
[11] A. Terry Rambo et al, eds., "The Challenges of Highland Development in Vietnam," East West Center, Center for Natural Resources and Environmental Studies, Center for Southeast Asia Studies, October 1995, page xvii; Sara Colm, "Land Rights: The Challenge for Ratanakiri's Indigenous Communities," *Watershed: People's Forum on Ecology*, Vol. 3, No. 1, Bangkok: Terra, July 1997.
[12] Gerald Cannon Hickey. *Free in the Forest: Ethnohistory of the Vietnamese Central Highlands, 1954-1976*. New Haven: Yale University Press, 1982, p. 36.
[13] Oscar Salemink, "The King of Fire and Vietnamese Ethnic Policy in the Central Highlands," published in Don McCaskill and K. Kampe, eds., *Development or Domestication? Indigenous Peoples of Southeast Asia*, Chiang Mai: Silkworm Books, 1997, p. 512.

The Dega People—An Oral History

Since God gave birth to the world, we ethnic minorities have always been in the same place. Since antiquity, our ancestors have always told us that this is our land. The Vietnamese never lived here. What we learned from our grandparents is that Vietnam started invading our land in 1930. In that year, the French started working in Dak Lak, and five Vietnamese went to work with them as cooks and helpers.

From the time the French left in 1954, bit by bit the Vietnamese increased their presence until they were all over the place. In 1958 because the Vietnamese were getting stronger and stronger in the Central Highlands all the ethnic minorities—Ede, Koho, Jarai, Stieng and Bahnar—stood up to make the first demonstration. All the ethnic minorities had one idea: we wanted our land back. At that time the Vietnamese promised to give us our land back so there would be no conflicts. They were not speaking the truth. Instead they put our leader, Y Bham Enuol, in jail in Hue for seven years.

In 1965 when they let Y Bham out of jail the ethnic minorities started the FULRO movement. It was based here in Mondolkiri [Cambodia], right near the spot where we are sitting today. I was twelve years old and carried a gun that was as long as me. Everyone, young and old, joined the struggle.

Later, in 1969, Nguyen Van Thieu, the president of South Vietnam, promised in the "O33" agreement to give us our land back. Y Bham would be in charge of the Central Highlands and the Vietnamese would go back to Vietnam. Instead, Vietnam received foreign aid and used the Dega to fight against North Vietnam. Thousands of us were killed.

In 1975 the [North] Vietnamese put our leader Nay Luett in prison for ten years. Vietnamese from both the north and the south took Dega labor to plant rubber and coffee. When the harvest came, they sent it to the lowlands. They used all sorts of tricks to destroy the ethnic minorities and take our land. Many Dega were sent to prison.

---

[14] Greg Booth, "RRA Report of Two Communes in the Se San Watershed," Regional Environmental Technical Assistance 5771—Poverty Reduction & Environmental Management in Remote Greater Mekong Subregion Watersheds Project (Phase I), Helsinki, 1999. Sara Colm, "Options for Land Security Among Indigenous Communities, Ratanakiri, Cambodia," Banlung: Non-Timber Forest Products Project, May 1997.

> *Beginning in 1980 they started turning all the land over to the Vietnamese. Each day more and more Vietnamese arrived, by the truckload. Especially since 1975, the Montagnards and the Vietnamese have not been happy together. We conducted a struggle in the forest [FULRO] to oppose them for many years. The life of Vietnamese and Montagnards together is like dogs biting each other; never easy.*
>
> *In 1988 the ethnic minorities started to become Christians. We'd been Christians for a long time before that but it was in 1988 when all the ethnic minorities believed; everywhere. Jesus changed our idea [from armed to peaceful struggle]. If we didn't have Christianity and the holy spirit within us, we would use violence to oppose the Vietnamese and we would all be dead.*
>
> —Mnong man, from Dak Lak, July 2001

Promises of Autonomy: The French

Resistance to Vietnamese central authority is not new among ethnic minorities in the Central Highlands. Highland ethnic groups sought and obtained pledges of autonomy not only from the French colonial government but also from both the North and the South Vietnamese governments during the Second Indochina War. While the various promises that these governments made to create such a zone were largely token gestures to gain the loyalty of the Montagnards, the idea garnered enthusiastic support among indigenous inhabitants of the highlands, who long felt persecuted, exploited, and alienated from the central government.

Much of the current debate over the highlanders' struggle for independence centers around the question of the legitimacy of Vietnam's sovereignty over the Central Highlands. This raises two questions—prior to French colonial rule, did Vietnam maintain political and administrative control over the Central Highlands, or did the highland groups exist as an independent state or states? Anthropologist Oscar Salemink argues that in pre-colonial times, the indigenous groups of the Central Highlands had little political organization beyond the village level.[15] However villages clearly made occasional alliances and maintained trade and political relations, according to Salemink, not only with other highland groups but with lowland communities, and not only in present-day lowland Vietnam, but Cambodia as well. Salemink and other historians argue that Vietnam's loose

---

[15] Oscar Salemink, "Mois and Maquis: The Invention and Appropriation of Vietnam's Montagnards from Sabatier to the CIA," in George W. Stocking, Jr. (ed.), *Colonial Situations: Essays in Ethnographic Contextualization* (History of Anthropology, Vol. 7), Madison: University of Wisconsin Press, 1991, p. 244.

administrative control and "nominal overlordship" over the Central Highlands dissolved in the late 1800s with the increased French role in the region and encroachment from Siam. The French assumed official control over the Central Highlands in 1893.[16]

Present-day claims by highlanders in Vietnam and abroad that both the French colonial administration and Vietnamese Emperor Bao Dai granted autonomous status to the Montagnards of the Central Highlands appear to be largely based on two documents. The first is a Federal Ordinance enacted in 1946 by the French colonial government in Vietnam, which created a special administrative commissariat for the highland populations (*les populations Montagnardes*) of South Indochina, separate from the Republic for South Annam.[17] This took place at a time of deteriorating relations between France and Ho Chi Minh's Viet Minh. In what some observers perceive was a cynical move to undermine the authority of Ho Chi Minh over all of Vietnam, the ordinance was enacted on May 27, 1946, three days before Ho Chi Minh left Vietnam for negotiations with the French in Paris.[18]

In July 1950, the French government issued an order establishing the Central Highlands as the Pays Montagnard du Sud (PMS) under the authority of Vietnamese Emperor Bao Dai, who the French had installed as nominal chief of state in 1949 as an alternative to Ho Chi Minh's Democratic Republic of Vietnam.[19] Terry Rambo notes:

> In order to win support from the highlanders, the French employed a divide-and-rule strategy, establishing Muong and Thai autonomous

---

[16] Oscar Salemink, "Mois and Maquis," p. 244.
[17] *Ordonnance fédérale du 27 Mai 1946 portant création d'un Commissariat du Gouvernement Fédéral pour les Populations Montagnardes du Sud Indochinois*, signed by Thierry d'Argenlieu, Saigon, May 27, 1946. Article 1 provided that the provinces of the Central Highlands would cease to be under the jurisdiction of the Commissariat of the Republic for South Annam, but would form a special administrative division called the "Commissariat of the Federal Government for the Highland Populations of South Indochina," with its seat established at Buon Ma Thuot.
[18] The French were attempting to circumvent an independent and united Vietnam under the Democratic Republic of Vietnam, which had been declared an independent state by Ho Chi Minh in September 1945. Instead, the French preferred a separate Indochina federation consisting not only of the Vietnamese states of Tonkin, Annam, and Cochinchina but also including Cambodia and Laos. In 1946 the French government provided Cambodia and Laos with limited autonomy under the Indo-Chinese Federation, with France maintaining control over the military, the economy, and the government. See Joseph Buttinger, *Vietnam: A Dragon Embattled*, New York: Frederick A. Praeger, Inc., 1967, p. 388 and p. 391.
[19] Bao Dai abdicated in 1945 when Ho Chi Minh established the Democratic Republic of Vietnam. D.J. Sagar, *Major Political Events in Indo-China, 1945-1990*, Oxford, Facts on File, 1991.

zones in the northwestern mountains, and separating the Central Highlands from Vietnam under the guise of the Pays Montagnard du Sud [PMS], which was administered as a "crown domain" directly under Emperor Bao Dai.[20]

The second document often cited by Montagnard autonomy advocates is a 1951 edict signed by Emperor Bao Dai establishing special status for the indigenous minorities of the Central Highlands (referred to as "des Populations des Pays Montagnards du Sud," or PMS). Known as the *statut particulier,* the edict guaranteed the highlanders all the rights of Vietnamese citizens as well as the right to "free evolution of these populations in the respect of their traditions and of their customs." Highland chiefs, whether hereditary or selected by native populations, would retain their titles and decision-making powers and customary tribal law would be retained. Article 7 guaranteed that "The rights acquired by the natives over landed property are guaranteed them in entirety."[21]

Part of the controversy over these documents revolves around the translation of the French term "des Populations des Pays Montagnards du Sud." Montagnard independence advocates translate this as "the Montagnard Country of the South," whereas some academics translate it as the "mountainous lands of the South" or the "lands of the Montagnard people in the south."

Promises of Autonomy: Hanoi

The French were not the only ones to promise special status to the highlanders. With the defeat of the French by the Viet Minh in 1954, several thousand highlanders sympathetic to the Viet Minh went to North Vietnam as part of the Geneva agreements. Many of them attended the Southern Ethnic Minorities school at Gia Lam, near Hanoi.[22] In January 1955 Ho Chi Minh announced plans for several autonomous zones to be set up in the Northern Highlands.

At the founding meeting in 1960 of the National Liberation Front of South Vietnam (NLF), more commonly known by the pejorative term Viet Cong, its political platform included recognition of the right to autonomy of the national

---

[20] A. Terry Rambo et al, eds., "The Challenges of Highland Development in Vietnam," East West Center, Center for Natural Resources and Environmental Studies, Center for Southeast Asia Studies, October 1995, page xxii.
[21] Edict No. 16/QT/TD, known as the *statut particulier*, signed by His Majesty Bao Dai, Chief of State, Dalat, May 21, 1951.
[22] Salemink states that many of the ethnic minorities currently within the provincial administrations in the Central Highlands are "Vietnamized" minority cadre who went North with the Viet Minh in 1954, after the Geneva Agreements. Salemink, "The King of Fire and Vietnamese Ethnic Policy in the Central Highlands," p. 499.

minorities. It called for the establishment of autonomous regions in minority areas and for the abolition of the "U.S.-Diêm clique's present policy of ill-treatment and forced assimilation of the minority nationalities."[23] The amended constitution of the Democratic Republic of Vietnam stated:

> Autonomous zones may be established in areas where people of national minorities live in compact communities. Such autonomous zones are integral and inalienable parts of the Democratic Republic of Vietnam.[24]

In the early 1960s the NLF sent agents to the Central Highlands to conduct propaganda and recruit highlanders. Minority-language broadcasts from Hanoi carried pledges of autonomy. During the mid-1960s minority leaders from the Central Highlands were regularly sent to visit autonomous zones in North Vietnam, with promises that autonomy would be granted to highlanders in the south when the country was liberated.[25]

The 1958 Bajaraka Movement

In 1955 the Central Highlands became part of the Republic of Vietnam, (South Vietnam). Trouble began to brew after President Ngô Dinh Diêm launched programs in 1956 to resettle ethnic Vietnamese to "land development centers" in the Central Highlands and assimilate the highlanders into mainstream Vietnamese society. In addition, thousands of ethnic minority refugees from the north were resettled in the Central Highlands as well.[26]

According to Hickey, the first "ethnonationalist" groupings in the Central Highlands started in 1955 in Buon Ale-A near Buon Ma Thuot, where the U.S.-based Christian and Missionary Alliance (CMA) church was located and where several Montagnard resistance leaders, including Y Thih Eban and Y Bham Enuol, were born.[27] In March 1955 the first group, a secret organization called Le Front pour la Liberation des Montagnards (the Montagnard Liberation

---

[23] Cited in Gerald Cannon Hickey. *Free in the Forest: Ethnohistory of the Vietnamese Central Highlands, 1954-1976.* New Haven: Yale University Press, 1982. p. 66.
[24] Viet Chung, "National Minorities and Nationality Policy in the D.R.V.," *Vietnamese Studies*, no 15 (1968), cited in Grant Evans, Internal Colonialism in the Central Highlands of Vietnam," Sojourn, volume 7, Number 2, 1992.
[25] Hickey, *Free in the Forest*, p. 70.
[26] Hickey, *Free in the Forest*, p. 17.
[27] Y Bham Enuol, born in 1913, studied at the Franco-Rhade School, the CMA Bible School, and the Ecole Nationale d'Agriculture. In the 1950s he worked as a civil servant in the provincial agriculture service in Darlac and Pleiku provinces. Y Thih Eban, born in 1932, was educated at the Franco-Jarai School in Pleiku and the College Sabatier. Hickey, *Free in the Forest*, p. 51.

Front), wrote to President Diêm with a list of demands, including the right of highlanders to fly their own flag.

In 1958, a highland resistance movement emerged called Bajaraka, an acronym for the four main Montagnard groups: Bahnar, Jarai, Rhade (or Ede) and Koho. In August of that year, Bajaraka leader Y Bham Enuol sent a letter to some of the main diplomatic missions in Saigon, outlining highlander grievances and their demands for autonomy, and requesting international intervention. There was no immediate response but in September 1958 two Bajaraka members were arrested north of Kontum, prompting Y Bham to send a letter to Diêm to resolve the problem. Instead, Y Bham and other Bajaraka leaders were arrested, including Y Thih Eban, Paul Nur, and Nay Luett. They were imprisoned in underground solitary cells in Dalat for three months.[28]

In a scenario reminiscent of the events of February 2001, one thousand highlanders signed a petition in 1958 requesting the release of the minority leaders and organized a demonstration attended by 2,000 people in Buon Ma Thuot, where a Bajaraka leader addressed the rally and outlined the highlanders' complaints. The government sent in armored units from the army's 23rd Division to break up the demonstration. According to Hickey, Diêm was incensed by the highlanders' call for autonomy, and immediately closed the Highlander Students' Section of the National Institute of Administration, relocated the Bureau for Highland Affairs from Dalat to Hue, and reassigned highlanders in the civil service from the highlands to posts in the lowlands. One hundred military officers were sent to Hue for reeducation and then reassigned to the lowlands. Montagnard army officers were ordered to take Vietnamese names and Montagnard traditional weapons such as crossbows were confiscated.[29]

In 1959 Y Bham Enuol and Paul Nur were released from prison. As soon as Enuol resumed his campaign for the Bajaraka movement he was quickly re-arrested and taken to police headquarters in Buon Ma Thuot, where he was reportedly tortured with electric shocks and imprisoned until early 1964.[30]

The Second Indochina War: 1960-1975

Much of the U.S. bombing campaign and many of the fiercest battles of the Second Indochina War, also known as the American War, were played out in the Central Highlands. The U.S. declared many parts of the Central Highlands as "free fire zones" targeted for aerial bombing raids and the use of chemical defoliants in order to smoke out North Vietnamese units, whose transportation

---

[28] Ibid.
[29] Hickey, *Free in the Forest*, p. 59.
[30] Ibid.

corridors—the "Ho Chi Minh Trail"—passed through the northern part of the Central Highlands en route from Laos and Cambodia.[31]

Both the U.S. and the North Vietnamese tried to recruit the indigenous minorities to their side. Repression of the Bajaraka movement by the Diêm administration in the late 1950s had turned many highlanders towards the National Liberation Front (NLF). In 1961, minority NLF members led by former Bajaraka leaders such as Y Bih Aleo, who had escaped arrest by Diêm and gone underground, formed the NLF's Montagnard Autonomy Movement.[32] U.S. counterinsurgency operations organized among indigenous minorities in the Central Highlands were in part a response to this.[33]

In the early 1960s, U.S. forces recruited highlanders for village defense units and reconnaissance teams to gather intelligence about North Vietnamese infiltration into the highlands and conduct propaganda in support of the Diêm regime.[34]

In 1961 the Central Intelligence Agency (CIA) established the "Village Defense" programs in Darlac (the former name of Dak Lak), followed by the "Mountain Scout" program (often called the Commando program). Highlanders were also trained by U.S. Special Forces Detachment A-35 to conduct paramilitary operations.[35] Given the earlier Bajaraka uprising, the Diêm government was uneasy about the U.S. arming highlanders, particularly under the CIA's Village Defense Program, in which 18,000 Montagnards were eventually armed.[36]

After the overthrow of Diêm in a coup in November 1963, the government of Nguyen Khanh released some Bajaraka leaders from prison (including Y Bham Enuol in February 1964) and upgraded the Bureau of Highland Affairs to a Directorate of Highland Affairs under the Ministry of Defense.

During this time Bajaraka resistance leaders began to link up with similar ethnonationalist movements brewing in Cambodia among ethnic Cham and Khmer Krom,[37] primarily through Lt. Col. Les Kosem, a Cambodian Cham and Col. Um Savuth, both officers in the Royal Khmer Army. In July 1964 the three

---

[31] UNHCR Centre for Documentation and Research, "Vietnam: Indigenous Minority Groups in the Central Highlands," Writenet Paper No. 05/2001, January 2002.
[32] Salemink, "Mois and Maquis," p. 270.
[33] Ibid.
[34] Ibid.
[35] Hickey. *Free in the Forest*, p. 78.
[36] Ibid, p. 80.
[37] The Cham are an ethnic group originating from the former Kingdom of Champa, which was located in present-day central Vietnam. It was absorbed into Vietnam over the course of three centuries, from 1471 until its assimilation by Vietnam in the 1830s. Khmer Krom are ethnic Khmers living primarily in southern Vietnam, in a region many Cambodians refer to as "Kampuchea Krom," or "lower Cambodia."

groupings merged as the Front Unifié de Lutte des Race Opprimées (FULRO, or the United Struggle Front for the Oppressed Races).

The FULRO Rebellions: 1964-1965

FULRO first made a name for itself as a militant group in September 1964 when it organized a rebellion among 3,000 Montagnard combatants in five U.S. special forces camps in the Central Highlands: Buon Sar Pa, Bu Prang, Ban Don, Buon Mi Ga and Buon Brieng.[38] Leaflets were distributed in Buon Ma Thuot on the first day of the rebellion, declaring that the Central Highlands had been invaded by "expansionist Vietnamese" following a "systematic genocidal policy." A number of Vietnamese special forces troops were killed and others taken hostage. After several days of negotiations between U.S. military advisors and the FULRO militants, and the deployment of Vietnamese military units near the camps, the rebels surrendered. Y Bham Enuol and approximately 2,000 FULRO followers fled across the border to Cambodia, where they established their headquarters near Camp Le Rolland (present-day Dak Dam) in Mondolkiri. Y Bham Enuol was to remain in Cambodia for most of the next decade.

After the revolt and at the urging of the Americans, the Nguyen Khanh government organized a conference of highland leaders in Pleiku in October 1964. Requests put forward by the highlanders included not only the institution of Bao Dai's *statut particulier* but economic development programs, reinstatement of customary highland law, use of minority languages in the schools, formation of a highland military force with its own flag, and Montagnard control over and administration of foreign aid to the highlands. Y Bham Enuol followed up on the demands in letters sent to the Khanh government as well as the U.S. Embassy, U.S. President Lyndon Johnson and the Secretary-General of the United Nations. Khanh reportedly agreed to many of the demands except for autonomy, highland control over foreign aid, and establishment of a highland military force.

Virtually none of the pledges were ever fulfilled however, in part because the Khanh government was overthrown in a coup in 1965. Political tensions rose again and in December 1965, a second FULRO uprising broke out, in which thirty-five Vietnamese, including civilians, were killed.[39] The rebellion was put

---

[38] According to Hickey, the revolts were planned by Col. Les Kosem and Col. Um Savuth with the assistance of several Montagnard leaders. Hickey, *Free in the Forest*, p. 99

[39] According to a document prepared in 1993 by the U.S.-based Montagnard Foundation, Inc., another armed uprising took place earlier in the year on July 29, 1965 at Buon Brieng. The revolt was reportedly put down by the Saigon government, which arrested 600 FULRO combatants. Montagnard Foundation, Inc., "Human Rights Violations—the People of the Dega Republic; Supplemental Materials for a Presentation Made to the

down in a day; four of the FULRO leaders were condemned to death and publicly executed, and fifteen others were imprisoned.[40]

Easing of Tensions in the mid-1960s

Relations between FULRO and the South Vietnamese government appeared to improve for a while under the government of Nguyen Cao Ky, who replaced Khanh after the 1965 coup. The government established a Directorate-General for Development of Ethnic Minorities, appointed Paul Nur, an ethnic Bahnar, as a cabinet member, and approved legislation entitling highlanders to own land.[41] Six highlanders, including a FULRO member, were elected to the National Assembly. FULRO forces in Cambodia began negotiations with the government about their return to Vietnam.

While 250 FULRO forces agreed to return in October 1966, Y Bham Enuol—who continued to insist on regional autonomy and an armed highlander force—was not among them. In 1968 Y Bham Enuol briefly returned to Buon Ma Thuot at the government's request to conduct negotiations over FULRO's possible return to Vietnam. An agreement reached in December 1968 specified that the highlanders could form their own political party and fly their own flag. Y Bham Enuol dropped some of his earlier demands, such as the right of highlanders to directly receive foreign aid.

In January 1969 more than 1,300 FULRO soldiers and their families rallied to the South Vietnamese government and left Mondolkiri. They were welcomed at an official ceremony in Buon Ma Thuot.[42] Y Bham Enuol, however, did not return with them. Several Cambodian army battalions surrounded the FULRO headquarters in Mondolkiri and escorted Enuol to Phnom Penh, where he was kept under virtual house arrest by Les Kosem and Um Savuth, who wanted to prevent him from leaving and cutting a deal with the Vietnamese government.[43] In Vietnam a less militant FULRO faction, led by Y D'he announced that

---

United Nations Workshop on the Rights of Indigenous Peoples, Geneva," July 19-30, 1993.
[40] The FULRO combatants who were executed were Nay Ry, Ksor Bleo, R'Com Re, and Ksor Boh. Montagnard Foundation, Inc., "Human Rights Violations—the People of the Dega Republic; Supplemental Materials for a Presentation Made to the United Nations Workshop on the Rights of Indigenous Peoples, Geneva, July 19-30, 1993; Hickey, *Free in the Forest*, p. 138. See also the accounts of the FULRO rebellions by First Lieutenant Roy C. Russell, "Their Time Has Come," *Typhoon* magazine, published by First Field Forces Vietnam of the U.S. Army Vietnam, October 1969.
[41] The Directorate-General was upgraded to a Ministry in 1966. Salemink, "Mois and Maquis," p. 272.
[42] Roy C. Russell, "Their Time Has Come," *Typhoon* magazine, published by First Field Forces Vietnam of the U.S. Army Vietnam, October 1969.
[43] Hickey, *Free in the Forest*, p. 190.

A History of Resistance to Central Government Control

FULRO was being formally dissolved and replaced with a highlander political party, the Ethnic Minorities Solidarity Movement, which advocated peaceful accommodation with the South Vietnamese government.[44]

In 1971 Nay Luett, an ethnic Jarai, was appointed as minister for ethnic minority development. He and colleagues such as Pierre K'Bruih worked to make the ministry a center for ethnonationalism, Hickey said, "where mountain country leaders gathered and participated in planning."[45] However as the war escalated in Vietnam, the struggle for minority rights was overshadowed by the highlanders' need for simple survival. Hickey estimates that at least 200,000 highlanders were killed during the Second Indochina War, and more than 85 percent of the population forced from their villages and displaced as refugees. The government relocated thousands of highlanders from their customary lands, moving them to "strategic hamlets" or regrouping them along major roads for defense purposes.

On March 10, 1975 North Vietnamese forces occupied Buon Ma Thuot in the final offensive of the war; a FULRO faction that supported the NLF agreed not to alert Saigon that North Vietnamese tanks were approaching.[46] In April 1975, a pro-U.S. FULRO group reportedly negotiated an arrangement with U.S. officials to continue guerrilla warfare against the Hanoi regime after the North Vietnamese victory. According to former FULRO members, although the U.S. reneged on promises of covert support, the group continued fighting until 1992.[47]

When the Khmer Rouge invaded Phnom Penh on April 17, 1975, Y Bham Enuol and other FULRO leaders living in Phnom Penh sought refuge in the French Embassy. They were all taken out by the Khmer Rouge and executed. Many of Enuol's most ardent followers, guerilla soldiers in the forests of Mondolkiri, were not to learn of his death for seventeen years.

The Highlands After 1975

With the reunification of Vietnam in 1975, Viet Minh pledges of autonomy never materialized. Instead, government officials launched programs to settle ethnic Vietnamese in New Economic Zones in the highlands while aiming to

---

[44] Russell, "Their Time Has Come," *Typhoon* magazine, October 1969.
[45] Hickey, *Free in the Forest*, p. xx.
[46] Until 1975 FULRO was made up of several different factions, some allied with the U.S. and other with the North Vietnamese. Mark Lioi, "The Montagnards—a 70-year saga of betrayal," *Phnom Penh Post*, June 8-21, 2001.
[47] Nate Thayer, "Montagnard Army Seeks U.N. Help," *Phnom Penh Post*, Sept. 12, 1992; Nate Thayer and Leo Dobbs, "Tribal Fighters Head for Refuge in USA," *Phnom Penh Post*, October 23, 1992; Oscar Salemink interview with Pierre K'Bruih, April 16, 1990; cited in "Mois and Maquis," p. 273.

relocate highlanders to the valleys to grow rice and industrial crops, rather than continuing their "unstable nomadic life" in the highlands.[48] Those who had worked with U.S. Special Forces or FULRO were sent to re-education camps. Hickey described the post-war situation:

> Peace, however, did not return to the highlands. It soon became apparent that the oft-promised autonomy for the highlanders was only a propaganda ploy. Worse still, Hanoi immediately began implementing plans to resettle large numbers of Vietnamese in upland "economic zones." There also were announcements in rhetoric reminiscent of the Diêm era about programs to settle the "nomadic" mountain people in "sedentary villages." At the same time all of the highland leaders from the ministry and those who had been active in provincial administrations and programs were captured and incarcerated either in jails or "reeducation camps." Those leaders who managed to elude captivity along with young highlanders from the Army, the Special Forces, and other paramilitary groups, fled into the forest where they organized a resistance movement.[49]

It was not long before FULRO forces, many of whom fled to the forests after the final defeat of South Vietnam, began to resurrect their guerilla movement. This time FULRO's resistance was directed against Hanoi. The re-emergence of the group was evident as early as the first session of the National Assembly in 1976, in which a parliamentarian referred to the use of "lackeys" by "imperialist" forces to conduct counter-revolutionary activities.[50]

By 1977 FULRO's primary supporters were the Khmer Rouge in Cambodia, with whom they had formed an uneasy alliance. In 1977 the two groups signed an agreement for the exchange of information and training, and in 1978 a FULRO combatant denounced Ho Chi Minh over Radio Phnom Penh.[51] Ieng Sary, then-Minister of Foreign Affairs for the Khmer Rouge, said in 1979: "The FULRO approached us for cooperation to exchange intelligence, military experience and get guerrilla warfare training."[52]

---

[48] Reported in FBIS-APA. 18 May 1976; FBIS-APA, 6 July 1976; cited in Hickey, *Free in the Forest*, p. 287 and 289. See also: UNHCR Centre for Documentation and Research, "Vietnam: Indigenous Minority Groups in the Central Highlands," Writenet Paper No. 05/2001, January 2002.
[49] Hickey, *Free in the Forest*, p. xxi.
[50] FBIS-APA, 6 July 1976; cited in Hickey, *Free in the Forest*, p. 289.
[51] Mark Lioi, "The Montagnards—a 70-year saga of betrayal," *Phnom Penh Post*, June 8 - 21, 2001.
[52] Nayan Chanda, "Ieng Sary: Unite for Our Country," *Far Eastern Economic Review* 104, no. 25, 1979.

By the early 1980s, FULRO forces numbered approximately 7,000. Forced to abandon their bases in Vietnam, they shifted their operation to Mondolkiri where they carried out small cross-border attacks against Vietnamese forces in the highlands. By 1986, however, the Khmer Rouge parted ways with FULRO and stopped supplying them with arms and provisions. "They had no political vision," a Khmer Rouge official said in a 1992 interview with the *Phnom Penh Post*. "Their fighters are very, very brave, but they had no support from any leadership, no food, and they did not understand at all the world around them."[53]

In 1986 several hundred FULRO soldiers and their families, who had escaped overland through Cambodia to Thailand, were relocated to the United States as refugees. The remnants of the army in Cambodia fell on especially hard time in the early 1990s. In 1992, demoralized and lacking food, ammunition and supplies, the remaining 400 FULRO combatants and their families in Mondolkiri surrendered to troops of the U.N. Transitional Authority in Cambodia (UNTAC). A major element in the combatants' decision to give up their struggle at that time was that when they asked for help contacting Y Bham Enuol, they learned he had been executed in 1975. The group received asylum in the United States and was resettled in North Carolina in late 1992.[54]

During the 1990s, land conflicts and religious repression escalated in the Central Highlands, as described in chapters below. In general, however, expression of dissent—either through peaceful means or guerilla movements such as FULRO—was virtually nonexistent until early 2001, when earlier demands exploded into view again.

---

[53] Nate Thayer, "Montagnard Army Seeks U.N. Help," *Phnom Penh Post*, Sept. 12, 1992.
[54] Human Rights Watch interview with former FULRO combatant, Greensboro, North Carolina, January 1999. For more information on FULRO see Charles Meyer, *Derrière Le Sourire Khmer*, Paris: Plon, 1971.

IV. GOVERNMENT POLICIES TOWARD ETHNIC MINORITIES

The Vietnamese national ethnic community may constitute, as one Kinh ethnologist has written, a garden in which a hundred flowers of different colors and perfume bloom, but the overall plan for the garden is exclusively determined by the head gardener (i.e., the state).
–A. Terry Rambo, East-West Center, Honolulu, 1995

There is a significant gap between rhetoric and reality in Vietnamese government policies towards ethnic minorities in the Central Highlands. On the one hand, the government is proud of its policies toward ethnic minorities and of constitutional provisions guaranteeing them the right to use their own languages, and to preserve and promote local identity and traditions. On the other hand, government policies are based largely on perceptions of highlanders as nomadic, in need of development and stability, and ultimately untrustworthy in the political sense because of the affiliation of some of them with the U.S. war effort and their longstanding desire for independence.

Historically, Vietnamese government policy toward the country's national minorities has been one that extols the rich diversity of Vietnam's fifty-four officially recognized ethnic groups and proclaims them the progenitor of the Vietnamese Communist Party, while stressing the overarching aim that all ethnic groups work together toward the common goals of national unity, defense, and building the nation.

Vietnam's long-fought struggle for national unity is proudly and rigorously defended, with the "crime of undermining the policy of national unity" bringing prison sentences of up to fifteen years under the 1999 Penal Code.[55] A 1993 government publication notes:

> The unity of the Vietnamese nation has been strengthened by the constant threat of invasion from feudalist or imperialist powers. In view of geographical position and natural resources, Vietnam has throughout its history been a focus of more powerful forces. Once settled in Vietnam, the ethnic groups realized the necessity of unity in order to safeguard the country and their own existence.[56]

---

[55] Article 87, Penal Code of the Socialist Republic of Vietnam, cited in *A Selection of Fundamental Laws of Vietnam*, the Gioi Publishers, Hanoi, 2001.
[56] *Ethnic Minorities in Vietnam*, The Gioi Publishers, Hanoi, 1993.

According to Vietnamese folklore, Vietnam's many different nationalities were hatched out of a hundred eggs from one set of parents, Lac Long Quan and Au Co. Half followed their mother to the mountains and the rest went with their father to the sea. They joined hands to build one nation stretching from the high peaks of Lung Cu in the north, to the hamlet of Rach Tau in the south, and from the Truong Son range in the west to the Truong Sa archipelago in the east.[57]

The 1992 Constitution affirms the rights of ethnic minorities. Article 5 states that the government forbids all acts of ethnic discrimination and guarantees the rights of ethnic groups to use their own language and writing systems, preserve their ethnic identity, and promote their own traditions and culture. Articles 36 and 39 authorize preferential treatment for national minorities in education and health care. Article 94 mandates the establishment of the Nationalities Council of the National Assembly to "supervise and control" the implementation of policies and programs in regard to ethnic minorities.[58]

Government institutions overseeing minority affairs include the Office of Mountainous Areas and Ethnic Minorities, established in 1990 and then upgraded to ministerial status as the state Committee for Ethnic Minorities and Mountainous Areas (CEMMA) in 1992. In addition, policy is formulated and coordinated by the National Assembly's Council of Nationalities and the Institute of Ethnology under the National Center for Social Sciences. Ethnic minorities currently hold seventy-eight seats, or 17 percent, of the 450-seat National Assembly, slightly higher than their proportion in the overall population (15 percent).[59]

"Mutual Respect, Participation, and Equal Rights"

Vietnam has been a party to the International Convention on the Elimination of All Forms of Racial Discrimination (CERD) since 1982. The U.N. Committee on the Elimination of Racial Discrimination, in its General Recommendation XXIII on Indigenous Peoples, calls on states parties to:

(a) Recognize and respect indigenous distinct culture, history, language and way of life as an enrichment of the State's cultural identity and to promote its preservation;

---

[57] Associate Professor Hoang Nam, "The Vietnamese Homeland in the Vietnamese Nation," published in Vietnam News Agency, "Vietnam Image of the Community of 54 Ethnic Groups," The Ethnic Cultures Publishing House, Hanoi, 1996.
[58] Constitution of the Socialist Republic of Vietnam 1992, *A Selection of Fundamental Laws of Vietnam*, the Gioi Publishers, Hanoi, 2001.
[59] Ninth periodic reports of States parties due in 1999, Addendum, Viet Nam, "Reports Submitted by States Parties under Article 9 of the Convention," International Convention on the Elimination of all Forms of Racial Discrimination, CERD/C/357/Add.2, 17 October 2000. United Nations Development Program, "Fact Sheet on Ethnic Minority Groups," December 2000, http://www.UNDP.org.Vietnam

(b) Ensure that members of indigenous peoples are free and 6equal in dignity and rights and free from any discrimination, in particular that based on indigenous origin or identity;

(c) Provide indigenous peoples with conditions allowing for a sustainable economic and social development compatible with their cultural characteristics;

(d) Ensure that members of indigenous peoples have equal rights in respect of effective participation in public life and that no decisions directly relating to their rights and interests are taken without their informed consent;

(e) Ensure that indigenous communities can exercise their rights to practice and revitalize their cultural traditions and customs and to preserve and to practice their languages.

A report submitted by the government of Vietnam in 2000 as part of its reporting duties as a state party to CERD stated:

For the Vietnamese people, racial discrimination is unfamiliar and does not exist in the country. In Viet Nam, all ethnic groups have, from time immemorial, coexisted peacefully without racial conflicts and discrimination. All ethnic groups in Viet Nam, regardless of their size, language, culture, history and level of development, have enjoyed the same rights in all aspects of life.[60]

In theory, official government strategy for ethnic minority development is based on the following elements, as outlined in a 1995 SRV policy document: a) targeting the poor, since ethnic minorities are disproportionately represented amongst those living in poverty; b) active participation of ethnic people in their own development; c) capacity building within ethnic minority communities; d) sustainable development; and e) mutual respect and responsibility between the parties involved:

The overall goal is to integrate ethnic minorities into wider society, and to create the conditions for all citizens, irrespective of ethnic

---

[60] Ninth periodic reports of States parties due in 1999, Addendum, Viet Nam, "Reports Submitted by States Parties under Article 9 of the Convention," International Convention on the Elimination of all Forms of Racial Discrimination, CERD/C/357/Add.2, 17 October 2000.

origin to enjoy equal rights in political economic, cultural and social domains.[61]

In practice, Vietnamese government policy has wavered from benevolent paternalism to repressive implementation of programs that clash with indigenous religious practices and customary approaches to agriculture and land use.[62] In some cases, the problem is poor implementation of national policies at the local level due to corruption, lack of resources, or poor communication of official procedures by the central government to the provincial, district, and commune authorities.

Fixed Fields, Fixed Settlements

Since the late 1960s, the official approach towards ethnic minorities in Vietnam has largely centered around having highlanders settle in permanent settlements and move from shifting or swidden cultivation, to paddy rice cultivation and cash crops.

The government has attempted to carry out these objectives through a number of programs that ostensibly bring new expertise and new population groups to the highlands. These have included the Fixed Cultivation and Permanent Settlement Program (FCPS, or *dinh canh dinh cu* in Vietnamese) and the New Economic Zones (NEZ) Program, which organized the migration of lowlanders to state-run agricultural farms, cooperatives and production collectives in the highlands.[63]

Launched in 1968, the FCPS, or "sedentarization," program sought to address environmental degradation allegedly caused by swidden cultivation by relocating "nomadic" highlanders to permanent settlements. The program sought to address twin goals of protecting watershed forests allegedly at risk of being destroyed by the highlanders while improving national defense by relocating

---

[61] Socialist Republic of Viet Nam, Committee for Ethnic Minorities and Mountainous Areas, UNDP, "Framework for External Assistance to Ethnic Minority Development," Hanoi, November 1995.

[62] A. Terry Rambo writes: "Granting of the constitutional right to minorities to preserve their cultures should not be mistaken for a genuine acceptance of cultural relativism.... Thus, the relationship between the Vietnamese state and its ethnic minorities remains a paternalistic one in which the ultimate authority to make decisions about appropriate directions for cultural change remains in the hands of the central government, not in those of the minorities themselves." A. Terry Rambo et al, eds., "The Challenges of Highland Development in Vietnam," East West Center, Center for Natural Resources and Environmental Studies, Center for Southeast Asia Studies, October 1995.

[63] Oscar Salemink, "Customary Law, Land Rights and Internal Migration," *Vietnam Social Sciences*, February, 2000, page 67.

ethnic minorities from isolated and sensitive border areas to regions under government control.[64]

In the early 1980s the government initiated transmigration programs to encourage lowland Vietnamese to resettle in New Economic Zones in the Central Highlands to address landlessness, overpopulation and high unemployment rates in others parts of the country, particularly the coastal areas. The programs also aimed to create a labor force to work on state agricultural farms and tree plantations (under Decree 82/CP) and to establish cooperatives and production collectives (under Decree 95/CP).[65]

These programs supported the aim of making Vietnam truly uniform, by having ethnic Vietnamese dispersed throughout the country, including the remote highlands. Migration of ethnic Vietnamese to restive border regions was seen to support both national defense and economic development goals. In theory, the underlying approach of the transmigration programs has been to try to take advantage of some of Vietnam's assets: an abundant labor force throughout Vietnam and the Central Highlands' "untapped land potential." Under these schemes, the labor force would be rationally redistributed according to land availability, relocating people from overpopulated areas to those with fewer people and more uncultivated land. The Director of the Department for Resettlement and Development of New Economic Zones at the Ministry of Agriculture and Rural Development outlined the official view of "rural to rural" migration at a 1998 conference:

> The legacy of history is an uneven distribution of the population from one area and region to another. While population density tops 1000 people/km^2 in some provinces of the Red River Delta, it is only slightly more than 30 people/ km^2 in parts of the northern uplands and Central Highlands....The Red River Delta has 21 percent of the country's population but only 14 percent of its arable land, while the Mekong Delta has less than 20 percent of the population but 30 percent of the farmland....
>
> In order to develop the country's potential and achieve rational utilization of its resources, the government has formulated a strategy to redistribute population and labor. Such a reallocation of the forces

---

[64] See Salemink, "The King of Fire and Vietnamese Ethnic Policy in the Central Highlands," p. 513.
[65] Huynh Thi Xuan, Vice-Chairwoman, Dak Lak Provincial People's Committee, "The Impact of Rural-Rural Migration to Resettlement Areas in Dak Lak Province," in *International Seminar on Internal Migration: Implications for Migration Policy in Vietnam*, Population Council, Vietnam, May 1998.

of production will allow these resources to be tapped and lead to equal development among different regions. Rural-rural migration in Vietnam is truly the will of the party and the people alike.[66]

Regreening the Barren Hills

In the 1990s, in part to address massive deforestation, the government instituted several new policies in regard to ethnic minorities and upland development. These included the 1992 Program 327 (known as the "Regreening of the Barren Hills Program"), which aimed to reforest barren areas, protect and exploit forests and unused land, and resettle ethnic minority swidden farmers. The 1998 "Five Million Hectare Reforestation Program" (Decree 661/QD-TTg), similarly aimed to induce families to reforest areas in exchange for certain user rights.[67] Both programs aimed to reforest "barren" land by resettling lowland farmers into the highlands while relocating highland shifting cultivators to permanent sites to practice fixed cultivation.[68]

In the mid-1990s a number of Vietnamese academics and researchers, such as those at Center for Natural Resources and Environmental Studies (CRES) at Vietnam National University in Hanoi, gained the support of progressive local officials and funding from the East-West Center and the Ford Foundation as they began to explore ways to promote sustainable natural resource management among highland communities. Several pilot projects were launched in the Northern Highlands that advanced a decentralized approach to sustainable forest use and protection, customary resource use, and community-based natural resource management.[69]

---

[66] Hoang Dong "Rural-rural Migration and Redistribution of Labor and Population in Accordance with Planning for Socio-Economic Development in Vietnam," in *International Seminar on Internal Migration: Implications for Migration Policy in Vietnam*, Population Council, Vietnam, May 1998.

[67] See Socialist Republic of Viet Nam, Committee for Ethnic Minorities and Mountainous Areas, UNDP, "Framework for External Assistance to Ethnic Minority Development," Hanoi, November 1995.

[68] Thomas Sikor, "Decree 327 and the Restoration of Barren Land in the Vietnamese Highlands," in A. Terry Rambo et al, eds., "The Challenges of Highland Development in Vietnam," East West Center, Center for Natural Resources and Environmental Studies, Center for Southeast Asia Studies, October 1995, p. 143.

[69] See: Jamieson, Neil, Le Trong Cuc and A. Terry Rambo, "The Development Crisis in Vietnam's Mountains," East-West Center Special Reports No. 6, 1998, and A. Terry Rambo et al, eds., "The Challenges of Highland Development in Vietnam," East-West Center, Center for Natural Resources and Environmental Studies, Center for Southeast Asia Studies, October 1995. UNHCR Centre for Documentation and Research, "Vietnam: Indigenous Minority Groups in the Central Highlands," Writenet Paper No. 05/2001, January 2002.

Despite innovative initiatives such as these, the overall approach by national and provincial authorities continues to call for sedentarization of the highlanders and an end to shifting agriculture and "nomadic lifestyles."[70]

---

[70] As the Ministry of Agriculture and Rural Development did in May 2001, and as President Tran Duc Luong did during his January 2002 visit to Kontum. *Viet Nam News*, May 5, 2001. "President Luong urges Kon Tum to reduce poverty," Vietnam News Agency (VNA), January 2002.

V. POPULATION EXPLOSION: THE IMPACT OF MIGRATION

One of the most significant problems is land disputes, since the traditional living space of local groups is shrinking more and more because of migration. This is particularly true for spontaneous migrants, who arbitrarily occupy the fields and forest land of the indigenous peoples.
—Huynh Thi Xuan, Vice-Chairwoman, Dak Lak Provincial People's Committee, 1998.

Over the last thirty years migration to the highlands has been both organized and spontaneous, with the new settlers consisting primarily of ethnic Vietnamese, or Kinh, but also including ethnic minorities from the poverty-stricken Northern Highlands, either moving voluntarily in search of land or to avoid planned hydropower projects.

At the beginning of the twentieth century, the population of the four provinces of the Central Highlands was around 240,000, the vast majority of which comprised indigenous ethnic minorities. The current population is now estimated at roughly four million, only 25 percent of which is indigenous.

Organized Migration

The impact of both planned and spontaneous migration of ethnic Vietnamese, who traditionally have lived in the lowlands and the Red River Delta in the north, has been dramatic. Between 1940 and 1989, the numbers of Kinh in the Central Highlands rose from 5 percent to 66 percent of the area's population.[71]

Lowland Vietnamese did not start to move into the region in significant numbers until the end of the Resistance War against the French (1946-1954).[72] The first to come were refugees from the north, who began to resettle in the Central Highlands in 1954. In the late 1950s the Republic of Vietnam's Land Development Program aimed to draw people from impoverished and heavily populated lowland regions, while creating a human buffer against NLF infiltration at the same time. More than 100,000 people—ethnic Vietnamese from the lowlands as well as refugees, including some ethnic minorities, from

---

[71] A. Terry Rambo, "Defining Highland Development Challenges in Vietnam," in A. Terry Rambo et al, eds., "The Challenges of Highland Development in Vietnam," East West Center, Center for Natural Resources and Environmental Studies, Center for Southeast Asia Studies, October 1995, p. 25.
[72] Neil Jamieson, "Ethnic Minorities in Vietnam: A Country Profile," Winrock, International, Hanoi, Vietnam, March 1996.

the north—had been resettled in 117 Land Development Centers in the Central Highlands by the end of 1962, where they farmed rubber and other crops.[73]

Since reunification of the country in 1975, the numbers have shot up, with hundreds of thousands of ethnic Vietnamese from the lowlands, as well as other minorities from the north, migrating to the Central Highlands. Much of the early migration (before 1991) was through the central government programs which established state Forest Enterprises, NEZs, and state coffee and rubber plantations.[74]

Spontaneous Migration

Since the initiation of *doi moi* (renovation), the liberalization process that began in 1986, government-organized transmigration has decreased while spontaneous migration has shot up. The new settlers include not only lowland Vietnamese but ethnic minorities such as Tai, Nung and Dao from the Northern Highlands. The Kinh have flocked to the Central Highlands both to farm cash crops and to work as traders in timber, forest products and cash crops; they also dominate the main urban markets. Northern minority people are moving to the Central Highlands because of poverty, population pressure, and depleted natural resources in the Northern Highlands, and the relative abundance of farm and forest land in the Central Highlands.

From 1990-1994, some 110,000 spontaneous migrants resettled in Dak Lak, more than 90,000 in Lam Dong, and smaller numbers in Gia Lai and Kontum.[75] While planned migrants receive some government assistance, virtually nothing is offered to those who resettle unofficially. "As a result, settlers have to destroy forest land in order to farm and build," noted the deputy people's committee chair of Dak Lak province.[76]

By encouraging hundreds of thousands of migrants to settle in the Central Highlands, the establishment of the New Economic Zones had the opposite effect in many areas from what had been envisioned. Rather than promoting economic development by bringing the highlanders into contact with lowlanders

---

[73] Hickey, *Free in the Forest*, p. 62.
[74] According to research by Jacqueline Desbarats, between 1976-79 Dak Lak province and its neighbor Song Be (presnt-day Binh Phuoc) received the largest number of NEZ settlers (more than 55,000), with Gia Lai-Kontum and Lam Dong receiving the next largest (more than 39,000). See Grant Evans, "Internal Colonialism in the Central Highlands of Vietnam," *Sojourn*, volume 7, Number 2, Singapore, 1992.
[75] Neil Jamieson, "Ethnic Minorities in Vietnam: A Country Profile," Winrock International, Hanoi, Vietnam, March 1996, p. 9.
[76] Huynh Thi Xuan, Vice-Chairwoman, Dak Lak Provincial People's Committee, "The Impact of Rural-Rural Migration to Resettlement Areas in Dak Lak Province," in *International Seminar on Internal Migration: Implications for Migration Policy in Vietnam*, Population Council, Vietnam, May 1998.

who were considered less "backward," the NEZs created competition over scarce land and natural resources. For the highlanders who were resettled from their ancestral lands to other areas, the resettlement programs often meant the destruction of traditional longhouses and customary agricultural practices.[77] Many highlanders who had not been resettled from their traditional lands were forced by dwindling access to farmland to abandon traditional farming systems.

Inevitably, the massive influx of new settlers resulted in land disputes. These included conflicts between migrants and indigenous residents, between managers of state-owned farms or forests and residents or migrants who have begun using land zoned for state use, and between earlier migrants who have staked out a plot of land and spontaneous migrants who arrived later.[78] Problems were also caused by unauthorized land sales to new migrants, as well as clearing of forest land by migrants for new farm plots.[79]

In fact, the end result of many of the government migration programs was often massive deforestation and clashes over lands traditionally inhabited by the ethnic minorities. Newcomers also encroached upon cattle grazing grounds and areas where ethnic minorities collected non-timber forest products such as bamboo, rattan, and bamboo shoots.

In the late 1990s government policy makers began to make occasional reference to the problems brought about by excessive migration to the Central Highlands. At a national workshop on the issue of internal migration in 1998 in Hanoi, the Vice-Chair of the Dak Lak People's Committee appealed for an end to migration to Dak Lak, bluntly stating that the Central Highlands could not handle any more migrants. Her plea did not fall on deaf ears: participants made various suggestions for ways to halt or decelerate the rate of migration and address the existing impacts, including the titling of ethnic minority lands.[80]

In September 1999, the Chairman of the Nationalities Council of the National Assembly stated that "the influx of unregistered migrants has brought many difficulties to local authorities in terms of the environment, social security, housing management, unemployment, and the overburdening of infrastructure

---

[77] According to Salemink, the use of traditional longhouses, which already began to dissipate under French rule, suffered a severe blow under the assimilationist programs of the South Vietnamese regime as well as the current government's policy of breaking up longhouses. Oscar Salemink, "The King of Fire and Vietnamese Ethnic Policy in the Central Highlands," p. 514.
[78] Dr. Do Van Hoa, "Resettlement in Vietnam: its Effects on Population and Production," *International Seminar on Internal Migration: Implications for Migration Policy in Vietnam*, Population Council, Vietnam, May 1998.
[79] Ibid.
[80] Salemink, "Customary Law, Land Rights and Internal Migration," *Vietnam Social Sciences*, February, 2000.

and urban services."[81] That same month, the Parliamentary Committee on Social Affairs acknowledged that rapid population growth among the minorities, coupled with the migration of several million of the Kinh majority, had resulted in "severe land shortages" in the highlands and the eruption of land disputes between the minorities and the newcomers.[82]

In November 1989 the Politburo partially admitted some of the shortcomings of the New Economic Zones in the highland regions and advocated that development programs operate on the basis of respect for local cultures and the "family economy."[83] No concrete changes were implemented, although the following year the Council of Ministers passed Decree No 72, which called for land to be returned to minority families and newer lowland settlers so that all could benefit from their own production.[84]

With the advent of market reforms in 1986 under *doi moi*—combined with the failure of the cooperatives—state enterprises and collectives were scaled back while the private sector and individual households were given a greater role in rural development. The VCP's Resolution No. 22 of November 1989 confirmed the importance of ethnic minorities for the nation and the development potential and strategic importance of the mountainous areas. It also criticized earlier policies which have failed to help ethnic minorities, such as the establishment of New Economic Zones, state farms, and cooperatives.

The Coffee Connection

Contributing to the unrest in the Central Highlands in 2001 was the fact that many highland farmers, already living below the poverty line, lost almost everything they had with the global plummet of coffee prices after 1999.

Vietnam is the world's largest exporter of robusta coffee. The economic base of the Central Highlands is centered on coffee production, with Dak Lak province alone producing nearly 60 percent of the country's output. During the last six years, low world prices combined with overproduction in Vietnam caused the domestic price to plunge from 40,000 dong (U.S. $3) per kilo in 1995 to 12,000 dong (less than U.S. $1) in February 2000, to as low as 4,250 dong (U.S. $0.27) in January 2002.[85]

---

[81] *Vietnam News*, September 15, 1999; cited in Salemink, "Customary Law, Land Rights and Internal Migration," *Vietnam Social Sciences*, February, 2000.
[82] Ibid.
[83] Salemink, "The King of Fire and Vietnamese Ethnic Policy in the Central Highlands," p. 508.
[84] Ibid.
[85] Oxford Analytica, "Vietnam: Rural Ructions," February 14, 2001. Reuters, "Vietnam Coffee—Trade slow despite good supply at harvest-end," January 15, 2002. Reuters, "Coffee rush returns to haunt protest-hit Vietnam," February 9, 2001.

Population Explosion: The Impact of Migration

As much as 80 percent of the population in the Central Highlands, both ethnic Vietnamese and highlanders, are thought to work in the coffee business, which can range from tending a small half-hectare plot to operating a state plantation.[86] Hardest hit by the coffee crisis were ethnic minority farmers, who had virtually no risk margin when they increasingly turned to farming coffee as a cash crop over the last decade on small plots of land, as an alternative to swidden agriculture, which requires more land. With the downturn in coffee prices, many of these smaller-holding minority coffee farmers were forced to sell their harvest at a loss or switch to other crops.

One private coffee trader in Dak Lak told Reuters in February 2001 that the plunge in coffee prices had exacerbated ethnic tensions in the region: once many highlanders realized that they had lost everything they had, their resentment toward larger growers—who are primarily ethnic Vietnamese migrants—increased, as did their requests to the government to return land to them that they had previously farmed before taking up coffee or being relocated by government programs. "They have been asking the authorities to return their land as their life has been miserable in areas they have been moved to," the trader told Reuters.[87]

The coffee yield for 2001-2002 was expected to be 30 percent lower than the previous harvest, as farmers held back their harvest as a speculative measure or switched to other crops.[88] Eleventh-hour efforts were made to bridge the gap between global supply and demand. In August 2001, plans were announced for key coffee growers in Dak Lak and Lam Dong to cut a total of 110,000 hectares of coffee trees in order to plant cocoa, cotton, or maize. Nationwide, the area under coffee cultivation is projected to drop by 250,000 hectares between 2000 and 2005.[89] While this type of large-scale adjustments may improve Vietnam's overall coffee market in the long term, many ethnic minority farmers need a more immediate solution to the economic blow they suffered by the downturn in coffee prices: how are they to make a living on extremely small plots of land?

Soaring Population: The Example of Dak Lak

The numbers of Vietnamese started getting bigger in 1990. During the last year [2000] they came day by day, month by month. There could be 100 new arrivals in a month, 500 in a month. We can't say how many have come to our area since 1979—perhaps 10,000

---

[86] Reuters, "Coffee rush returns to haunt protest-hit Vietnam," February 9, 2001.
[87] Ibid.
[88] Luu Phan, "Coffee output forecast to fall by 30%," The Saigon Times Daily, January 17, 2002.
[89] Reuters, "Vietnam coffee—trade slow despite good supply at harvest-end," January 15, 2002.

people. They come with their families, borrow money from the government, and try to buy some land from the minorities. They control the village committee. There's only one Ede on the committee now.
—*Ede man from Buon Cuor Knia, Dak Lak, April, 2001*

The province of Dak Lak, where the population has more than quadrupled with the absorption of 623,000 new settlers between 1976 and 1998, is one example of skyrocketing migration.[90] In 1921 the province reportedly had only twenty ethnic Vietnamese residents. By 1943, the province's population of 80,000 included 4,000 Kinh. During the French and American wars in the 1950s and 1960s there was a steady flow of Kinh to the province. By the end of war, this had become a flood; by 1978 Kinh constituted 61 percent of the population of the province.[91]

Between 1976 and 1996, Dak Lak resettled 311,764 planned migrants. Spontaneous migrants compounded the flow, with approximately 350,000 arriving during the same interval.[92] The period of sharpest increase in spontaneous migration was between 1991 and 1995; the numbers subsequently dropped in 1997 as a result of several government decrees and a message from the prime minister warning new migrants they would face serious consequences if they destroyed forest land.

By 1997, the province's population was close to 1.5 million. Indigenous minorities such as the Ede and the Mnong, who had made up 48 percent of Dak Lak's population in 1975, now only comprised 20 percent of the population.[93] Ethnic Kinh comprised about 70 percent, with miscellaneous others, including ethnic minorities from the Northern Highlands, making up the remaining 10 percent.[94] The government's plan for the period through 2010 is for Dak Lak to accept another 260,000 people from other parts of the country.[95]

The arrival of an average of 30,000 new migrants a year, together with economic growth, has necessitated the formation of new districts and administrative groupings. In 1975, Dak Lak had ninety-six administrative units

---

[90] Huynh Thi Xuan, Vice-Chairwoman, Dak Lak Provincial People's Committee, "The Impact of Rural-Rural Migration to Resettlement Areas in Dak Lak Province," in *International Seminar on Internal Migration: Implications for Migration Policy in Vietnam*, Population Council, Vietnam, May 1998.
[91] Jamieson, "Ethnic Minorities in Vietnam: A Country Profile," March 1996, p. 8.
[92] Huynh Thi Xuan, "The Impact of Rural-Rural Migration to Resettlement Areas in Dak Lak Province," May 1998.
[93] Ibid.
[94] Neil Jamieson, "Ethnic Minorities in Vietnam: A Country Profile," March 1996, p. 8.
[95] Huynh Thi Xuan, "The Impact of Rural-Rural Migration to Resettlement Areas in Dak Lak Province," May 1998.

(communes or wards) in seven districts and one city. By 1997 the province had 192 administrative units (towns, communes, wards) in eighteen districts. Each year the province needs at least 1,000 new classrooms and thousands of teachers.[96] Medical facilities and social services are stretched to the limit. While government authorities credit the arrival of the new migrants with helping to break up the remnants of FULRO in the early 1990s, provincial authorities also note that spontaneous migration has caused its own law and order problems because close to one-quarter of the new migrants are not officially registered with local authorities.[97]

A 1996 survey in Dak Lak found that planned and spontaneous migrants occupied an average of 1.26 hectares of land per household. At that rate, provincial authorities said, the new migrants could have destroyed as much as 100,000 hectares of forest for agricultural clearing during the prior twenty years.[98] Land conflicts were inevitable, particularly since most migrants to the province have settled in upland rural areas where the indigenous ethnic minorities have traditionally lived.[99] Jamieson described the impact of migration on Dak Lak:

> The towns, settlements along major roads, and much of the best land are dominated by Kinh. As Kinh flowed into the province, the Ede were even further marginalized. In combination, sixty-four state Farms and forty-two state Forest Enterprises controlled 86 percent of the land in Dak Lak, including virtually all of the high quality land, but encompassed only 20 percent of the population. The remaining 80 percent of the population, including most of the ethnic minority population, had to eke out a living on less than 14 percent of the land.[100]

---

[96] Ibid.
[97] Ibid.
[98] Ibid.
[99] Ibid.
[100] Neil Jamieson, "Ethnic Minorities in Vietnam: A Country Profile," Winrock, International, Hanoi, Vietnam, March 1996, p. 8.

VI. THE 1990s: ESCALATION IN LAND CONFLICTS

The authorities confiscate our swidden fields or rice paddies and say it's the property of the government. Just when our fields are ready for harvest, they take the land, plowing it over during the night to make coffee or rubber plantations. Sometimes they even want to demand money from us after they've taken our land and plowed it over. All we can do is cry. The Montagnards want to fight back.
—Jarai man from Gia Lai, March 2001

As land in the Central Highlands increasingly became occupied by immigrants and agribusiness, the question of land use rights became one of the most pressing problems facing the indigenous highlanders. Most Montagnards say the land issue emerged around 1975-1977, worsened in the mid-1980s, and then hit crisis levels during the second half of the 1990s.

A 1957 report by the Agricultural Division of the U.S. Operations Mission was a harbinger of conflicts to come. It noted that "the Montagnard tribes by tradition have certain rights to the land…it is our understanding that such rights have never been formally defined and recorded." The result could be disastrous if not promptly dealt with, the report said, offering several recommendations, including allocation of ownership rights, opening newly-cultivated lands to highlanders as well as ethnic Vietnamese "in a manner suitable to their customs," and indigenous language instruction in permanent farming techniques.[101] The report was virtually ignored by government officials from the Republic of Vietnam as well as most American advisors in Vietnam at the time.

Since 1975 all land was deemed to officially belong to the state. Agriculture was organized into cooperatives, and forests and plantations were taken over by state enterprises.[102] It took at least two years before government land experts from Hanoi were able to take that message to the far flung regions of the country. State cooperatives and enterprises were more fully established in the highlands in the early 1980s.

With the implementation of reforms under *doi moi* in the late 1980s, the cooperatives' role in managing and controlling land began to ebb. Legislation formalizing the movement to "decollectivize" land ownership was passed, such as Instruction No. 10 of 1988, which provided for allocation of land to households and enabled individual people to lease or buy part of the

---

[101] "Policy Regarding Land Development Projects," mimeographed, U.S. Operations Mission, Saigon, January 1957; cited in Hickey, *Free in the Forest,* 1982. p. 36
[102] UNHCR Centre for Documentation and Research, "Vietnam: Indigenous Minority Groups in the Central Highlands," Writenet Paper No. 05/2001, January 2002.

cooperative's land. Within five years the cooperatives did not really exist except in name; the reality was that some form of private ownership was possible, particularly for those who had connections and could pay for it.

Lack of Land Security

According to the 1993 Land Law, while all land still belongs to the state, individuals can acquire right to use and occupy land and they are allowed to buy, sell, inherit, and lease land use rights. Farm land can be leased for twenty years, with an automatic renewal of the lease if the land user has abided by the land law.[103] However the legal framework for land usage rights and transactions is extremely weak and guarantees little security for land users, even if they hold official land use certificates.

Indigenous minority land remains particularly vulnerable not only because official policy discourages rotational agriculture, but because the land law only covers so-called "permanent agriculture" and not swidden plots left fallow.[104] Plots of land customarily used by highlanders and left fallow to restore fertility are difficult to title and instead are often distributed to new settlers.

In addition, the law does not accommodate the customary communal ownership of land by many highlanders, many of whom are not accustomed to the idea of applying for title to individual plots of land.[105] The land law is weighted toward privatized, individual claims rather than recognition of communal resource management traditionally used by the indigenous minorities.[106]

Indeed, this may have been a factor in many highlanders selling the small plots of land to which they were able to establish claims, or turning those plots themselves into quick-cash crops such as coffee and pepper. Those crops, while providing needed income, are risky endeavors because of the vagaries of the international market in such commodities. In other cases, highlanders who have gained land use certificates to small plots of land may end up selling their land

---

[103] Article 20, 1993 Land Law, published in *A Selection of Fundamental Laws of Vietnam*, The Gioi Publishers, Hanoi, 2001.
[104] UNHCR Centre for Documentation and Research, "Vietnam: Indigenous Minority Groups in the Central Highlands," Writenet Paper No. 05/2001, January 2002.
[105] Sara Colm, "Land Rights: The Challenge for Ratanakiri's Indigenous Communities," *Watershed: People's Forum on Ecology*, Vol. 3, No. 1, Bangkok: Terra, July 1997.
[106] John V. Dennis, PhD, "A Review of National Social Policies, Viet Nam," Poverty Reduction & Environmental Management in Remote Greater Mekong Subregion (GMS) Watersheds Project (Phase I), 2000. See also UNHCR Centre for Documentation and Research, "Vietnam: Indigenous Minority Groups in the Central Highlands," Writenet Paper No. 05/2001, January 2002.

because they lack the capital and labor to work in profitably.[107] Farmers who sell their land may have money in hand for a while, but that can quickly disappear, leaving nothing to support their livelihood or for their progeny to inherit.

The land law tends to recognize only one name per household on land use certificates, which are primarily issued to men, who are usually classified as head of household. This not only denies women land use rights but also stands in stark contrast to traditional customs of many of the highland ethnic groups, in which landowners are always women and land is inherited through the female line.[108]

Land allocation and the issuance of land use certificates began in the mid-1990s. Government statistics show that as many as eight million households have been allocated agricultural land. However, the process of land allocation in highland areas has been slower and more problematic, not only because of lack of technical cadastral expertise but because of difficulties highlanders have in obtaining equitable access to government departments because of their physical isolation from provincial towns, lack of money for fees and bribes, language problems, and discrimination by local authorities.[109]

In the past, many highlanders supported themselves on at least one or two hectares of land per family, on which they practiced swidden agriculture. As lowlanders or ethnic minorities from other parts of Vietnam began to encroach on their land, or as state plantations displaced them, such practices became untenable.[110] An Ede man described the situation:

---

[107] Salemink, "Customary Law, Land Rights and Internal Migration," *Vietnam Social Sciences*, February, 2000.

[108] Rita Gebert, Gender Issues in the MRC—GTZ Sustainable management of Resources in the Lower Mekong River Basin Project, Dak Lak Province, Vietnam," Deutsche Gesellschaft für Technische Zusammenarbeit (GTZ) GmbH and Mekong River Commission Secretariat, Hanoi, 1997. Greg Booth, "RRA Report of Two Communes in the Se San Watershed," Regional Environmental Technical Assistance 5771—Poverty Reduction & Environmental Management in Remote Greater Mekong Subregion Watersheds Project (Phase I), Helsinki, 1999.

[109] Ministry of Agriculture and Rural Development, *Report on Land Situation*, Hanoi, 1998. Cited in Roger Plant, "Indigenous Peoples, Ethnic Minorities and Poverty Reduction (Working Draft)," ADB RETA No. 5953, Manila, October 2001. UNHCR Centre for Documentation and Research, "Vietnam: Indigenous Minority Groups in the Central Highlands," Writenet Paper No. 05/2001, January 2002.

[110] In neighboring Ratanakiri province of Cambodia, where the population density is much lower, indigenous highlanders have an average of one to two hectares per family under active cultivation plus another five or six hectares of fallow fields to plant swidden and cash crops on a rotational basis. Sara Colm, "Land Rights: The Challenge for Ratanakiri's Indigenous Communities," *Watershed: People's Forum on Ecology*, Vol. 3, No. 1, Bangkok: Terra, July 1997.

The 1990s: Escalation in Land Conflicts

My grandfather had more than five hectares of land. The government took the land and gave only part of it to me—less than a hectare. In the past we did shifting agriculture, moving our farm plots around. The fallow land was part of our land. Now we just farm in one place. I have just enough land to feed my family, but nothing left over.[111]

Today, most highlanders eke out a living by farming rice and perhaps a small home garden of coffee and peppers on less than a hectare of land, making ends meet by trading in the market or working as laborers for the growing population of ethnic Vietnamese in the region.[112] Any disruption of the household economy—be it a fine imposed for attending a church service or having a third child, or confiscation of a portion of a rice field—can have disastrous consequences on a family's economic survival.[113]

Over the past ten years, local authorities have acquired vast swathes of agricultural land for commercial development, sometimes forcing farmers to sell or buying from indebted peasants at prices far below market value.[114] Farmers' loss of livelihood, inadequate payment for land, and confiscation of property by local authorities have fueled intense anger by indigenous highlanders, particularly in the last seven to ten years.

State Confiscation of Land

As in many countries, land can be confiscated by the state, if it is deemed necessary for government infrastructure projects such as roads or state agricultural plantations, although advance notification must be given to the user of the land, and proper compensation paid. The 1993 Land Law states that the government can "recover possession" of land if it is needed for purposes of "national defense, security, national or public interest." The law stipulates that prior to state appropriation of the land, the land user shall be notified of the reasons why the land is to be recovered, the timeframe, the plan for transfer, and the methods of compensation.[115]

The U.N. Committee on the Elimination of Racial Discrimination in its General Recommendation on Indigenous Peoples, calls upon states parties to:

---

[111] Human Rights Watch interview with Ede man from Buon Cuor Knia, Dak Lak, April 22, 2001.
[112] Most highlanders interviewed by Human Rights Watch stated that they only had one or two *sao* of land in Vietnam. One *sao* is 360 square meters.
[113] Many highlanders report being forced to pay fines of 600,000 dong (about U.S. $46) when their third child is born, with fines rising for the fourth and fifth, as part of government family planning programs. See section, "Pressure to Limit Family Size," below.
[114] "Cuu Long farmers sell their land to survive," *Vietnam News,* July 2, 1997.
[115] Articles 27 and 28, 1993 Land Law, The Gioi Publishers, Hanoi 2001.

...recognize and protect the rights of indigenous peoples to own, develop, control and use their communal lands, territories and resources and, where they have been deprived of their lands and territories traditionally owned or otherwise inhabited or used without their free and informed consent, to take steps to return those lands and territories. Only when this is for factual reasons not possible, the right to restitution should be substituted by the right to just, fair and prompt compensation. Such compensation should as far as possible take the form of lands and territories. [116]

However, in many cases of state land expropriation or compulsory land sales in the Central Highlands, farmers receive inadequate compensation after local officials have taken their cut. This has sparked protests, such as in Ea H'leo in Dak Lak in August 2000,[117] D hamlet in Buon Ma Thuot City in 1985 and 2000 (see below),[118] and Buon Cuor Knia in Dak Lak in 1993 and again in 1996.[119] Many highlanders fall into debt, and so are obliged to sell their land, often at artificially low prices, for short-term economic gain. As increasing numbers of farmers in the Central Highlands lose their land, they have little choice but to work as tenant farmers or occasional hired labor for more wealthy ethnic Vietnamese landowners, with no labor rights or legal associations to represent their interests.

In interviews and in complaint petitions to government departments obtained by Human Rights Watch, highlanders described how local authorities—often the provincial Education Department—have confiscated their small one hectare coffee fields, ostensibly to construct schools or other government buildings, without paying any compensation.[120]

In some cases, as in Dak Doa district of Gia Lai, streams that ethnic Jarai had used to water their fields were diverted in the early 1980s to irrigate state tea

---

[116] Vietnam has been a party to the International Convention on the Elimination of All Forms of Racial Discrimination (CERD) since 1982. Committee on the Elimination of Racial Discrimination, General Recommendation XXIII on Indigenous Peoples (Fifty-first session, 1997) U.N. Doc. A/52/18, annex V.

[117] Reuters, "Vietnam district stable after ethnic clash," August 17, 2000. Radio Free Asia, "Ethnic minority attack on Vietnamese settlers in Central Highlands," August 15, 2000

[118] See Appendices A and B, pages 174-178, for full translations of Vietnamese language petitions in regard to the land conflict in D Hamlet, whose name has been withheld to protect the security of petitioners.

[119] Human Rights Watch interview with Ede men from Buon Cuor Knia, April 23, 2001.

[120] Human Rights Watch interviews with Jarai men, March and June 2001; Ede families, April, 2001; Mnong and Ede families, July, 2001.

The 1990s: Escalation in Land Conflicts 47

and coffee plantations, hampering the Jarai's farming. "In the dry season they redirect the water so it's difficult for us to grow our crops," said a Jarai man from Dak Doa. "Then right before the rice is ready for harvest, our fields get completely flooded out. This has been happening since 1981." [121]

"A Plea for Help"

In a document obtained by Human Rights Watch from a highland region in Phu Yen province, which borders Gia Lai and Dak Lak, an ethnic minority petitioner described how on July 27, 2000, government bulldozers razed the small plot of land (less than a hectare) he had cleared and farmed for nine years.[122] The explanation given by local officials at the time was that the land was needed for public purposes and that he would be compensated. The petitioner wrote an official complaint but one year later had received no response—or compensation.

In a second complaint dated July 25, 2001, entitled "Plea for Help," the man requested intervention from the provincial bureau of religious affairs. The complaint is signed not only by the man whose land was confiscated but by his hamlet chief, who wrote "Certification of the Chief of [name withheld] Hamlet. All of the foregoing is true."

Describing the history of the case, the petition stated that in April 2001 the man was invited to meet village authorities, who said he would be compensated two million dong (about U.S. $153) for the land that had been razed the previous year. "I refused, because I had spent more than seven million dong razing and clearing the land and planting trees and vegetables, and I was only being offered two million," the man wrote in his complaint.

A month later, on May 30, village and district policemen stopped by the man's house and told him to take down his house and move somewhere else. During the course of that conversation the police reportedly also asked him why he was a Protestant. The next morning, eighty people—including village police, district soldiers and local officials, appeared at the man's house in two vehicles and dozens of motorcycles. The petitioner described what happened:

> [They] were fully equipped with guns and ammunition, a movie camera, and handcuffs. They ordered me to take the house down. [Name of official withheld] began, and then all of the soldiers, police

---

[121] Human Rights Watch interviews with Jarai men from Dak Doa district, Gia Lai on June 26, 2001 and December 9, 2001.
[122] "Plea for Help," (*Don Keu Cuu*) to Bureau of Religious Affairs, Phu Yen Province and Protestant Church of [city name withheld], Phu Yen Province, July 25, 2001. Vietnamese-language document and translation on file at Human Rights Watch.

and local defense force joined in. They forced me to help with the work, telling me that if I didn't, I would go to jail.

Afterwards, government officials accused the man of illegally propagating the Protestant religion and opposing the Vietnamese Communist Party. He was told: "This land belongs to the state, gained by the sacrifice of untold numbers of revolutionaries, and doesn't belong in the slightest to America. Here you are practicing an American religion—why should you expect the state to come up with money for you?"

Lack of Government Action

Many grievances have to do with the fact that local authorities seldom respond to written or oral complaints about land conflicts submitted by ethnic minorities. An ethnic Bahnar described the problem to anthropologist Oscar Salemink:

> The authorities do nothing; they put the Kinh in the right. The Kinh are never punished for their conflicts with the Bahnar, only the Bahnar are punished. We are very often punished, since 1975 every family in our village has been fined at least once.[123]

The 1993 Land Law stipulates that land disputes are to be resolved through conciliation by the provincial, district, or municipal People's Committees. If any party disagrees with the decision of the People's Committees they can appeal to higher government administrative bodies, or to the courts.[124]

Despite the provisions of the law, it appears that many highlanders—if they complain at all to local authorities—rarely succeed in moving beyond the district level People's Committee, which almost never takes action on the complaints. "They dutifully write down a report," said an Ede man from Buon Cuor Knia in Dak Lak. "But the problem continues."[125] A Jarai from Chu Se district in Gia Lai had a similar complaint:

> The authorities take and sell land to ethnic Vietnamese that is already in use by the ethnic minorities. The Vietnamese get the land title documents, and then they evict the highlanders. It is the commune

---

[123] Salemink, "The King of Fire," p. 511.
[124] Articles 28.3, 38, and 38.2.c of the 1993 Land Law, published in *A Selection of Fundamental Laws of Vietnam*, The Gioi Publishers, Hanoi, 2001.
[125] Human Rights Watch interview with Ede men from Buon Don district, Dak Lak, April 22, 2001.

authorities who are selling land. In other cases, ethnic Vietnamese occupy land that Jarai have left fallow to let it become fertile again. When we complain afterwards, we face intimidation from the authorities. At the same time, there is little point in complaining to the authorities because they are heavily involved.[126]

No Response after Five Years: The Conflict in D Village[127]

Official documents obtained by Human Rights Watch from the Central Highlands, including citizen complaint petitions filed with national and local level government departments, reflect the concerns of many highlanders about government inaction over confiscation of village lands.

One longstanding conflict dates back to the mid-1980s in D village, a hamlet of some 113 Ede families (644 people) on the outskirts of Buon Ma Thuot City, which is recorded in two citizen complaint petitions submitted in 1995 and 2000.[128]

The first document, dated April 27, 1995, was sent to the Nationalities Council of the National Assembly and copied to the Ministry of Interior and the district and commune Peoples Committees in Dak Lak province. It described how in 1985 villagers followed a government relocation order and moved their village to a new site. At that time, the petitioners stated, villagers received a pledge from the first secretary of the Communist Party in their commune that their former village lands were still theirs to cultivate.

However beginning in 1986 the government began to appropriate the village land, with much of it going to a state tree nursery operated by the provincial forestry service. The villagers proposed that the forestry service enter into a contract in which villagers could plant trees on the land in order to at least partially support their livelihood, but the forestry service did not agree.

In 1990, the petitioners stated, the forestry service turned over forty hectares of land to an ethnic Vietnamese person from another province, who planted trees and cashews on the land. Additional land was turned over to the state nursery, leaving less and less for the villagers to support their livelihoods. In 1995, the petition stated, the forestry unit employed armed units to further confiscate village land.

---

[126] Human Rights Watch interview with Jarai man, May 18, 2001.
[127] The name of the village has been withheld to protect the security of petitioners.
[128] See Appendices A and B, pages 174-178, for the full translation of the following citizen petitions: "Resolution of the People of D Hamlet, Re: Loss of land needed to make a living to Central Committee on Nationalities of the National Assembly," April 27, 1995. "Supplemented Petition, regarding the wrongful exploitation of land of D hamlet, Buon Ma Thuot City, Dak Lak Province," October 24, 2000.

The villagers of D hamlet stated in their first petition that they did not oppose the government's underlying goals in planting nurseries—but not at the expense of local peoples' livelihoods, and not when confiscated land was subsequently sold to people from other regions to plant cash crops. The 1995 petition stated:

> As far as the nursery goes, we agree with the economic plan of the state as it was set out in the beginning. But [instead] the trees are being cut down and the land has been leased out and rent collected on it. In the meantime we villagers are not allowed to work the land....
>
> Therefore we are sending this petition to you and ask you to investigate the situation and find a resolution that satisfies the hopes of our people. At present, the forestry service is not using the land for its intended purpose but rather has sold the land taken from the local people to people from other regions to plant coffee and sugar cane.[129]

The 1995 petition ends with a plea for government action: "As a result of this situation the people in the hamlet of D are in desperate straits, and before long, deaths are going to result either as a result of starvation or struggles to make a living."

Apparently there was little, if any, response from government officials. A second petition from D village obtained by Human Rights Watch, dated October 24, 2000, noted that "five full years have gone by, and we have received no reply. Our difficult economic situation has become even worse. Indeed, we have gotten to the point where we may die of starvation. We are losing all of our confidence."[130]

Intersection of Land Conflicts and Religious Persecution

Montagnards interviewed by Human Rights Watch said that often those singled out by the government for confiscation of their land were minority Christian leaders, and that such discriminatory action has been going on for years. This is supported by some of the documents obtained by Human Rights Watch, such as a 1993 order from commune police in Dak Lak confiscating the

---

[129] "Resolution of the People of D Hamlet, Re: Loss of land needed to make a living, to: Central Committee on Nationalities of the National Assembly," April 27, 1995. See Appendix A, page 174, for full translation of Vietnamese language document.
[130] "Supplemented Petition, regarding the wrongful exploitation of land of the hamlet of D, Buon Ma Thuot City, Dak Lak Province," October 24, 2000. See Appendix B, page 176, for full translation of Vietnamese language document.

The 1990s: Escalation in Land Conflicts 51

property of a church leader on the grounds that she was illegally propagating religion.[131]

In one case from Dak Mil district of Dak Lak, a Mnong named T[132] told Human Rights Watch that when local authorities bulldozed his small coffee farm in May 2001, he perceived the act as very much linked to his role in his village as church leader:

> It was because I was the leader of the youth religious group that they took my land. They didn't do this to my followers. The authorities had been monitoring me for some time.[133]

For years T had conducted regular church services in his home as well as a weekly youth group on Thursday nights in the village church, which was built by the villagers over the objections of local authorities in 1997.

In May 2001, local authorities announced that they needed T's land to build a school and confiscated his one-hectare farm. The conflict had started about a year earlier, when two Vietnamese commune officials—the same ones who had prepared legal land use documents for T for his land in 1997—came several times to inspect and measure his land.

> When they first came, in 2000, I went to talk with them. They said it was the land of the government already. I told them not to take my land: "I'll struggle with you even if I die, because it's my land." They said, "You can't work it because the district government has decided already. You have no power to oppose us."

T complained verbally and in writing to the district and commune authorities. While both the district and commune responded in writing, they did not solve the problem, he said. Instead, on May 8, 2001, a Vietnamese worker from the commune office arrived with a tractor and began to plow over his land:

> I tried to stop him. I wanted to fight him so he called four others—all Vietnamese, including one Vietnamese policeman. The policeman came to watch because we were fighting. I asked him to help me. He said, "I don't have the ability to help you—I can't help you." The

---

[131] *Bien Ban Tam Giu Do Vat Tai San*, or Receipt for Temporarily Confiscated Goods and Property, [village and commune withheld], Dak Lak, July 9, 2001. Vietnamese language document on file at Human Rights Watch.
[132] The name of the villager has been withheld to protect his security.
[133] Human Rights Watch interview, July 16, 2001.

police and my relatives stopped me from burning the tractor. Everyone in my village saw this happen.

T, who had farmed the one-hectare plot since 1997, said the land was unused when he took it over and cleared it. In 1999, he obtained legal land use rights for land from the district office, paying a one-time fee of 20,000 dong (about U.S.$1.50) for the land certificate and then 40,000 dong a year in tax.[134]

T explained his understanding of the land use certificate he had obtained: "It means that my whole life I will have the land."

After the confiscation of his land, T struggled to support his family and came under increased surveillance and harassment from local officials for his religious activities. He eventually fled to Cambodia, seeking asylum there.

> When they plowed my land I was devastated. The coffee was to support my life. When they plowed it, it was like they killed me. They plowed it all—500 coffee plants, one well, and eighty-seven pepper plants. Afterwards, I had nothing left.

A number of people in his village, including T himself, supported the February 2001 demonstrations, although most were unable to actually participate because of police barricades along the road to Buon Ma Thuot. While T's initial calling appears to have been as a church leader, the confiscation of his land made him a stronger supporter of the land rights movement: "My understanding of the movement is that it's the struggle to demand the land of the ethnic minorities and control it ourselves," he said.

Escalating Tensions over Land

Throughout the Central Highlands, conflicts over land rose sharply in the mid to late 1990s, as described by an Ede woman church leader from Dak Lak:

> Since the Communists came in 1975, they said all land belongs to the state. There's no land that we can own, even if we have the papers. I had title to my soybean farm since 2000, but the authorities took it anyway. They said they had authorization from the province to give

---

[134] The land use document that he acquired in 1999, entitled "*Giay Quyen Su Dung dat dai*" entitles the person to use and occupy a plot of land. According to the land law, these rights are good for twenty years, and then renewable after that if the person has abided by the land law—unless the state deems it necessary to repossess the land for infrastructure purposes, national defense, etc. See articles 20, 27, and 28 of Vietnam's 1993 Land Law.

The 1990s: Escalation in Land Conflicts 53

> my land to the government. Then they gave it to a Vietnamese family who had resettled there.
>
> The conflicts over land have been strongest since the early 1980s, when Vietnamese people started moving to my village. Now there are more Vietnamese than ethnic minorities in my village, or more than 1000. There are daily arguments between the two groups.
>
> Vietnamese people would forcibly occupy land that ethnic minorities had cleared but were not yet occupying. They took over our land, bit by bit. The minorities who had farms told the Vietnamese to go back to their place, in Hanoi. The conflicts occurred daily.[135]

An Ede man said that when conflicts first arise, often it is just a small spat between a couple of highlanders and ethnic Vietnamese people over a patch of land. "The next day many more Vietnamese come—how can we fight with them?" he said. "When we report to the government authorities they don't do anything. Usually these conflicts are between four or five of us and twenty or thirty Vietnamese."[136]

Some highlanders described how even village cemeteries had been confiscated and plowed over for state plantations or private farms, as described by a Mnong from Dak Mil district:

> In my village from 1994-2000 the Vietnamese took our land—even plowing over our cemetery to build their houses. People were very unhappy when they plowed over the cemetery but did not dare oppose them. The felt the district officials would do nothing to help.[137]

A Mnong asylum seeker in Cambodia summarized the land concerns of many of the highlanders:

> We consider ourselves the owners of the land and natural resources. Forestry and agricultural enterprises take over an area by official decree, and then it belongs to the state. The government explains to us that the Forestry Enterprise is supposed to benefit us—but then we see Vietnamese buying off the plots. Suddenly agricultural land that

---

[135] Human Rights Watch Interview with Ede woman from Dak Lak, April 22, 2001.
[136] Human Rights Watch interview with Ede man from Dak Lak, April 22, 2001.
[137] Human Rights Watch interview with Mnong man from Dak Mil district, Dak Lak, July 16, 2001.

used to belong to us belongs to Vietnamese people who have the proper stamps and papers. It happens through the administration. We freely withdraw or are told we can't live there anymore. In the end there are threats: you must move for development.[138]

"One Day We Will be the Ones in Charge"

The story of M,[139] an illiterate Jarai farmer from the Central Highlands who fled to Cambodia in June 2001, exemplifies the type of simmering anger that many highlanders felt.[140]

In April 2001 M's rage exploded, which landed him in prison for two months. He was arrested after he confronted a local Vietnamese businessman who had cheated him out of part of his week's wages as a laborer. After clearing farmland for the businessman for a week, at 15,000 dong (about U.S. $1) a day, M was furious when the man short-changed him:

> I got angry with him, and said "Just wait—one day we'll have our own [Montagnard] country and we will be the ones in charge then."

M, who was not active in the MFI organization and did not attend the February 2001 demonstrations, had heard of the land rights movement from A.S., an MFI organizer who had passed through his district some months before.

> He met me in my farm field. I didn't know him before. I don't know what the movement is called-I only heard "Dega"-the struggle to get our land back. In my village no one but me followed the movement as far as I know. As for Kok Ksor, I had only heard of him, but not so clearly-from A.S. I knew that Kok Ksor was in America and that he would come in the future and help us.

The Vietnamese man who had cheated M went to the police, who then immediately arrested M and took him to jail. He was interrogated and beaten twice, first during his arrest and then during an interrogation about a month later. Both times he told the police that he supported the movement for highlanders "getting their land back."

> The first time they beat me, they hit me on my back and legs with a long stick during interrogation. The reason was because I told them I

---

[138] Human Rights Watch interview with Mnong man from Dak Lak, July 12, 2001.
[139] The name of the villager has been withheld to protect his security.
[140] Human Rights Watch interview with Jarai man from Gia Lai, June 27, 2001.

wanted to protest about the land and wanted to take our land back. There was no blood, only bruises, which disappeared after two or three days. The second beating was the same. They asked me if I was going to stop [demanding land]. I said I will continue. When I said I wanted to struggle against them, they began beating me. I said one word about that and they beat me. I told them I would do whatever I could to oppose them; even if it meant I die, I wasn't afraid. That caused them to hit me even more.

While M was by no means an active MFI member, it appears that his one interaction with a MFI organizer encouraged him to take action to recover land that he saw as having been unfairly taken away by the government:

In the past, during the time of my grandparents, my family's land was larger. We had about three hectares. I had that land during the war, and my grandparents before me. It was enough to support my family, planting rice. Later, after liberation, they plowed it for rubber. From 1977 until now, they started taking my land. They keep squeezing me. In 1977 they took a little bit and then in 1978 they took the rest. It was for a state rubber plantation. Since 1978, I've had less than half a hectare.
When we protested about the land problem, the authorities told us to complain to the province. But we don't know how to write-how can we protest. Many people in my village have the same problem. Their land has been taken away. My current plot of land is not enough to support my family, so I work as a laborer, cutting trees and grass for others.

When the Vietnamese businessman cheated him out of his wages, that was the last straw. M had no prior association with or knowledge of MFI, but his own frustrations over land made him receptive to the MFI organizer's message. His confrontation with the authorities landed him two months in jail before he was able to flee to Cambodia.

VII. REPRESSION OF ETHNIC MINORITY PROTESTANTS

The communists will not let us pray. They say that Christianity is an American and French religion, so we came to live in the jungle. In our land under the communists, people pray at home secretly or in the rice fields. They cannot worship together like we do in the jungle. Here we are free.
—FULRO liaison officer in an interview with the *Phnom Penh Post*, just before surrendering to U.N. forces in Cambodia, 1992

The discontent in the Central Highlands arises not only out of the encroachment on Montagnard traditional lands but official harassment and discrimination against ethnic minorities who are evangelical Christians. For many of the highlanders who participated in the February 2001 protests, both issues—land and religion—are linked to their aspirations for independence.

The combination of mounting frustration and tight government controls on political expression has led to increasing politicization of religion in the Central Highlands. Protestant prayer and worship services provide a space for Montagnard expression not controlled by the authorities.

While article 70 of Vietnam's constitution and the ICCPR call for the right to freedom of religion, Vietnam's overall record on religious rights is poor.[141] The government's 1999 decree on religion, while purporting to guarantee freedom of religion, provides for extensive government regulation of religious organizations. It requires government approval of religious seminaries and appointments of religious leaders and bans religious organizations that conduct activities contrary to "structures authorized by the prime minister."[142] The decree calls for punishment of members of any religious organization that is "used to

---

[141] Article 18 of the International Covenant on Civil and Political Rights (ICCPR), to which Vietnam is a state party, provides:

1. Everyone shall have the right to freedom of thought, conscience and religion. This right shall include freedom to have or to adopt a religion or belief of his choice, and freedom, either individually or in community with others and in public or private, to manifest his religion or belief in worship, observance, practice and teaching.

2. No one shall be subject to coercion which would impair his freedom to have or to adopt a religion or belief of his choice.

3. Freedom to manifest one's religion or beliefs may be subject only to such limitations as are prescribed by law and are necessary to protect public safety, order, health, or morals or the fundamental rights and freedoms of others.

[142] Decree No. 26/1999/ND-CP, "Decree of the Government Concerning Religious Activities" (translation on file at Human Rights Watch), articles 8 and 18-26.

oppose the State of the Socialist Republic of Vietnam," as well as those who participate in undefined "superstitious activities."[143]

The government does not allow the existence of independent associations or nongovernmental organizations, including church groups.[144] In Vietnam, for worship services to be legal, a religion must be formally approved by the VCP and its leaders vetted and approved by government authorities. The VCP-run Vietnamese Fatherland Front officially recognizes only six religious organizations—one each for Buddhists, Roman Catholics, Protestants, Hoa Hao and Cao Dai followers, and Muslims. Until 2001 the only Protestant churches recognized by the government were some fifteen churches in northern Vietnam that fell under the rubric of the northern branch of the Protestant evangelical Church, based in Hanoi.

In April 2001, the Bureau of Religious Affairs recognized the Evangelical Church of Vietnam (ECVN) in the south.[145] One observer described this as a "modest concession after years of repression."[146] While the decision theoretically extends to all the southern provinces of Vietnam, including the Central Highlands, it is doubtful that it will legalize the unregistered Protestant "house churches" in minority areas or any churches deemed to be *Tin Lanh Dega* (Dega Protestants).[147] Religious freedom advocates have expressed concerns that the decision is another effort by the government to bring more Protestants under state control, and perhaps to bar minority Protestants from gathering to worship in house churches.[148]

---

[143] Decree No. 26/1999/ND-CP, articles 5 and 7. Article 5 states: "All activities which threaten freedom of religious belief, all activities using religious belief in order to oppose the State of the Socialist Republic of Vietnam, to prevent the believers from carrying out their civic responsibilities, to sabotage the union of all the people, to go against the healthy culture of our nation, as well as superstitious activities, will be punished in conformity with the law."

[144] See Human Rights Watch, "Vietnam: Repression of Dissent," vol. 12, no. 1 (C), May 2000.

[145] Decision No. 15 QD/TGCP, "Concerning the approval of legal recognition of the Evangelical Church of Vietnam (south)," Government Bureau of Religious Affairs, Hanoi, March 16, 2001 (translation on file at Human Rights Watch).

[146] Vietnam Observer, "Opportunity and Danger: Prospects for Vietnam's Protestants in 2001," March 26, 2001.

[147] Nguyen Minh Quang, "Evangelism," *Religious Problems in Vietnam*, The Gioi Publishers, 2001. Freedom House, Center for Religious Freedom, "Correct Thinking in Vietnam: New Official Vietnam Documents Revealing Policy to Repress Tribal Christians," July 2001.

[148] David Brunnstrom, "Hanoi recognizes southern Protestant church branch," Reuters, April 3, 2001. See also Vietnam Observer, "Analysis of Decision No 15," March 30, 2001. Confidential religious policy guidelines issued by the VCP in 1999 cautioned against linking ethnic minority Protestant churches in the Northern and Central Highlands with ethnic Vietnamese Protestant churches in the lowlands: "Local-level conferences of

While the ECVN historically included Montagnard churches in the Central Highlands as two-thirds of its members, authorities have been very reluctant to extend this recognition to the Montagnard congregations, which have exploded in number, and have all been considered illegal. The February 2001 demonstrations, involving many Christians, made the authorities even more wary. In late 2001, it appeared the authorities were going to grant some kind of recognition to a small number of Montagnard churches, particularly those congregations that were clearly non-political and which had had permanent church buildings in the past. However, as of February 2002, there were only two officially-recognized pastors for a congregation of 100,000 in Gia Lai.[149] In Dak Lak, authorities had recognized only two individual churches as of March 2002, according to church sources there.

In March 1999, the U.N. Special Rapporteur for Religious Intolerance issued a highly critical report on religious freedom in Vietnam, based on his October 1998 visit to the country.[150] The Vietnamese government subsequently repudiated the findings and announced it would no longer allow independent human rights monitors to visit Vietnam. The Vietnamese government reacted equally defensively to testimony in February 2001 by critics alleging religious repression in Vietnam before the U.S. Commission on International Religious Freedom, which later concluded that "the Vietnamese government continues to suppress organized religious activities forcefully and to monitor and control religious communities."[151]

---

the Evangelical Church are to be conducted only in the churches which are in a state of normal and stable operation among the Vietnamese ethnic group in the lowland areas. These conferences cannot be extended to the areas inhabited by minority tribes in Western Highlands, Southern Truong Son Mountains [i.e. Central Highlands] as well as where there are the new converts to the religion...It is not yet our policy to allow evangelical church organizations in tribal and mountainous areas to be related with evangelical denominations in provinces and cities in the lowland plains areas." Steering Committee 184, "Top Secret; Program 184A: Development of Policy on Protestantism in some Provinces and Cities," Hanoi, March 5, 1999. Published by the Center for Religious Liberty of Freedom House in November 2000 under the title *"Directions for Stopping Religion."*

[149] David Brunnstrom, "Pastors say some curbs eased in Vietnam highlands," Reuters, February 18, 2002.
[150] Commission on Human Rights, "Civil and Political Rights, Including the Question of Religious Intolerance; Addendum: Visit to Vietnam," Report submitted by Abdelfattah Amor, December 12, 1998.
[151] U.S. Commission on International Religious Freedom, "Congress Should Demand Religious-Freedom Improvements As it Considers Bilateral Trade Agreement With Vietnam," September 12, 2001.

Christianity in the Highlands

Protestantism is said to be the fastest growing religion in Vietnam, particularly among ethnic minorities in the Northern and Central Highlands. The largest concentration of Protestants in Vietnam is in the latter.[152]

Prior to the arrival of Christianity in the Central Highlands, most Montagnards' metaphysical beliefs centered around animism. Animist Jarai, Mnong, and Ede call the main spirits that they respect *yang*, with individual *yang* responsible respectively for the village, water, mountains, agricultural fields, large trees, rocks, and other natural phenomena. These spirits are believed to hold immense powers and, if properly treated, watch over the village and can ward off disease, poor crop harvests, or other calamities. Many highlanders believe that when the spirits are not treated properly there can be severe consequences to villages and crops as well as to individuals.[153]

Catholicism took root in the highlands with the establishment of the French mission at Kontum in 1850. Protestantism started to become popular in the mid-1950s, when American missionaries affiliated with the Christian and Missionary Alliance (CMA), the Seventh Day Adventists, and the Summer Institute of Linguistics took up residence to conduct missionary activities, linguistic studies, and translate the Bible into Montagnard languages.[154] After the reunification of Vietnam in 1975, the practice of Christianity had initially appeared to wane. Many Christian churches and religious schools were closed and ethnic minority pastors imprisoned. Despite these obstacles, the number of converts steadily rose, in part because of Christian radio programs in minority languages broadcast from the Far Eastern Broadcasting Corporation in the Philippines.

Since 1975, Protestant membership has quadrupled throughout Vietnam, to an estimated 600,000 to 800,000 adherents today. The numbers of Protestants in the Central Highlands is currently estimated at 229,000 to 400,000, with those in

---

[152] Vietnam Observer, "Dimensions of the Protestant Movement in Vietnam and Religious Freedom Restrictions and Abuses They Suffer," October 15, 2001.

[153] For additional information on animist religious practices of indigenous highlanders in Cambodia and Vietnam, see: Gerald Cannon Hickey, *Shattered World: Adaptation and Survival among Vietnam's Highland People's during the Vietnam War*, Philadelphia: University of Pennsylvania Press, 1993. Georges Condominas, *We Have Eaten the Forest: The Story of a Montagnard Village in the Central Highlands of Vietnam*, New York: Kodansga International, 1994. Joanna White, "The Indigenous Highlanders of the Northeast: An Uncertain Future," Center for Advanced Study, 1996. Sara Colm, "Sacred Balance: Conserving the Ancestral Lands of Cambodia's Indigenous Communities," *Indigenous Affairs*, International Working Group on Indigenous Affairs, No. 4, October-December 2000.

[154] According to the website of the Vietnamese Communist Party, www.vcp.org.vn, CMA first based missionaries in Vietnam in 1911 and started its evangelical missions in the Central Highlands in 1932.

Dak Lak province alone increasing from 15,000 in 1975 to as many as 150,000 members today.[155]

Government Statistics: Protestantism in the Central Highlands (1975-2000)

Province	Prior to 1975 (persons)	1999 (persons)	Increase (persons)	Increase rate (%)
Kon Tum	7,940	9,430	1,490	2.7
Dak Lak	11,738	98,938	87,200	742
Gia Lai	8,125	60,250	52,125	641
Lam Dong	25,000	60,000	35,000	140
Total	52,803	228,618	175,815	432

Source: Government Committee for Religious Affairs, VCP Webpage, September 2001.

In the past, Montagnard traditional animist religious practices and rituals were discouraged by the government for being "superstitious" activities, or removed from the village context and commodified: costumed minority dancers were put up on stage to perform for visiting officials from the lowlands or foreign tourists.[156] Ironically, in recent years highlanders who have converted to Christianity have complained about local officials forcing them to reinstall traditional ancestral altars in their homes and take down the sign of the cross. The "goat's blood ceremonies" employed in Dak Lak to secure pledges from highlanders not to continue any political activity consisted of a crude approximation of an animist ceremony (See Case Study XVI, "The Goat's Blood Oath Ceremonies in Ea H'leo," p. 163.)

Christianity among highlanders was largely dormant from the installation of the Communist regime in 1975 until the late 1980s, when reforms were implemented under *doi moi* and the FULRO resistance movement finally fell apart. Many Montagnards turned back towards Protestantism when they abandoned the armed struggle against the Hanoi regime in the early 1990s. "If we didn't have Christianity and the holy spirit with us, we would still use

---

[155] Vietnam Observer, "Opportunity and Danger: Prospects for Vietnam's Protestants in 2001," March 26, 2001.
[156] Salemink refers to this as the "folklorization of culture." Salemink, "The King of Fire and Vietnamese Ethnic Policy in the Central Highlands," p. 498.

violence to oppose the Vietnamese, and we would all be dead," a former FULRO fighter told Human Rights Watch.[157]

Part of the appeal of Christianity during its resurgence was that it served as an underground, alternative outlet for Montagnard political aspirations and an avenue for protest in a context where all other forms of dissent were prohibited. Anthropologist Oscar Salemink noted: "Nowadays, the most conspicuous act of covert resistance is in the field of religion. With their traditional religious practices branded as superstition and outlawed, many Montagnards have turned to Christianity as an act of protest."[158]

The House Church Movement

Government restrictions on churches and organizations not recognized by the state means that despite the large numbers of Christians, there are few churches in the highlands. Most minority Protestants worship quietly in small groups in their homes. However, prior to the February 2001 demonstrations, it was not uncommon for minority church leaders to occasionally organize large religious gatherings in forests or farm fields, attended by as many as 200 people. Police would often break up the ceremonies and impose fines or other penalties on the participants, such as forced labor clearing fields, cutting grass or working on state coffee plantations.

Dedication or construction of buildings for use as churches is not only discouraged, but often actively banned, with reports of local authorities destroying churches. Human Rights Watch has received a number of reports of officials destroying Christian churches in the Central Highlands, such as the 1996 burning of a church in Dak Mil district, Dak Lak;[159] the bulldozing of Tanh My church in Lam Dong province in December 1997;[160] the destruction of a church in December 2000 in Dak N'Drung commune, Dak Song district, Dak Lak;[161] and the burning down of the church in Plei Lao village, Gia Lai in March 2001.[162] (See Case Study XV, "The Church Burning and Killing by Security Forces in Plei Lao," p. 150.)

---

[157] Human Rights Watch interview with Mnong man, July 17, 2001.
[158] Salemink, "The King of Fire," p. 521-522.
[159] Human Rights Watch interview with Mnong people from Dak Mil district, Dak Lak, July 13, 2001.
[160] Commission on Human Rights, "Civil and Political Rights, Including the Question of Religious Intolerance; Addendum: Visit to Vietnam," Report submitted by Abdelfattah Amor, December 12, 1998.
[161] Human Rights Watch interviews with Mnong people from Dak Song district, Dak Lak, October 29, 2001.
[162] In addition, at least four ethnic Mnong and Stieng churches in Binh Phuoc (former Song Be) province, which is south of Dak Lak, were reportedly demolished in 1999. International Christian Concern, Vietnam Country Report, October 2001.

Most ethnic minority Christians in the Central Highlands have joined a nationwide movement to form independent, and thus unregistered evangelical "house churches," with prayer services held in private homes. Larger prayer meetings and church services are often held late at night in people's homes from 2:00 a.m. until dawn— "the sleeping time for police," as Montagnards call it— to lessen the chance that authorities will monitor the gatherings.[163]

"All the pastors have to work in homes," said an Ede woman church leader from Dak Lak. "If you are seen having visitors to your house you have a problem, even if only two or three people have gathered."[164]

The house church movement began to gain popularity in 1989, when several congregations left the Evangelical Church of Vietnam (South) after four popular pastors were expelled or left. It is now estimated that house churches make up one-fourth of Vietnam's evangelical Protestants.[165]

Although officials in some lowland towns and cities have turned a blind eye to some ethnic Vietnamese house churches, most in the Central Highlands are closely monitored. As mentioned above, the government's recognition of the Evangelical Church of the South in February 2001 does not appear to apply to ethnic minority house churches.[166]

Particularly since the emergence of an activist Montagnard movement in early 2000, the practice of *Tin Lanh Dega*, or "Dega Christianity", combines aspirations for independence and the particular type of evangelical Christianity many highlanders practice. Montagnard preachers often use Biblical stories of the lost tribes of Israel and the promised land to illustrate the political struggle for independence, and prayer meetings are often followed by political discussions. While many minority Christians in the Central Highlands would reject the label of "Dega Christians," others use the term with pride. A Jarai village Bible teacher offered this explanation of the *Tin Lanh Dega*:

> We call our church "Dega." The reason we want our own religion is because in the past there were Vietnamese leaders who controlled the church. They would come into our villages and take photographs of poor people in the Central Highlands to raise charity money from abroad. None of that money ever reached us. We started the Dega

---

[163] Human Rights Watch interview with Mnong church leader from Dak Lak, July 16, 2001.
[164] Human Rights Watch Interview with Ede woman church leader from Dak Lak, April 22, 2001.
[165] Vietnam Observer, "Dimensions of the Protestant Movement in Vietnam and Religious Freedom Restrictions and Abuses They Suffer," October 15, 2001.
[166] David Brunnstrom, "Hanoi recognizes southern Protestant church branch," Reuters, April 3, 2001.

religion in 2000. We wanted to make our own church to contact directly with international supporters, not through Vietnam. The authorities charge that we believe in politics and that it's not religion we are doing.[167]

The Ede woman church leader from Dak Lak summed up "Dega Christianity" this way: "We want our own religion. It's our culture—if you kill it, our soul will still live."[168]

Not all Montagnard Protestants support "Dega Christianity," which is seen as mixing religion and politics. Two Montagnard pastors who spoke to a government-sponsored press tour to Pleiku in February 2002 expressed criticism of Protestants who had joined the pro-independence protests a year earlier. "Many of the protesters were very young and had not learned the true message of Protestantism," Montagnard pastor Siu Pek told reporters. "Some people mistakenly associated Protestantism with politics."

Siu Pek and another pastor, Siu Y Kim, said they believed most minority Christians in the Central Highlands belonged to more "orthodox" churches and did not support the idea of an independent state.[169] In an interview with the VCP daily, *Nhan Dan* (The People), Siu Y Kim said: "In Vietnam, there is only one Protestant religion, only one State, the Socialist Republic of Vietnam. There is no so-called 'Dega State' and of course Protestant followers do not recognize the so-called 'Dega Protestant Church.'"[170]

Vo Than Tai, the chief of Dak Lak's bureau of religious affairs, put it more strongly: "Dega Protestantism is not a religion. It is a political organization," he said. "The abuse of religion that encroaches [on] the interest of the nation must be dealt with.[171]

While the numbers of Dega Protestants are difficult to determine, it appears that the religion has grown increasingly popular over the last several years. Both "Dega Christianity" and the Protestant house church movement more broadly provide a way for highlanders themselves to carve out their space in which to develop their own ethnic and religious identity. This is in defiance of the repressive strictures of the VCP, which insists that the national minorities

---

[167] Human Rights Watch interview with a Jarai Bible teacher from Gia Lai, June 28, 2001.
[168] Human Rights Watch interview with Ede woman church leader from Dak Lak, April 22, 2001.
[169] David Brunnstrom, "Pastors say some curbs eased in Vietnam highlands," Reuters, February 18, 2002.
[170] Hong Thanh, "Aspirations for family reunion," *Nhan Dan* (The People), March 5, 2002.
[171] Amy Kazmin, "Tensions rise over Vietnam's highland refugees," Financial Times, March 12, 2002.

and their church assimilate with lowland Kinh under the rubric of the party. Salemink summed this up succinctly:

> What Protestantism does provide…is an organizational and ideological autonomy which allows space for a separate Montagnard (Jarai, Ede) ethnic identity in a context of increasing discipline, surveillance and governmentalization…. By redrawing the boundary between the *Yuan* (Kinh) and themselves *(Dega*, Montagnards) in the one field where the current regime leaves some space in the form of a theoretical freedom of religion, Montagnards reclaim some spiritual autonomy after their political defeat in the construction of a Montagnard homeland with a fixed territory and *statut particulier* [i.e. Bao Dai's 1951 Edict].[172]

Protestant prayer and worship services provide a space for Montagnard expression not controlled by the authorities. In part for this very reason, the government has become increasingly suspicious of Protestants in the region, fueling a vicious cycle. To minority Christians, the fact that the government seeks to monitor and suppress house church services is proof that the government is not serious about respecting rights to freedom of religion. To government officials, the fact that highlanders attending house services sometimes speak about political matters is proof that the religion is a conduit for political subversion.

Party Directives to Suppress Minority Christians

The growth in Protestantism in the highlands, particularly during the last decade, is viewed with intense suspicion by the VCP and seen as a major challenge to the party's authority. The government's actions to suppress expression of independent political and religious ideas has not been subtle: it has banned churches in many villages, barred ministers from preaching, monitored private worship services, required that applicants abandon their faith as a condition of obtaining government jobs, and otherwise trampled on ethnic minority religious freedom.

Confidential government directives issued between 1999 and 2001 show a centrally directed national campaign and special bureaucratic infrastructure to target and suppress Christians in ethnic minority areas in the Northern and Western Highlands.

In 1999, for example, an official VCP body known as *Ban Chi Dao* 184, or the Committee for the Guidance of Correct Thought (hereafter referred to as

---

[172] Salemink, "The King of Fire," p. 523.

Committee 184), released internal religious policy guidelines, which included an analysis of the perceived threat posed by evangelical Protestants in the highlands. After 1975, Committee 184 said, Protestantism was "abused by the evil-minded" in the region when FULRO members exploited religion in an effort to rebuild their rebellious force. Since 1980, when a number of evangelical pastors and followers were released from re-education camps, they resumed their proselytizing activities. Thus evangelical religion continued to grow, especially after renovation (*doi moi*), when Protestantism "literally exploded" in the Central Highlands:

> Our administration proposed powerless psychological tools. The evangelical religion spread from one village to another, people began gathering together openly—creating a problem for the masses.[173]

In response, authorities closed churches and banned religious activities in some areas; fining, detaining or imprisoning those who persisted. Committee 184 documents described its successful effort to contain Protestantism:

> When we pursued and drove away the FULRO and the rebellious groups, evangelical churches in some places had to be closed...After a few years of taking measures against Protestantism—such as suspending religious activities of Protestantism, dismissing the governing board of deacons, re-educating clergies in detention camps, closing churches, dealing forcefully with unauthorized religious activities and agitating for the masses to defect from their own religions—in fact, Protestants activities have been narrowed and prevented from operating in a normal way.[174]

Committee 184's guidelines stated that Protestant religious activities in the south were neither officially banned nor recognized. In some areas a more lenient approach was possible: followers were able to practice their religion unhindered, allowing the importing of Bibles and rebuilding of churches.[175]

The 1999 documents acknowledge the problems arising from the fact that the government lacked a unified policy in regard to Protestantism, leading some

---

[173] Steering Committee 184, "Top Secret; Program 184B: Developing the Economy and Culture, Normalizing Society and Building Political Infrastructure in the Mountainous Regions where the Minority Peoples are Christian Believers," Hanoi, May 3, 1999. Published by the Center for Religious Liberty of Freedom House in November 2000 under the title *"Directions for Stopping Religion."*
[174] Ibid.
[175] Ibid.

local authorities to crack down on the religion because they did not distinguish between the motivation of "true Protestants" and "unauthorized missionary activities as well as the abuse of Protestant religion by the evil-minded persons." That confusion, concluded Committee 184, "makes the believers feel repressed and alienated."[176]

Elements of a propaganda campaign for the Central Highlands were outlined in the VCP's "Program 184B." Re-education classes for pastors, evangelists and lay workers were to be organized to provide information about government policies and the "enemy's" scheme of "peaceful evolution," a term used to refer to anti-government forces abroad conspiring with internal dissidents to overthrow the regime.[177] Plan 184B advised local cadre to categorize religious leaders on the basis of the potential danger to the state in order to take appropriate action:

> Using the re-education classes and careful surveillance, put the religious leaders into appropriate categories, as follows:
> - Those with a bad political history and who currently are in a resistance mode—keep track of them and don't let them go out to propagate religion.
> - Those who take advantage of religion to go after individuals quietly, and practice superstition, etc.—ask them to confine their religious activities to their own home.
> - A number who practice pure, orthodox religion, decide clearly how long, exactly where, and to what extent they may practice religious activities publicly.
>   a. Stop all propagation of religion to new areas that do not have government permission for this…
>   b. Propagandize and explain so that the citizens can chose for themselves.[178]

Program 184B ends with exhortations to "completely stop all the negative manifestations [of religion], and fight against the bad elements which are causing unrest…" Finally, in order to "reduce the damage that comes from abroad and handle in a timely manner any complications that may come up," the army, security police, government departments and mass party organizations are to identify cadres to be on alert, should intervention be needed.[179]

---

[176] Ibid.
[177] Ibid.
[178] Ibid.
[179] Ibid.

Program 184B details the perceived threat to the regime posed by Protestantism and mirrors what many minority Protestant have been told by local authorities in the villages:

> According to the Christians, if you follow America you get help, the Soviet Union has collapsed, socialism is about finished—follow the party and the revolution and you will always be poor. Only by following the Lord can you escape your poverty. The highland peoples need their own land and need to establish their own country and resist the invasion of the Vietnamese, and so on…Because of this, the development of Christianity in the minority areas seems exploitative and takes on the appearance of political opposition and is fraught with the danger of causing social unrest, dividing the peoples, and alienating them far from our regime. The minority peoples, for a whole variety of reasons, have followed the Christian religion and don't understand the poisonous plot of the evil gang…[180]

This and other internal VCP documents show that Vietnam's leadership is aware of minority grievances in the Central Highlands but will allow no organized expression thereof. Given the government's extremely heavy-handed response to the February 2001 demonstrations, it is ironic that the documents indicate a certain awareness by some in the party that too much repression can be counterproductive, attracting people to the forbidden religion:

> …Using methods of fighting the contagion of Christianity in the minority areas (such as using force to make people renounce their religion, fining people, arresting and confining missionaries to prevent their activities) has the opposite effect of making the people even more curious…Actually the numbers grow slowly if we have a relaxed policy, and if we crack down hard, Christianity grows faster.[181]

Pressure on House Churches

Interviews with highlanders and citizen complaint petitions show that the repression of ethnic minority Christians in the Central Highlands has been going on for a long time, particularly since the resurgence of Protestantism after 1992. Catholics have generally been under less pressure in the Central Highlands. After the February 2001 demonstrations, however, ethnic minority Catholics in

---
[180] Ibid.
[181] Ibid.

Kontum were called to a number of meetings in which local authorities warned them not to repeat the mistakes of the "Dega Protestants."[182]

A Jarai from Gia Lai described the atmosphere for minority Protestants: "When we meet, the police watch and walk around and listen to what we say. They try to listen to what we're praying for and see if it's political. They do this all the time, but especially at Christmas."[183]

One Jarai man, who was a Bible teacher for five villages in Ea H'leo district of Dak Lak, described numerous attempts by officials to intimidate him since 1993, when police reportedly fired a gun over his house and detained him at the commune headquarters for a night. Christians in his village needed to constantly change location of the house church, out of fear of arrest. In 1996 he was arrested again, during a prayer service in a house church. Another time he was beaten in the village. Other times he was threatened, sometimes at gunpoint. In December 2000 the police tried to break up a Christmas celebration in his village. "We asked the police why lowland Vietnamese can celebrate Christmas, but not us," he said. "They didn't arrest anyone, so after they left, we continued the ceremony."[184]

An Ede church leader from a hamlet near Buon Ma Thuot town said that after being arrested and imprisoned in a dark cell for a year in 1985 for FULRO activities, she left the armed group and turned towards Christianity. The official harassment continued:

> When I was released from prison I started to preach the gospel. The Communists arrested me and took me to the provincial police station where I was beaten and put on probation. They say that our religion is FULRO and not a real religion, and don't allow us to follow it.[185]

The Ede church leader described how penalties increase with each infraction committed by evangelical pastors. For the first offense police impose fines of 1 million dong (about U.S. $77) and confiscate all documents and Bibles. The second time, they call the pastor to the commune or provincial police station and put the pastor on probation, often accompanied by forced labor cutting grass or clearing fields. After that, a jail sentence is a definite possibility, she said. She herself was put on probation and detained at the commune police station for fifteen days in 1987 and again in 1994, when four

---

[182] Human Rights Watch interview with Jarai and Bahnar residents of Sa Thay district, Kontum, October 16, 2001.
[183] Human Rights Watch interview with Ede man from Dak Lak, April 22, 2001.
[184] Human Rights Watch interview with Jarai man from Ea H'leo, Dak Lak, March 2001.
[185] Human Rights Watch Interview with Ede woman church leader from Dak Lak, April 22, 2001.

truckloads of armed police broke up a Christmas celebration she was leading. "Every Christmas they would come," she said. "We would hide the books and hymnals. They'd ask us why we continued to worship and ask us if we wanted to go back to jail."[186]

Arbitrary Fines and Forced Labor

In addition to fines, many Montagnard Christians have been subjected to forced labor as penalties for organizing or attending religious gatherings or refusing to denounce Christianity. "Many of the known prominent Christians have experienced this in Kontum and Gia Lai," said an aid worker.[187] While the work is relatively mild—having to use a scythe to cut the grass around provincial buildings or clearing scrubland by hand—the number of days can be significant, reducing farmers' time in their fields, and therefore their ability to make a living.

One Jarai man from Gia Lai said that since becoming a Protestant in 1997 he had been called to meet with local authorities more than 100 times in efforts to pressure him to renounce Christianity. Each time that he did not agree, he was forced to work. The man had copies of official citations from the police in his commune showing that he had been forced to work a total of 129 days from mid-1997 until mid-2001, when he fled from Vietnam.[188]

"Each time they asked me if I was still a Protestant, and when I said yes they made me cut the grass around the People's Committee building," he said. "I got used to it over the years. They won't change, and I won't change. It's part of my life."

This particular man's case appeared to be unusual. While others who have converted to Protestantism since 1995 told Human Rights Watch that they have been exposed to forced labor, most had been forced to work much less, with many estimating they had worked eight to ten penalty days a year. The Ede woman church leader, however, described another severe case of forced labor penalties in Dak Lak:

> The police came while we were having a religious meeting. Some of the people ran away. The police asked who the preacher was. I said I was. They gave me an invitation to the subdistrict office for the next

---

[186] Ibid.
[187] Human Rights Watch interview with international aid worker, November 2, 2001.
[188] In 1997 he was summoned by police five times and worked as forced labor for thirty days, in 1998 he was summoned seven times and worked thirty-six days, in 1999 he was summoned seven times and worked thirty days, in 2000 he was summoned four times and worked seventeen days, and in 2001 he was summoned seven times and worked twenty-four days.

day. There were lots of questions. I was forced to work for three days to cut grass and clear the grounds near the police station. The whole congregation came to help.

The police let me stay home for two days but then they called me again. They kept asking me about FULRO and the church. They'd send me home but then the city and provincial police would call me in. Sometimes they'd just hit the table and yell at me. One day they took me to a special place with a flag out front. I thought they'd brought me somewhere to kill me but they didn't. This happened for three years—every two or three days they would call me in. They were watching me the whole time.[189]

---

[189] Human Rights Watch Interview with Ede woman church leader from Dak Lak, April 22, 2001.

VIII. ETHNIC DISCRIMINATION

Human Rights Watch research revealed widespread perceptions among highlanders that Vietnamese government agencies discriminate against them in education, health, and the provision of other social services. Highlanders interviewed by Human Rights Watch claimed they were treated worse than lowland Vietnamese by government officials and ethnic Vietnamese civilians in all aspects of their lives—not only access to land, but education, medical care, government services, and even allocation of trading stalls in the markets. Christians, they asserted, face additional discrimination: they are often not considered for government jobs because their loyalty to the state is questioned, and local officials often impose arbitrary fines and forced labor on them in an effort to pressure them to renounce their religion. Many are asked to renounce their Christian beliefs in order to have their children advance in school.[190]

Some of the claims—such as widespread allegations of forced sterilization of Montagnard women in government family planning programs—are difficult to substantiate. Other complaints are commonly heard elsewhere in Vietnam. The fact that ethnic minority people have to pay in advance for medical care or cover their children's school fees, for example, are the same for ethnic Vietnamese people in other parts of the country.[191] "Their isolation, and mistrust of the government, makes them think many of the policies that make them unhappy apply only to them," said a Western development worker with experience in the Central Highlands.[192]

There is substantial evidence, however, to support some of the highlanders' claims of unequal treatment.[193] At a minimum, the highlanders'

---

[190] Article 26 of the International Covenant on Civil and Political Rights, which Vietnam ratified in 1982, provides: All persons are equal before the law and are entitled without any discrimination to the equal protection of the law. In this respect, the law shall prohibit any discrimination and guarantee to all persons equal and effective protection against discrimination on any ground such as race, color, sex, language, religion, political or other opinion, national or social origin, property, birth or other status.
[191] Since *doi moi*, or the "renovation" policy launched in the late 1980s, the government has stopped full subsidy of social services. This means that citizens throughout Vietnam now have to pay some of the costs of educational and medical services. National policies granting preferential treatment for ethnic minority communities are not always implemented in practice.
[192] Human Rights Watch interview, July 16, 2001.
[193] Lack of sufficient food, medical care, and the prevalence of diseases such as malaria, dysentery, and cholera in the Central Highlands—as well as fees for medical care—may all be factors in the relatively low life expectancy of the indigenous minorities of the Central Highlands and the fact that infant and child mortality there is the highest in the country. UNHCR Centre for Documentation and Research, "Vietnam: Indigenous Minority Groups in the Central Highlands," Writenet Paper No. 05/2001, January 2002.

perceptions of being discriminated against, combined with their massive mistrust of state authorities, is a major issue the government must face in its efforts to address the unrest in the Central Highlands.

Poverty

The annual gross domestic product in Vietnam is approximately U.S. $400,[194] making Vietnam one of the poorest countries in the world. The Central Highlands is considered to be one of the most impoverished regions in Vietnam. While the national economy has grown over the last decade, with the number of poor households decreasing nationwide, 40 percent of the minority population in the Central Highlands continues to live below the poverty line.[195] In a June 2001 report, the United Nations Children's Fund (UNICEF) said that as many as 45 percent of ethnic minority children in the Central Highlands suffer from malnutrition.[196] A 1989 study found that the life expectancy of ethnic Jarai in the Central Highlands was on average fifty-four years, as opposed to sixty-eight years for ethnic Vietnamese.[197]

Most highlanders support themselves by farming, with many households holding less than half a hectare of agricultural land. Much of the farmland is not irrigated and the yield per hectare is low (estimated at less than one ton of rice per hectare). Many families suffer a food shortage for three to five months every

---

[194] UNHCR Centre for Documentation and Research, "Vietnam: Indigenous Minority Groups in the Central Highlands," Writenet Paper No. 05/2001, January 2002.
[195] Some international development organizations define poverty based on the "hunger-poverty line," in which a family is defined as poor if their monthly per capita income is not enough to provide a daily calorie intake of 2,100 calories per person. The Vietnamese government considers households in mountainous areas to be poor if they have less than thirteen kilograms of rice per person per month (which corresponds to about 1,500 calories per person per day). This does not address other necessary expenditures such as education, clothing, transportation, and health care. The World Bank uses the "2,100 calorie plus poverty line," which not only evaluates whether people have enough food or income to avoid starvation but enough income to meet other essential non-food expenses, including education, health care, culture and travel. See Decision N. 59/DOLISA of November 6, 1998, cited in Tran Ngoc Thanh, "A Study of the Rural Poverty in Dak Lak Province—Vietnam; Constraints and Opportunities for Alleviation," Dissertation submitted in partial fulfillment of the requirements for the MSc in Rural Resources and Environmental Policy, Wye College, University of London, 1999. See also: United Nations Development Program, "Fact Sheet on Ethnic Minority Groups," December 2000, http://www.UNDP.org.Vietnam
[196] Reuters, "Vietnam's population growing by a million a year," July 12, 2001.
[197] Study cited in a report by the UNHCR Centre for Documentation and Research, "Vietnam: Indigenous Minority Groups in the Central Highlands," Writenet Paper No. 05/2001, January 2002.

year.[198] While the government has policies and programs directed at alleviating poverty in the Central Highlands, setting ambitious targets from the national and provincial levels, implementation is poor.[199] A national initiative known as Program 135 targets Vietnam's 1,700 lowest-income communes nationwide, particularly minority communities in the highlands.[200] In 1999 the Vietnamese press began to carry reports of corruption within CEMMA's administration of Program 135, particularly in the Northern Highlands, which led to reprimands for CEMMA's director in December 2000 and the dismissal of several provincial officials.[201]

A study conducted in Ea Sol commune of Ea H'leo district of Dak Lak in 1999 found that families' average monthly income ranged between 200,000 to 500,000 dong (U.S. $15-$38) per month, with the first group considered "poor" and the second group considered "better off." That annual income is derived from farming, animal husbandry, collecting forest products, or working as laborers.[202] The ability to grow rice is often critical, as rice is often used as a means of exchange in ethnic minority areas. Ethnic minority people earn 15,000-20,000 dong (about U.S. $1) a day for casual labor working on plantations or clearing fields. The women sometimes sell vegetables in the market, although they are sometimes chased off by ethnic Vietnamese vendors.

"If we have fresh vegetables we want to sell in the market, individual Vietnamese often smash our produce or overturn our baskets and don't let us

---

[198] Tran Ngoc Thanh, "A Study of the Rural Poverty in Dak Lak Province – Vietnam; Constraints and Opportunities for Alleviation," Dissertation submitted in partial fulfillment of the requirements for the MSc in Rural Resources and Environmental Policy, Wye College, University of London, 1999.
[199] According to the official Viet Nam News Agency (VNA), in 2002 Gia Lai province will spend 64 billion dong (or U.S. $5 million) in an effort to reduce its poverty rate from 22 percent to 20 percent during the year through hunger eradication and poverty alleviation programs. These will include 20 billion dong spent on sedentary farming and resettlement programs in NEZs and 30 billion dong for construction of schools, irrigation projects, water and electricity supply facilities, and medical stations. The remainder will be granted as soft loans to poor households to develop agricultural production and traditional handicrafts. "Vietnam's Central Region Aims to Reduce Poverty Rate in 2002," Asia Pulse, January 21, 2002.
[200] UNHCR Centre for Documentation and Research, "Vietnam: Indigenous Minority Groups in the Central Highlands," Writenet Paper No. 05/2001, January 2002.
[201] Vietnamese press sources from 1999-2001 (*Viet Nam News*, *Dai Doan Ket*, *Thanh Nien*, *Lao Dong*, and *Tuoi Tre*), and *The Nation*, February 7, 2001, cited in UNHCR Centre for Documentation and Research, "Vietnam: Indigenous Minority Groups in the Central Highlands," Writenet Paper No. 05/2001, January 2002.
[202] Tuyet Hoa Nie Kdam, Pham Van Hien, Nay Ky Hiep, "An Assessment of Households' Economic Conditions Participating in Pilot Project of FLA in Ea Sol Commune, Ea H'leo District," MRC/GTZ, October 1999.

sell," said an Ede woman from Dak Lak. Even on a good day a woman might make 5,000 to 10,000 dong (less than a U.S. dollar) in the market.

Poverty combined with political vulnerability has made highlanders particularly susceptible to extortion and petty corruption. Highlanders interviewed by Human Rights Watch said that when they complain, authorities have proven unwilling or unable to stop such practices.

The constant levying of fines adds to the financial burden. Highlanders claim that they are often fined for violating the local market law when they bring their vegetables in to sell, or are asked by police to show their residency cards, which many people do not have. One relatively educated and articulate Ede man told Human Rights Watch that it took him two years and 600,000 dong (U.S. $43) in bribes to obtain his residency card, which is required for every Vietnamese citizen by law.[203]

Highlanders interviewed by Human Rights Watch said that often they are stopped by police and fined right before lunchtime. "Are you ready to denounce your religion?" they are asked. If not, it's a 50,000 dong fine—enough for the policeman's lunch. One informant from Lam Dong was constantly fined, to the effect of 1.5 million dong (U.S. $104) a year, equivalent to the cost of keeping three children in elementary school.[204]

Teenage highlanders said they no longer dared to leave their villages after dark because often the police stop them, ask them what they are doing and charge them with violating the law. Their choice is to pay a 50,000 dong (U.S. $3.50) fine the next day at the police station, or 10,000 dong (U.S. $0.69) on the spot. "We have to bow to the policeman as we hand over the money," one Ede youth said.[205]

Such practices can be devastating for Montagnard families, who must be extremely careful to avoid being fined by the police or incurring extra medical or school fees, if they want to make ends meet. Most families can just about survive on the poverty level, said a foreign relief worker—unless there are any mishaps. "That means, however, that often there's only one meal a day," he said. "If there are two or three children who are school age and the family needs to pay school fees, it's very difficult. Either the children don't go to school, or there's less to eat. On top of that, any other fines or fees or forced labor days or travel bans that take a farmer away from his fields or casual labor job can be

---

[203] Human Rights Watch interview with Ede man from Dak Lak, July 16, 2001.
[204] Human Rights Watch interviews with Ede, Koho and Jarai men, July 12-17 2001.
[205] Human Rights Watch interviews with Ede men from Dak Lak, July 17, 2001.

catastrophic. You can see why the loss of a family's rice field—even if it's less than half a hectare—can be devastating."[206]

Education

The ethnic minorities of the Central Highlands have among the highest rates of illiteracy in Vietnam. Illiteracy among the Bahnar and Jarai is estimated at 70 to 72 percent of males and 88 percent of females.[207] The government has sought to address the problem by establishing special ethnic minority boarding schools. Theoretically ethnic minority students are entitled to full or partial exemption from school fees, according to state education policies and the Law on Education.[208] In practice, school fees are imposed.

The set fees to attend school in Vietnam are 300,000 to 500,000 dong (U.S. $23-33) per year per child for elementary school, 1 million dong (U.S. $66) per child per year for lower school, and 1.5 million dong (U.S. $100) per child per year for high school. School supplies such as books, pens and paper are not included, which can add another 50,000 to 100,000 dong per year. With annual incomes often considerably less than U.S. $200 a year, such costs make school attendance prohibitively expensive for many highlanders. As a result, very few Montagnard children attend school past seventh grade. A Montagnard woman explained why so many minority children drop out of school before graduating from twelfth grade:

> When a student gets to eighth or ninth grade, there's always difficulty trying to get to a higher level of education. When you're a member of a different religion, or have a different background, or your father was a member of FULRO, you're not allowed to go to a higher level of education because they don't want you to know anything. If you're in a religion that's not accepted, like Protestantism, it's really difficult. They line the kids up and ask them what religion they are. They'll find a way to drop the kid—either by taxing them more or

---

[206] Other costs include government taxes levied on rice harvests, which can run from 70,000 dong (U.S. $5) for one harvest on a 400 m² soybean field to a flat fee of two million dong (U.S. $154) per harvest for those growing coffee. Human Rights Watch interview with international aid worker based in Vietnam, July 17, 2001, and with an Ede woman from Dak Lak, April 22, 2001.
[207] United Nations Development Program, "Fact Sheet on Ethnic Minority Groups," December 2000, http://www.UNDP.org.Vietnam
[208] Ninth periodic reports of states parties due in 1999, Addendum, Viet Nam, "Reports Submitted by States Parties under Article 9 of the Convention," International Convention on the Elimination of all Forms of Racial Discrimination, CERD/C/357/Add.2, 17 October 2000.

making them pay more money. The families are already very very poor, so the kids have to drop out.[209]

Many schools in the highlands typically close at noon, which means that in order to get a good education, highlanders would need to pay for extra classes provided after hours by school teachers, who take on extra jobs offering tutoring or special classes for extra fees. Tutoring one child individually can cost 20,000 to 25,000 dong (about U.S. $2) per hour or 30,000 to 35,000 per hour (or about U.S. $2.50 per student) for a group of five students. For a child attending seventh grade, those figures suggest that a family could easily spend three to five million dong (U.S. $200-$380) a year to see that the child gets a reasonable education. If a family had three or four school-age children, the costs are prohibitive for all but the wealthiest Montagnard families.

The government is aware of the burden of school costs and has made some efforts to help alleviate them for minority students—particularly since the February unrest—but those efforts have not gone nearly far enough.

Despite provisions in the Vietnamese Constitution for instruction in minority languages (Article 5), the vast majority of primary schools in the Central Highlands conduct their classes in Vietnamese.

Montagnard Christians claim that their children are often discriminated against in school, particularly if it is known that their family supports the independence movement or formerly supported FULRO. One young Ede girl was able to make it to the tenth grade because she spoke good Vietnamese, but she was told she was no longer welcome at school after she attended the February 2001 demonstration in Buon Ma Thuot.[210]

Other people interviewed by Human Rights Watch said that even those who are able to graduate from high school find that government jobs are unavailable to them because of ethnic discrimination as well as suspicions that "Dega Protestants," or families of former FULRO members, would not be loyal to the government.

"Even if we study to grade twelve, we can't work as doctors or government workers because they say we are following a 'U.S. religion' and not real Christianity," an Ede woman told Human Rights Watch.[211]

Human Rights Watch has also received reports of highlanders being pressured to abandon Christianity in order to obtain government jobs. In one document obtained from Ea H'leo district, a Jarai woman who had undergone

---

[209] Interview conducted by Scott Johnson and Tim Johnson for film, "America's Forgotten Allies," Scorpion Productions, 2001.
[210] Human Rights Watch interview with Ede girl from Buon Ma Thuot, June 16, 2001.
[211] Human Rights Watch with Ede woman from Dak Lak, July 14, 2001.

teacher training in Dak Lak was required to sign a pledge that she would not oppose party policies in order to be considered for employment at an elementary school. Nonetheless the local People's Committee decided against approving her hire by the school, stating in an official memorandum: "If she undertakes in writing to abandon Protestantism, then the Commune Committee will permit the school to hire her."[212]

Pressure to Limit Family Size

Highlanders interviewed by Human Rights Watch claimed that government family planning programs were particularly coercive in the highlands, but the evidence is unclear. Vietnam's official family planning policy aims to limit families to no more than two children. The U.S. State Department describes the policy as one that "emphasizes exhortation rather than coercion," in which penalties such as fines or denial of promotions to government employees are rarely imposed.[213]

While "exhortation rather than coercion" may be the rule for most of Vietnam, fines appear to be common for highlanders who have more than two children. Out of twenty Ede and Mnong women interviewed by Human Rights Watch specifically about this issue, those who had had more than two children had either had their most recent births at home and not in the hospital to avoid detection, or were forced to pay 600,000 dong (about U.S. $46) when the third child was born, with fines rising for the fourth and fifth.[214]

A Mnong woman from Dak Mil said: "They tell us not to have too many children. They say the ethnic minorities should only have two. They pressure us to have an operation, or if we have too many children, they don't get medical treatment." Her third child, which she delivered despite pressure not to from local health workers, became ill after being born. She blames the fact that the child is now partially blind and appears to be developmentally disabled to the fact that local health workers refused to give her and the baby any postnatal medical treatment.[215]

"I had my third baby at home because I was afraid the authorities would fine me," another Ede woman told Human Rights Watch. "I had a friend help

---

[212] "Written Guarantee to Peoples' Committee of [name withheld] village, Ea H'leo, Dak Lak, signed and stamped by the commune People's Committee. Date illegible. Vietnamese-language document and translation on file at Human Rights Watch.
[213] "Vietnam," Country Reports on Human Rights Practices, 2000, released by the Bureau of Democracy, Human Rights, and Labor, U.S. Department of State, February 2001.
[214] Human Rights Watch interviews with Ede and Mnong women, July 2001.
[215] Human Rights Watch interview with a Mnong woman, November 1, 2001.

me. She's not a midwife, and we did not have any medicine. I was afraid. There was only God to help me."[216]

Distrust of authorities is so pronounced that many highlanders are convinced that government family planning programs are designed to reduce the numbers of highlanders so that ethnic Vietnamese have more land to occupy. A petition submitted to provincial authorities by villagers from a hamlet in Dak Lak in December 2000 included the following complaint in regard to birth control programs:

> Child birth issues: The Hanoi government has used false propaganda in talking about birth control with the Dega. They strongly encouraged our people to participate in birth control plans so that they can destroy the life of the baby and also to exterminate the whole Dega population. By doing this, they hope that they can have more land to occupy. As a result, those who participated in birth control program have suffered too much pain and dizziness. Their bodies no longer functioned normally as they used to function, and the government did not pay any attention at all to their health.[217]

Many highlanders in the refugee camps in Cambodia, as well as Montagnard advocacy groups in the United States, have alleged that the government engages in forced sterilization.[218] Human Rights Watch, which is unable to conduct investigations in Vietnam, has no evidence to support that allegation.[219]

Out of dozens of highlanders interviewed by Human Rights Watch, none had been sterilized against their will; most said they were fined, pressured to join family planning programs, or warned that they would not be eligible for family medical care if they had more than two children.

A woman from a hamlet near Buon Ma Thuot said that when her younger sister became pregnant in December 2000, the doctors pressured her to have an

---

[216] Human Rights Watch interview with group of Ede women, July 14, 2001.
[217] "A report of the cruel action against the tribal people in the Highlands," Citizens' petition from [village name withheld], written in December 2000. The Ede-language document, obtained by Human Rights Watch in July 2001, is on file at Human Rights Watch.
[218] See "Vietnam Ambassador Admits Sterilizations of Montagnard Hill Tribes," Montagnard Foundation, Inc. Media Release, August 2001.
[219] The overall focus of Human Rights Watch research was not specifically on the family planning issue, but on human rights conditions in the Central Highlands more generally.

Ethnic Discrimination

abortion. She did not agree. "When the child was born, the doctor did not give it proper care. They wanted her to do an operation, but she refused."[220]

"When we refuse to have the [sterilization] operation, the medical workers say if we get sick later, they won't treat us in the hospital," said an Ede woman from Buon Dha Prong in Dak Lak. "They call us hard headed troublemakers."

Another woman was fined when she went to the hospital to deliver her third baby. "They wanted to operate on me so I couldn't have more children, but I didn't agree," she said.[221]

Western observers with long experience in Vietnam said they find it highly unlikely that any forced sterilization programs are going on in Vietnam, and especially not any that are targeted specifically at the Central Highlands. "Since the 1980s there's been mass birth control programs throughout Vietnam, and even forced abortion and forced birth control programs, but not forced sterilization," said one Hanoi-based diplomat. "Vietnam isn't sophisticated enough to enact a sterilization program—plus it lacks the facilities."[222] However, the Vietnamese government's refusal to allow independent investigations by human rights organizations or the U.N. makes assessment of any allegations difficult.

The government has, however, set national sterilization target figures as part of its family planning program that may account for the pressure, although Human Rights Watch has no data to suggest the campaign is being directed more against minority women than against ethnic Vietnamese. As part of the program, the government has hired "birth control promoters," who receive commissions (about U.S. $3 a piece) for each individual they recruit to the program. In addition, village volunteers, officially called "collaborators," monitor married couples to ensure they do not have more than two children.[223]

In Vietnam, voluntary national sterilization programs such as tubal ligation procedures and the use of a controversial drug called quinacrine, have been employed since at least 1993.[224] Between 1993 and 1999 Vietnam accelerated

---

[220] Human Rights Watch interviews with Ede and Mnong women, July 14, 2001.
[221] Ibid.
[222] Human Rights Watch telephone interviews with a Hanoi-based western diplomat and a western relief worker, both with long experience in Vietnam, May and July, 2001.
[223] Doctors who perform sterilization procedures also receive commissions (about eight cents per person), while women throughout Vietnam who agree to tubal ligations receive between U.S. $7 and $20 and men receive U.S. $28 for a vasectomy. See Mark McDonald, "Capping Vietnam's Baby Boom: A government drive takes family planning's gospel to a fast-growing nation," *San Jose Mercury News*, February 11, 1999. See also Margot Cohen, "Trauma Ward," *Far Eastern Economic Review*, June 29, 2000.
[224] Quinicrine, which was banned in India in 1998, is inserted in pellet form into the uterus, where it causes sterilization through a chemical scarring of the fallopian tubes. In addition to Vietnam, it has been used in Pakistan, Bangladesh, Morocco, and Chile. See

the use of sterilization, increasing the numbers of women who had tubal ligations to approximately 750,000 within that time period. In addition, an estimated 30,000 to 50,000 women were sterilized through the use of quinacrine.[225] The use of quinacrine was discontinued from the national program, in part because of bad side effects in 1990.[226] The national program now relies more on the use of condoms and contraceptive pills, as well as intrauterine devices (IUDs).

Having more than two children can lead to other forms of harassment. An Ede man who was summoned to district police headquarters in Dak Lak after participating in the February 2001 demonstrations said that part of his interrogation revolved around the size of his family:

> They called me to the district in July. At that time they asked me how many children I had. I said four. They asked "Why so many?" I answered that the Bible doesn't forbid us from having many. The policeman said if I have so many children it makes it difficult for me to make a living and difficult for my wife. "The reason you have difficulties in your life is your own fault [not the government's]," he

---

Alix Freedman, "Two Americans Export Chemical Sterilization to the Third World," Wall Street Journal, June 18, 1998; Express News Service (New Delhi), "Gov't Bans Quinacrine," August 17, 1998; Marge Bere, "The Quinacrine Controversy One Year On," Reproductive Health Matters, No. 4, November 1994.

[225] Alix Freedman, "Two Americans Export Chemical Sterilization to the Third World," Wall Street Journal, June 18, 1998.

[226] Tran Tien Duc, a director of the National Committee for Population Control and Family Planning, told a reporter in 1999: "Some studies now show there were bad side effects. I think it was a mistake to use it on such a large scale." Mark McDonald, "Capping Vietnam's Baby Boom: A government drive takes family planning's gospel to a fast-growing nation," *San Jose Mercury News*, February 11, 1999.

said. "That's the reason you have organized and joined the demonstrations."[227]

---

[227] Human Rights Watch interview with Jarai man from Ea H'leo district, Dak Lak, October 30, 2001.

IX. THE MOVEMENT FOR LAND RIGHTS AND RELIGIOUS FREEDOM

The main reason we demonstrated was to demand the land of the Jarai that the Vietnamese had occupied. We had asked peacefully for our land back for a long time. The pressure was increasing. We could not live in one group [with the Vietnamese]. There was increasing repression from the Vietnamese so we decided to demonstrate.
—Jarai man from Dao Doa district, Gia Lai, March 2001.

The February 2001 protests—involving thousands of people from dozens of villages in three provinces marching for miles to the provincial towns—were not spontaneous outbursts of peasant dissatisfaction. They appear to have been planned long in advance by a network of organizers who built popular support for a peaceful movement to demand minority lands back from Vietnamese control. The government's security forces apparently became aware of the movement as much as six months before the protests, when they began to call in suspected members for questioning.

The Run-up to the Protests

By the late 1990s, the Central Highlands region was a powder keg ready to explode. Longstanding Montagnard grievances over land and unmet political aspirations dating back to the first and second Indochina wars were fueled by increasing repression of Protestant churches and confiscation and encroachment on Montagnard lands by new settlers. Tensions increased in January 2001 with reports that as many as 100,000 more people, mostly ethnic minorities from the North, could be resettled in Gia Lai and Dak Lak to make way for the Son La hydropower project. Endemic poverty in the region was worsened by the plummet in the price of coffee, which had made up much of the economic base of the highlands.

In early 2000, members of the Montagnard Foundation, Inc. (MFI), an indigenous rights organization based in the U.S. state of South Carolina led by Jarai-American Kok Ksor, began to recruit supporters in the Central Highlands to spread the word about a movement to gain independence. They found a receptive audience in many parts of the highlands.

Former FULRO members who had resettled as refugees in the U.S. in the 1980s and 1990s returned to their home villages as tourists, quietly spreading the word about MFI and Kok Ksor.[228] Other MFI members in the U.S. contacted

---

[228] Kok Ksor was born in 1944 in Bon Broai village in the present-day province of Gia Lai, Vietnam. According to a self-published biographical statement, Kok Ksor joined the

The Movement for Land Rights and Religious Freedom 83

a growing network in the highlands through telephone calls, faxes, and smuggled letters and tape cassettes.

"I'd known Kok Ksor since 1978, but he was in the U.S. and I was in the forest," said one former FULRO member who was recruited in Ia Grai district of Gia Lai in early 2000. "We had renewed relations with him since 2000."[229]

Starting in the Pleiku area with a meeting in March 2000, a local network was set up, which then extended to Chu Se and Cheo Reo, and on to Ea H'leo in northern Dak Lak. Further south, organizers living in hamlets near Buon Ma Thuot began to spread the word to outlying districts such as Ban Don, Dak Mil and Ea Sup, and further south to Lam Dong province. Meanwhile the Pleiku activists began to quietly recruit supporters in neighboring Kontum, to the north.

In Chu Se district, Gia Lai, villagers said they became aware about the movement for independence—or as they put it, "the struggle to get our lands back" —in early 2000 when local organizers and church leaders began to talk about it.

"I heard about it in church," said one villager from Chu Se district. "Ama X told us we have a new leader, named Kok Ksor, the leader of us all. "According to Ama X, we would ask for approval to ask for our land back. Many people in the village supported that idea."[230]

By mid-2000, meetings had been held in dozens of villages, and an informal network had been established for communication—both within the highlands and with supporters abroad. In some areas leaders were appointed and loose-knit district, commune and village organizations established. Organizers began to go village by village to disseminate information about the movement, which consisted of three main points: 1) Kok Ksor was the Dega president and had supposedly received international support to lead the new country; 2) the Montagnards living in "Dega land" should ask that their country,

---

Bajaraka movement in 1958 and FULRO in 1964, when he went to Mondolkiri with Y Bham Enuol. In addition to serving as FULRO representative for the Pleiku—Cheo Reo area, Ksor served with U.S. military units of the Fourth Infantry Division in Pleiku and the Fifth Special Forces group. In 1974, according to Ksor, he was appointed by Y Bham Enuol as his chief of staff. Between 1971 and 1974 Ksor was sent on three occasions by Cambodian Prime Minister Lon Nol to U.S. Intelligence Officers School in Okinawa and to Transportation Officer Training in the United States. Ksor was in the United States when the Khmer Rouge took over Cambodia and executed Y Bham Enuol and other FULRO leaders in Phnom Penh. A naturalized U.S. citizen, he now lives in Spartanburg, South Carolina. Since 1993 Ksor has advocated on behalf of Montagnard people at various international gatherings, including the U.N. Workshop for Indigenous People in Geneva and the Second Summit Meeting for Indigenous Peoples in Oaxtepec, Mexico. See: Kok Ksor, "Narrative Biography of Ksor Kok," July 19, 1993.
[229] Human Rights Watch interview with Jarai man from Gia Lai, March 2001.
[230] Ama "X"'s name has been changed to protect his security. Human Rights Watch interview with a Jarai man from Chu Se district, Gia Lai, June 27, 2001.

currently under the "oppressive yoke of the Vietnamese," be returned to them; and 3) the struggle would be peaceful and eschew violence, which would diminish respect for the cause.[231]

In some areas organizers distributed copies of Ede-language documents on Montagnard history, the U.N.'s Universal Declaration of Human Rights, and audio cassette recordings of Kok Ksor.[232]

In August 2000, in what may have been an unplanned, impromptu clash, several government officials and policemen were reportedly injured during a confrontation over land between Ede and Vietnamese migrants in Ea H'leo district of Dak Lak. That conflict, which appears to have been small and short lived, received little press coverage and did not spread beyond Ea H'leo.[233] At about the same time, movement organizers commenced activities in Ea H'leo.

Contacts were made with supportive church leaders in Lam Dong province in August 2000 as well.[234] In September and October, organizers from Chu Se district of Gia Lai began contacting villages in neighboring Cheo Reo district, further to the east.[235] Plans were soon underway to conduct a peaceful mass demonstration, with target dates set for September or December 2000.

Government Surveillance

Months before the February 2001 protests it appears that Vietnamese government authorities had been able to obtain intelligence about the movement, most likely through intercepted faxes and telephone calls, as well as possible infiltration of the group. Beginning in August 2000, local police began to summon dozens of the suspected members to police stations for interrogation. In early October, more than twenty-seven MFI members from many districts in Gia Lai were summoned for questioning by police in Pleiku.[236]

One member from Gia Lai, a former FULRO member, said he was called in thirty times by police during 2000 and early 2001. Each time he was detained for two or three hours, or a half a day. "The high-ranking police officer would interrogate me, ask me what we were doing. They didn't beat me but they threatened to kill me," he said.[237]

---

[231] Handwritten Vietnamese-language document outlining the activities of MFI in Gia Lai, dated March 12, 2001. Document and translation on file at Human Rights Watch.
[232] Vietnamese-language handwritten document outlining the activities of MFI in Ea H'leo, dated March 12, 2001. Document and translation on file at Human Rights Watch.
[233] Reuters, "Vietnam district stable after ethnic clash," August 17, 2000. Radio Free Asia, "Ethnic minority attack on Vietnamese settlers in Central Highlands," August 15, 2000.
[234] Human Rights Watch interview with Montagnard from Lam Dong, October 30, 2001.
[235] Human Rights Watch interview with Jarai man from Cheo Reo, Gia Lai, March 2001.
[236] Human Rights Watch interview with Jarai man from Gia Lai, March 2001.
[237] Human Rights Watch interview with Jarai man from Gia Lai, March 2001.

The Movement for Land Rights and Religious Freedom 85

A supporter in Kontum told Human Rights Watch that he was issued a written warrant by the police in August 2000. He was summoned again on January 31, 2001, right before the protests in Pleiku and Buon Ma Thuot, and again in late February. The police citations he received referred to both his belief in Christianity and his political work.[238]

In Dak Lak, police called organizers from several districts for questioning numerous times, as described by a Montagnard from Dak Lak:

> The government was following me. They started summoning me to the province in December [2000], when I was called four times, and then twice in January. Each time they would ask me why I was an opponent of the government. I told them straight that we wanted our own country. I was honest. They said if you do this, it's not real, it's a trick [of Kok Ksor]. I responded that it was not a trick—we were all standing up to oppose the Vietnamese government in order to have our own government for the ethnic minorities. The police were angry. They threatened and intimidated me but didn't beat me.[239]

The police surveillance caused the organizers to postpone plans for a late-2000 demonstration for the time being.

At the end of the year, monitoring of suspected organizers increased. On December 16, 2000, three people—an Ede, a Koho from Lam Dong, and a Hmong who was visiting from the north—were arrested in another organizer's home in Dak Lak. An eyewitness told Human Rights Watch that at 12:00 a.m. forty provincial police in two large army trucks arrested the three men, who were kept at the district for one night, where they were beaten and kicked during interrogation. They were then sent to the provincial police station for five days and nights before being released.[240]

On December 19, 2000, police summoned ten people in Lam Dong province for interrogation. They were released that night but police were subsequently posted in the home of at least one of the leaders, who was required to obtain written permission in order to leave his village. "From December when they arrested me the police were guarding throughout the province and not allowing us to organize," said the man. Shortly afterwards telephone service from Lam Dong to other provinces was terminated.[241]

---

[238] Human Rights Watch interview with Montagnard from Kontum, October 11, 2001.
[239] Human Rights Watch interview with Montagnard from Dak Lak, October 30, 2001.
[240] Human Rights Watch interview, April 22, 2001.
[241] Human Rights Watch interview with Montagnards from Lam Dong, , October 30, 2001.

The January 2001 Crackdown

In early January 2001 Prime Minister Phan Van Khai and VCP Secretary General Le Kha Phieu both made strong statements attacking "hostile forces" who they alleged were attempting to destabilize the country and sabotage the regime by taking advantage of "hot spots" and "complicated issues such as religious and ethnic issues to cause disturbances." They did not give any details.[242]

Afterwards, police increased the surveillance, interrogation and detention of highlanders suspected of supporting the independence movement. On January 8, 2001, a Mnong couple from a hamlet near Buon Ma Thuot, who were key MFI organizers, were arrested. The wife was interrogated and detained for four nights at the district jail, and the husband was held at the provincial police station for five nights.[243] Then, on January 12, 2001, district police in Ea H'leo arrested another local leader, Siu Un, in Blec village. As a result, 300 people demonstrated in Ea H'leo district town two days later. That protest, which did not receive any press coverage at the time, apparently did not involve any violence by the protesters or police, who released Siu Un the same day.[244]

Meanwhile, in Lam Dong the local Montagnard leader who was already under modified house arrest was pressured to renounce his alleged wrongdoings in front of his whole village on January 15:

> I didn't sign the documents that the police wanted me to sign. They were very angry. The police asked me if I wanted to live or die and did I want to go to jail. I didn't agree to any of their demands.[245]

The February 2001 Demonstrations

While much of the impetus for the demonstrations may have come from abroad, it is clear that by early 2001, the pressures that had built up in the Central Highlands—over land, livelihoods, and religious freedom—had become intense. Even without external support and encouragement from outside, the situation had become explosive, with conflicts over religious practices and land occurring in many parts of the highlands on a daily basis.

---

[242] Reuters, "Vietnam party chief warns of subversion attempts," January 4, 2001; Reuters, "Vietnam PM sees threats in religion, rights issues," January 5, 2001.
[243] Human Rights Watch interview with Mnong man from Dak Lak, July 16, 2001.
[244] Human Rights Watch interviews with Jarai men from Ea H'leo, March and June 2001.
[245] Human Rights Watch interview with Montagnard from Lam Dong, October 30, 2001.

The Movement for Land Rights and Religious Freedom 87

February 2: Pleiku

On January 29, 2001 Rahlan Pon and Rahlan Djan, two highlanders from Cu Prong district in Gia Lai were arrested. In an official statement released on February 8, the Vietnamese government said that the two men had violated the law by "instigating some ethnic tribes to use violence against the local governments and national unity."[246]

Word about the arrests quickly spread through Montagnard networks in Gia Lai, where organizers decided to seize the opportunity to launch a public demonstration to call not only for the release of the two men but also for an independent state and greater religious freedom. On January 31, 2001, approximately 500 villagers marched to the district center in Cu Prong to demand the release of the two men, while plans were made to conduct larger demonstrations in Pleiku and Buon Ma Thuot.[247]

The demonstration in Pleiku was planned for February 2. It was clear that the Vietnamese intelligence service was aware of the plans beforehand. On February 1, police surrounded the homes of MFI organizers in Gia Lai, including Bom Jena and Ksor Kroih.[248] That morning troops were deployed to surround many villages near Pleiku and put up roadblocks on the roads leading to the provincial town. At 4:00 p.m. that day telephone lines were cut in Pleiku. Despite these obstacles, a number of activists were able to get word to dozens of villages the night of February 1, urging them to demonstrate in Pleiku the next day.

On Friday, February 2, thousands of highlanders from dozens of villages marched towards the provincial town, where they filled the streets in front of the provincial offices of the VCP and the People's Committee.

Eight hundred people from four communes in Mang Yang and Chu Pah districts gathered before dawn on February 2 to march together to Pleiku, as described by one Jarai eyewitness:

> We left home at 4:00 a.m., walking for twenty kilometers. We got to the provincial [People's Committee] hall in Pleiku at 8:30 a.m. Along the road there were many police, who had put up roadblocks. The city streets were filled with barbed wire barricades and four fire trucks were parked in front of the gate to the provincial compound, prepared

---

[246] Embassy of the Socialist Republic of Vietnam in the United States, "Two Fact Sheets on religious freedom in Vietnam," February 9, 2001. In a press interview in March 2001, Nay Lan, deputy director of the Gia Lai People's Committee, stated that Rahlan Pon and Rahlan Djan had "violated Vietnam's regulations on border areas." Deutsche Presse-Agentur, "Unrest questions unanswered in Vietnam highlands," March 16, 2001.
[247] Human Rights Watch interview with Jarai men from Gia Lai, March 2001.
[248] Human Rights Watch interview with Jarai man from Gia Lai, March 2001.

to use force against the people. The people fought with the police and tried to climb the barricades.

At the second intersection near the provincial hall, many people were wounded. As the people approached, the police used lengths of barbed wire to hit the people, and also hit them with wooden batons and electric prods, causing many to be injured. The fighting happened at the barricades and again near the provincial hall. The police started the fighting and at first the people didn't fight back. We wanted to speak to the provincial governor. Then more people gathered.

By 10:00 or 10:30 a.m. there were thousands of people at the provincial hall, and the police began to beat people. That's when the people fought back. It was essentially a riot. The Vietnamese police ran off; only Jarai police were left to fight with the people. Around 11:00 or 12:00 p.m., the provincial leaders came out to hear the concerns of the people. They met with several of us, with government photographers crowding around to take our pictures. We presented the proposal for the independent state and religious freedom. We asked why they had arrested the two highlanders, and asked for their release.[249]

In the plaza in front of the Pleiku People's Committee office, several highlander leaders spoke over hand-held microphones and bullhorns, outlining the demands for independence and religious freedom. As the crowd swelled, a number of government officials came out of the building to address the crowd. According to Voice of Vietnam radio, the officials explained government policy in regard to land and listed their "achievements in consolidating the national unity bloc and boosting socioeconomic development in not only the province but also the entire Central Highlands regions."[250]

After signing affidavits admitting their wrongdoings, Rahlan Pon and Rahlan Djan were released during the demonstration; as of late February 2002, they were thought to be back in their village.

A businessman in Pleiku described the demonstrations in a telephone interview with Agence France-Presse: "On Friday and again throughout the weekend, lines of protesters stretching as far as the eye could see marched along

---

[249] Human Rights Watch interview with Jarai man from Gia Lai, March 2001.
[250] "Vietnam radio reports 'unrest' in Gia Lai, Dak Lak provinces," Voice of Vietnam radio, Hanoi, in Vietnamese 23:00 gmt 8 Feb 01, BBC Monitoring Asia Pacific - Political, February 9, 2001.

the roads leading into Pleiku...The mood of the demonstration was strikingly peaceful." He added that some of his staff had even asked for time off work to take part.[251]

Highlanders from some districts farther from the provincial town were unable to make it all the way to Pleiku in time for the demonstration. A Jarai from Chu Se district (thirty kilometers from Pleiku), marched with a thousand people from his district. The group turned back midway to Pleiku when they realized the demonstration had dispersed:

> There were police all along the road. They asked why we were there. We said because two people had been arrested and also because of the land [problems]. They tried to stop the people from going to the demonstration but the people didn't listen and continued on. We were halfway to Pleiku when we saw people on bicycles returning from the demonstration. They told us that the demonstration had happened and that the two people had been released and the authorities promised to solve our problem. At 4:00 p.m. we heard the news and turned back.[252]

February 3: Buon Ma Thuot

Security forces were well prepared for the February 3 demonstration in Buon Ma Thuot. On February 2, as protesters were marching on Pleiku, Dak Lak authorities summoned several prominent Protestant pastors in Buon Ma Thuot to "help solve a problem" because of their influence with the population.[253] That night, police officers surrounded the homes of key MFI organizers in a hamlet near Dak Lak, escorting them to the district police station the next morning as a warning for others not to join the protests.[254]

Activists in Ea H'leo district of Dak Lak, which is approximately halfway between Pleiku and Buon Ma Thuot, received word on February 2 about the demonstrations that had taken place that day in Pleiku. At midnight, a group of 200 villagers from Ea H'leo town started off on Highway 14 for Buon Ma Thuot, some forty kilometers away. Some walked, others rode bicycles, motorcycles or motorized carts pulled by farm tractors. A member of that group described the scene to Human Rights Watch:

---

[251] Steve Kirby, "Huge protests as ethnic unrest sweeps Vietnam's central highlands," February 7, 2001.
[252] Human Rights Watch interview with Jarai men from Chu Se, Gia Lai, March 2001.
[253] Vietnam Observer, "Opportunity and Danger: Prospects for Vietnam's Protestants in 2001," March 26, 2001.
[254] Human Rights Watch interview with Ede man from a hamlet near Buon Ma Thuot, July 16, 2001.

> The police cut the cables on the tractor-pulled trailers that many people were riding—otherwise there would have been more people. People got off and walked even without the trailers. When we got to Buon Ho, which is halfway to Buon Ma Thuot, many trailers were cut so people walked. The police hit and scuffled with the people but not seriously. At 9:00 a.m. we got to Buon Ma Thuot. Out of three thousand people [from Ea H'leo], only 500 were able to enter the town. Near the provincial town, in Dak Li commune, the police had erected barricades. The people climbed over them, tore them down, and continued. The police beat one person badly there and kept many from going on.[255]

Another participant, traveling from Buon Kdun, a hamlet four kilometers southwest of Buon Ma Thuot, gave this description:

> The police blocked the road, but we pushed over the barricades. There were six places where there were barricades. The police pointed their guns at us and threw tear gas. We shouted that we want our Dega land back, and we want independence. We were carrying signs. When we entered town they fired water cannons at us. I took a stone and threw it at the water truck. Near the town center they had special police with helmets, plastic shields and electric batons. They threw tear gas. We had documents to give to the authorities, who told us to go home, wait fifteen days, and they would solve the problem.[256]

Despite these impediments, several thousand people, from at least half a dozen districts, were able to make it to the town center of Buon Ma Thuot. A prominent Ede pastor, one of the Montagnard church leaders who had been called in by provincial authorities the night before, spoke to the crowd over a bullhorn, urging the demonstrators to disperse. An eyewitness described the scene:

> At the protest the Vietnamese took Pastor [name withheld] to come up to talk to the demonstrators and tell us to stop. He tried to use the police microphone but we told him to use ours. He told us not to

---

[255] Human Rights Watch interview with Jarai man from Ea H'leo, Gia Lai, March 2001.
[256] Human Rights Watch interview with Ede man from Buon Kdun, Dak Lak, July 13, 2001.

protest and said he had not been arrested. But the people didn't believe him. We trust him but think he was coerced.[257]

As in Pleiku, a group of protesters was able to meet briefly with local officials and hand over documents requesting a solution to highlander land and religion problems and an independent state.[258]

The Vietnamese Embassy in Washington, D.C. acknowledged in a public statement on February 8 that social unrest continued from February 3-6 in Buon Ma Thuot and other parts of Dak Lak:

> Although small, [the incidents] affected security and social order, caused traffic congestion and hindered children going to school. Most of the petitioners were minority people misled about the situation in Pleiku and incited by extremists. Several extremists took the opportunity to destabilize security and social order and attack those who were on duty. They damaged administration offices at hamlet, commune and district levels, causing property losses and destabilizing social order.[259]

Clashes Between Police and Protesters

Some press accounts reported that police clashed with protesters and that not only demonstrators, but also some police officers were injured.[260] Highlanders who attended the protests told Human Rights Watch that their intent was to conduct peaceful demonstrations, although some admitted they fought with police. A protester from a hamlet near Buon Ma Thuot said that people from his village attacked six police cars and some people threw stones:

> Along the road the police tried to stop people from coming by hosing them down with water and beating them with batons. The police fired tear gas and water cannons. The people got angry and fought back. In

---

[257] Human Rights Watch Interview with Ede woman from Dak Lak, April 22, 2001.
[258] Human Rights Watch interview with Ede man from Dak Lak, July 13, 2001.
[259] Embassy of the Socialist Republic of Vietnam in the United States, "Security returns to normal in Central Highlands," February 8, 2001.
[260] An account in the French-language newspaper *Libération*, based on interviews with ethnic Vietnamese in Ratanakiri province, described hundreds of highlanders slipping quietly into Pleiku the night before the February 2 demonstration, "armed with sticks, daggers and shovels." No other accounts by eyewitnesses interviewed by journalists or Human Rights Watch confirmed that highlanders carrying sticks, knives or shovels arrived in Pleiku the night before the demonstrations, although on the day of the protests some did have slingshots. Arnaud Dubus, "La révolte des Montagnards au Viet-nam," *Libération*, April 11, 2001.

the beginning it was the police who were beating. Protesters who came later in the day from Gia Lai and Ea H'leo were fighting.[261]

Film footage on state television in Vietnam showed glimpses of protesters in Buon Ma Thuot using slingshots and featured an interview with one protester who confessed he had destroyed vehicles of the city's security forces. Had the protesters used serious violence or weapons, or caused serious injury to police or officials, the television coverage—carefully produced and edited for national broadcast more than a month later—would likely have shown this.[262]

For the most part the protests in Pleiku and Buon Ma Thuot appear to have been peaceful. A Hanoi-based diplomat with long experience in Vietnam commented that it was surprising that not more people were hurt by being crushed or trampled in the crowd, considering the sheer numbers that gathered in the provincial towns.[263]

At 3:00 p.m. on February 3, three army tanks were sent into Buon Ma Thuot. After receiving pledges from the authorities that their complaints would be addressed, the crowds eventually dispersed.

February 5-6: Ea H'leo

Two days after the demonstrations in Pleiku and Buon Ma Thuot, several smaller protests were held in Ea H'leo district in Dak Lak after a number of local Jarai leaders in Ea H'leo received summonses to report to the police station. On February 5, approximately one thousand people gathered at the district police station and People's Committee headquarters.[264] There are conflicting accounts about this demonstration. Foreign reporters, who were not on the scene but filed wire services reports based on telephone interviews with witnesses, reported clashes between police and demonstrators. According to these accounts, some protesters seized truncheons from the police and waved them in the air; they also reportedly stripped and tied up one of the policemen until security forces regained control.[265]

---

[261] Human Rights Watch interview with Ede man from Buon Ma Thuot, April 22, 2001.
[262] Videotape of Vietnam Television coverage of the demonstrations in Pleiku and Buon Ma Thuot, March 27-28, 2001; on file at Human Rights Watch along with a translation of the transcript.
[263] Human Rights Watch telephone interview with Hanoi-based Western diplomat, May 31, 2001.
[264] Human Rights Watch interview with Ea H'leo resident, March 2001.
[265] Deutsche Presse-Agentur, "Unrest questions unanswered in Vietnam highlands," March 16, 2001. David Thurber, "Vietnamese officials prevent journalists' access to protesters," Associated Press, March 16, 2001.

The official Viet Nam News Agency stated in an account of the events at Ea H'leo that "many provocateurs damaged administrative offices and public property, opposed law enforcement forces, and undermined political and social order in the locality for several days. The provocative acts were organized as part of a scheme of 'peaceful evolution' and subversion by hostile and reactionary forces."[266] State media alleged that two Jarai from Ea H'leo, Nay D'Ruc and Y Phen Ksor "raided local State offices, opposed State employees and destroyed public property."[267]

Jarai present at the protests in Ea H'leo, however, told a different story. They said that on the orders of the deputy chief, police officers beat the demonstrators and ordered ethnic Vietnamese civilians, who carried knives, machetes, and hoes, to also attack the crowd.[268] About thirty demonstrators were injured, they said.

On February 6, approximately 2000 people gathered in Ea Hral commune of Ea H'leo.[269] Jarai informants said that during that demonstration, the police and local Vietnamese "did not dare" beat the protesters. A local official in Ea H'leo told Reuters that protesters attacked the post office on February 6 but that police and military units had restored order there.[270]

February 14: Kontum

Western wire services carried additional reports of demonstrations in Ea Sup district of Dak Lak, Cu Prong district of Gia Lai, and Kontum provincial town during the ten days following the main protests in Gia Lai and Buon Ma Thuot.[271]

Despite the crackdown in Gia Lai and Dak Lak after the demonstrations, MFI organizers were able to conduct a sizable protest in Kontum on February 14. This received little press coverage, other than a brief mention in the state People's Police newspaper, which was picked up by Reuters.[272] Eyewitnesses

---

[266] Viet Nam News Agency, "Seven Sentences for Security Destablisers in Central Highlands Province," September 26, 2001.
[267] Viet Nam News Service (VNS), "Stiff jail terms mandated for saboteurs of public security," September 28, 2001.
[268] Cambodia Office of the High Commissioner for Human Rights, interviews with asylum seekers from Ea H'leo, May 24, 2001. Human Rights Watch interview with Ea H'leo resident, March 2001.
[269] Human Rights Watch interview with Jarai man from Ea H'leo, March 2000.
[270] David Brunnstrom, "Military patrols Vietnam highlands after protests," Reuters, February 8, 2001.
[271] Steve Kirby, Agence France-Presse, "Huge protests as ethnic unrest sweeps Vietnam's Central Highlands, February 7, 2001. David Brunnstrom, "Vietnam coffee belt reported calm after unrest," Reuters February 11, 2001.
[272] David Brunnstrom, "Officials differ over religion in Vietnam unrest," Reuters, March 16, 2001.

told Human Rights Watch that 3,000 to 4,000 people participated in a one-day demonstration in Kontum on February 14, which lasted from 3:00 to 8:00 p.m. There was some scuffling between protesters and police, who used water cannons and electric batons on the crowd.[273]

Coerced or Willing Participants?

While exact numbers of demonstrators at the main protests in Pleiku and Buon Ma Thuot are difficult to determine, it is clear that the total, certainly in Pleiku, was in the thousands. Highlanders who attended the demonstrations said that thousands participated, but they may have been referring not only to the protesters who reached the provincial towns but those who tried to attend but were blocked by police along the way, or who arrived too late. Government officials interviewed by Western wire service reporters put the numbers at 4,000 highlanders in Pleiku and several hundred in Buon Ma Thuot. Shopkeepers and local residents interviewed by telephone shortly after the demonstration estimated the numbers in Pleiku at 4,000 and in Buon Ma Thuot at 2,000.[274]

The Voice of Vietnam radio attributed the protests in Pleiku to "misleading comments and a lack of information concerning the arrest of two locals on 29 January." Other sources, such as the state newspaper *Lao Dong* (Labor), stated that people had been promised the cost of bus tickets as an incentive to attend the demonstrations; other government newspapers alleged that demonstrators were paid the equivalent of U.S. $5 to join the protests.[275]

In Buon Ma Thuot, the state press reported that some participants joined the demonstrations because they were under the impression that several minority pastors—including one who later addressed the crowd over the bullhorn at the government's request—had been arrested. The *Army Daily* quoted an Ede man from Buon Cuor Knia as saying:

> On the morning of 3 February, while preparing to go to work, some people told us that we must go to Buon Ma Thuot to demand the local authorities to release a priest. When we followed them over there, we found out that they lied and cheated us. No priest had been arrested.

---

[273] Human Rights Watch interview with Jarai and Bahnar men from Kontum, October 11, 2001.

[274] See David Brunnstrom "Officials differ over religion in Vietnam unrest," Reuters, March 16 2001. David Thurber, "Vietnamese officials prevent journalists' access to protesters," Associated Press, March 16, 2001. Deutsche Presse-Agentur, "Vietnam blames war-era exiles for preaching bad religion," March 15, 2001.

[275] *Lao Dong* (Labor) newspaper, March 23, 2001, cited in UNHCR Centre for Documentation and Research, "Vietnam: Indigenous Minority Groups in the Central Highlands," Writenet Paper No. 05/2001, January 2002.

> They told us to demand the establishment of "The Autonomous Government of Dega." If we had known this, we would not have come. We are religious followers....We do not want bad people exploiting religion to harm our people and country. We all see that our government always tries to provide our people with a prosperous life.[276]

The *Army Daily* quoted another ethnic minority man with a similar story:

> On my return from the market, I was asked to join other people in demanding for the release of Priest [name withheld]. I did not know the priest but I followed other people anyway. We found out in Buon Ma Thuot that no priest had been arrested. Some people just cooked up the story to cheat the local religious followers. Then, my friends and I returned home. We are regretful and ashamed...[277]

---

[276] "Vietnam: Army daily cites U.S.'s 'active support' of ethnic unrest in highlands," *Quan Doi Nhan Dan* (Army Daily), Hanoi, in Vietnamese, March 16, 2001, translated by BBC Worldwide Monitoring, March 29, 2001.
[277] Ibid.

X. GOVERNMENT RESPONSE: THE INITIAL REACTION

Outside troops have been mobilized. We have battle plans. Pleiku is ready for any military actions if needed.
—Military official in the Gia Lai provincial army base, February 9, 2001, in an interview with Deutsche Presse-Agentur

Following the protests, Vietnamese authorities responded with a mixture of repression and new policy initiatives, some aimed at addressing highlander grievances. Their initial reaction was to dispatch thousands of police and army units to disperse the protesters. Police conducted village-to-village sweeps and arrested dozens of highlanders, in a number of cases using torture to elicit confessions and public statements of remorse or renunciation of Christianity by protest organizers and church leaders. Those singled out included former FULRO and church leaders, as well as demonstrators. Authorities also stepped up surveillance and propaganda activities throughout the Central Highlands. They banned religious gatherings in many places and tightened existing controls on association, assembly, and movement. They also virtually barred outside access to the region, allowing only a few strictly controlled government tours.

At the same time, the Vietnamese government moved to increase its minority language broadcasting, although much of this was directed to programs extolling the virtue of the party and its policies. It pledged to increase educational opportunities for minorities and initiated a review of economic development policies in the Central Highlands.

Repression, however, continued throughout 2001, with further arrests and the destruction and closure of minority churches. In June 2001, the party issued an internal analysis of the causes of the February unrest, concluding that political enemies were using ethnicity and religion to weaken national unity. Beginning in September 2001 and continuing through early 2002, at least thirty-four highlanders were brought to trial for their role in the protests. As the first anniversary of the protests approached in February 2002, the presence of security forces in the region was increased with the deployment of additional 2,300 soldiers to Gia Lai, Dak Lak, and Kontum.[278]

The Immediate Response: Arrests and Police Sweeps

Even before the February 2001 demonstrations started, elite military troops and riot police were sent to Gia Lai and Dak Lak, where police set up checkpoints along the main roads to block protesters from entering the

---

[278] Reuters, "Vietnam to send extra police to Central Highlands," January 29, 2002. Reuters, "Hanoi troops sent to teach highlanders about plots," February 25, 2002.

Government Response: The Initial Reaction

provincial towns. At least three tanks were sent into Buon Ma Thuot on February 3. Immediately following the Buon Ma Thuot demonstration, four units of troops from Vietnam army's 95th Regiment were sent to Dak Lak, and helicopters circled the area for days.[279]

Despite the troop build-up, it appeared at first as though the authorities might choose not to take action against the demonstrators. During and after the demonstrations in Pleiku and Buon Ma Thuot, provincial authorities met with some of the protest leaders to discuss their concerns. "They told us to wait fifteen days, go home and stop demonstrating, and they would decide," said an Ede man who was in the delegation that met with officials in Buon Ma Thuot. "We said if the problem isn't solved within fifteen days we will demonstrate again. They said don't worry."[280]

The demonstrators agreed to disperse, with most returning to their villages that night. Instead, beginning as early as midnight on February 3, security forces began to arrest suspected movement leaders. Police began fanning out into hundreds of villages, where they conducted searches and interrogated villagers. They used photographs of marchers taken during the demonstrations or at the police barricades erected on the roads to the provincial towns the day of the protests to identify suspected organizers. One Ede man described what happened:

> Within days of our meeting with the People's Committee they started the arrests. Soldiers and police came to the villages in Russian jeeps with name lists. Tanks were parked outside the villages.[281]

Late on the night of February 3-4, three jeeps carrying provincial policemen entered a hamlet on the outskirts of Buon Ma Thuot. "They surrounded my house," said one man who was arrested that night. "My wife was crying. I was wearing only shorts, no shirt. They beat me and gave me shocks with an electric baton. They tied me up and threw me in the jeep. They accused me of organizing the demonstrations, and sent me to the prison in Buon Ma Thuot." He was released three months later.[282]

On the night of February 6-7, tanks moved from the center of Buon Ma Thuot along the road to Buon Cuor Knea, about fifteen kilometers east of the provincial town.[283]

---

[279] Reuters, "Vietnam tense after protests," February 8, 2001. Deutsche Presse-Agentur, "War-era FULRO thought to be fueling Vietnam unrest," February 9, 2001.
[280] Human Rights Watch interview with Ede man from Dak Lak, July 13, 2001.
[281] Ibid.
[282] Ibid.
[283] Human Rights Watch interview with Ede man from Buon Ma Thuot, July 13, 2001.

On February 6 in Gia Lai, police surrounded and ransacked the homes of suspected leaders including Bom Jena and Ksor Kroih and took them off in late-night abductions.[284] A Jarai man from Gia Lai described the arrests:

> At 2:00 a.m. on February 6, the police, government cadres and ordinary Vietnamese beat gongs and drums and surrounded the villages. They entered the villages, damaged houses, rifled through belongings, and arrested people. Everyone was really afraid. My own house was destroyed, and I had to flee.[285]

In Dak Lak, sixty police and soldiers stormed Buon Ea Sup village at midnight on February 6, firing into the air and throwing tear gas canisters as they entered. They surrounded the homes of people suspected of leading others to the demonstrations, including Y Nuen Buon Ya (Ama El) and Y Nong (Ama Cong). The police dragged the two men out of their homes in their underwear and arrested them.[286] Several hundred young ethnic Vietnamese teenagers holding burning torches in their hands accompanied the police and soldiers.

"The Vietnamese were screaming and shouting and threatened to burn down our houses," said an eyewitness from Buon Ea Sup. "They were mocking our 'stupid' ideas and said, 'It is our land, not yours—you will see. We can kill you all within an hour.'"[287]

At 3:00 a.m. on February 6, police surrounded the homes of several organizers in neighboring Ea H'leo district of Dak Lak. Many had already gone into hiding but Siu Un, who had been briefly detained in January, was again arrested.[288] The next day the police returned, this time with written arrest warrants for three people, two of whom had already fled.[289] At least ten people in Dak Lak were arrested immediately after the protests, according to Vietnamese officials interviewed by Reuters.[290]

---

[284] Bom Jena was later sentenced to twelve years of imprisonment and Ksor Kroih was sentenced to eleven during a trial conducted on September 26, 2001 in Pleiku.
[285] Human Rights Watch interview, Jarai man from Gia Lai, March 2001.
[286] Y Nuen Buon Ya, whom Vietnamese state media later alleged had persuaded thousands of highlanders to demonstrate, was sentenced to eleven years in prison on September 26, 2001 on charges of "undermining public security." Y Nong was reportedly sentenced to four years in prison after a trial in October or November 2001.
[287] Eyewitnesses from Buon Ea Sup said in October 2001 said that it appeared that the police had mobilized the Vietnamese youth to raid the village because they arrived at the same time as the police and military, who made no efforts to control them.
[288] Human Rights Watch interview with Jarai man from Ea H'leo, March 2000. Siu Un was sentenced to eleven years imprisonment on charges of undermining security at a trial on September 26, 2001.
[289] Human Rights Watch interview with Jarai man from Ea H'leo, March 2000.
[290] Reuters, "After unrest, Vietnam paper publishes riot code," March 28, 2001.

Government Response: The Initial Reaction

By February 9, a military official at the Gia Lai provincial army base announced that additional troops had been mobilized and that Pleiku was prepared for any necessary military action. On February 10, the party newspaper *Nhan Dan* (The People) reported that 1,300 military reinforcements had been sent to the Central Highlands since late January, where authorities were employing "proper security measures" in order to "encourage local people to return to their hamlets."[291]

As the arrests were taking place, provincial authorities in Gia Lai again summoned ethnic minority church leaders on February 6, to remind them that their role was to promote solidarity and warn them about attempts by "wicked elements to exploit religion to make propaganda, distort the situation and sow disunity among local inhabitants."[292]

By February 8, the Foreign Ministry announced that twenty people had been arrested in Gia Lai alone for "provocative acts" and damaging state property during the demonstrations. "They were people who caused social instability and damage, destroyed schools and resisted the authorities," Foreign Ministry spokeswoman Phan Thuy Thanh told reporters.[293] A provincial official in Gia Lai said that the suspects were former FULRO members who were spreading Protestantism and advocating autonomy.[294]

At least eight people were arrested immediately after the February 14 demonstrations in Kontum provincial town. Some were released from the provincial prison in August 2001 and placed under house arrest.[295]

The arrests continued during the second half of February in Ea H'leo, Krong Buk, Krong Nang, and Ea Sup districts of Dak Lak. On February 14, forty police and soldiers entered a village in Ea H'leo in Dak Lak to carry out arrests. "At my house they beat me on my head and on my back and arms with a stick," said a man who was arrested. "I passed out, and they threw me in a vehicle. When I came to I was in the prison in Buon Ma Thuot. They asked if I wanted to follow Kok Ksor or the government of Vietnam. I said Kok Ksor, and they hit me again." He was released on May 19, 2001.[296]

---

[291] Agence France-Presse, "Vietnam signals determination to crack down on ethnic unrest," February 10, 2001.
[292] *Quan Doi Nhan Dan* (People's Army Daily), cited by Tini Tran, "Ethnic Minority Protest in Vietnam," Associated Press, February 7, 2001. Steve Kirby, "Vietnam warns religious leaders over ethnic unrest," Agence France Presse, February 7, 2001.
[293] Reuters, "Vietnam says 20 arrested over ethnic unrest," February 8, 2001. David Brunnstrom, "Officials differ over religion in Vietnam unrest," Reuters, March 16, 2001.
[294] Tini Tran, "Vietnam Era Group Accused," Associated Press, February 10, 2001.
[295] Human Rights Watch interviews with Jarai and Bahnar men from Kontum, October 30, 2001.
[296] Human Rights Watch interview with Jarai man from Ea H'leo, Dak Lak, October 11, 2001.

Hearing of the arrests and police sweeps, other Montagnard leaders and members of the movement immediately went into hiding; some in underground pits in villages, others in the forest. By mid-February, a handful had crossed the border from Gia Lai to Ratanakiri in Cambodia, followed by dozens more in early March who had fled from Dak Lak further south across to Mondolkiri, Cambodia.

Surveillance and Interrogations

Throughout the Central Highlands, highlanders were subjected to surveillance and interrogation after the February protests. A villager from Chu Se district, Gia Lai described the situation there:

> After the demonstrations there was no freedom in our village. Police went to each house to interrogate the people and patrolled on the roads near our homes. At night there were soldiers around the village—some with guns, others with batons. We were afraid all the time.[297]

Police and local authorities went village by village to search for suspected organizers and conduct community meetings to pressure people to sign loyalty oaths and persuade them not to support independence. A resident of Ea H'leo described a session that took place in early February:

> In these meetings, the Vietnamese communist cadre would state: what kind of person is this Kok Ksor that people would follow him? They said he was a person who stole villagers' cattle, that he had only finished fourth or fifth grade, and what right did he have to declare an independent Dega nation? The world only accepted Ho Chi Minh as the leader of the Vietnamese nation. By historical tradition the whole world recognized the nation of Vietnam; no one in the world recognized a Dega nation.[298]

A Jarai man described the atmosphere in Dak Doa district, Dak Lak:

> After we saw others arrested, many people went into hiding. The government and police forced families of those who had fled to turn in their husbands. They took pictures of the houses of the men who

---

[297] Human Rights Watch interview with a Jarai man from Chu Se district, Gia Lai, June 27, 2001.
[298] Human Rights Watch interview with Jarai man from Ea H'leo, Dak Lak, March 2001.

Government Response: The Initial Reaction

had fled and of their wives. They searched and ransacked the houses. Then they called village meetings, in which they included children and youth. The government asked, who do you want to follow: Ho Chi Minh or Kok Ksor? They made the people sign and thumbprint statements and forced the people not to follow Kok Ksor. In my commune the chief of commune called adults and teenagers alike and told them not to follow Kok Ksor. The youth did not know why they were called.[299]

Another man from Ia Grai district in Gia Lai said:

After the demonstrations there was a lot of pressure and intimidation. People didn't dare go to their fields alone. The police were everywhere. They called meetings every day, telling people not to follow Kok Ksor. Before the demonstrations there were no soldiers in my village; afterwards, they guarded everywhere. If we went to see the water level in our rice field the soldiers wouldn't let us go after dark but told us to wait until morning. If I left my home, soldiers watched my house to see if I'd return.[300]

Former members of FULRO came in for particular scrutiny. They were subject to police interrogation and monitoring regardless of whether they had participated in the protests.[301] An eighty-nine-year old Mnong man from Dak Lak who had left the FULRO movement in 1992 described the situation:

After the demonstrations three policemen and about twenty soldiers entered my village to investigate people, especially former FULRO. I fled to my farm field. Three policemen came to my house looking for me. They questioned my neighbors as well but they were especially looking for me. They knew I'd been a FULRO member three times [in the late 1950s, mid-1960s, and from 1975-92] so they were really

---

[299] Human Rights Watch interview with Jarai man from Gia Lai, March 2001.
[300] Human Rights Watch interview with Jarai man from Ia Grai district, Gia Lai, June 26, 2001.
[301] A June 2001 internal VCP document alleged that many evangelical pastors and church workers are former FULRO members who have been manipulated by the United States to oppose the Vietnamese government. Confidential VCP Advisory, "Mobilization to Strengthen the Masses and the Traditional Life, the Revolution, and the Solidarity among all Ethnic Peoples and Oppose the Forces who are Active in Order to Destroy the Progressive Forces and the Protection of our Fatherland, the Socialist Republic of Vietnam," June 2001. Vietnamese language document and English translation on file at Human Rights Watch.

interested in finding me. The police came six or seven times to my house. Finally in June I was able to escape to Cambodia.[302]

A Montagnard from Dak Lak who had been a FULRO member until his arrest and imprisonment in 1985 said that government officials were searching for former FULRO both before and after the demonstrations:

> They summoned me six times to the police station, beginning in December 2000. Each time I didn't agree with their demands to join with them. My neighbors and relatives warned me that the government was getting ready to arrest me and send me to prison or secretly kill me because I'd been a member of FULRO in the past. When I joined Kok Ksor's organization in 2000, I already had a name as an opponent of the government.[303]

On February 8, police summoned forty villagers in Buon Ea Sup in Dak Lak who were suspected of supporting MFI to the commune police headquarters for interrogation, but released them that evening. The police sessions in Buon Ea Sup continued every day, including Sundays, for weeks. Participants in the demonstrations were pressured to sign written statements promising to end all contact with MFI and other "foreign organizations" and to abandon Christianity.

"They wanted us to say that Vietnamese and ethnic minorities were one people, not separate," said a villager from Buon Ea Sup. "They also wanted us to do a special ceremony to seal the pledge, in which we were to drink wine mixed with goat's blood."[304]

Police Torture

Some people—particularly those suspected of being key supporters of Kok Ksor—were beaten and tortured during their "working sessions" with the police, as described by one villager from Buon Ea Sup:

> Three police interrogated me in a room. They asked me whether I had documents from Kok Ksor and I said no. Then they beat me. They used an electric baton near my eyes [he has a small scar there still]. I don't know how many times they shocked me; I lost consciousness. When I came to, I realized my back and my stomach hurt badly and that I had probably been kicked many times.

---

[302] Human Rights Watch interview with Mnong man from Dak Lak, June 23, 2001.
[303] Human Rights Watch with Montagnard from Dak Lak, October 30, 2001.
[304] Human Rights Watch interviews with residents of Buon Ea Sup, October 20, 2001.

> They brought me to the police station for such sessions—beating and interrogation—fifteen times over the next fifteen days. In some of the sessions the policeman pinched my ears and twisted my eyelids, and slammed his elbow into my ribs. He was angry that I'd shown other villagers the map and documents [about the proposed Dega state] and demanded that I confess.
>
> They beat me so badly that I finally gave up the documents to them. They still continued to pressure me about religion and tried to get me to sign a document renouncing Christianity. I said I couldn't write. The policeman took my hand in his and forced my hand. The interrogations went this way every time, every day, until March 9 when I fled.[305]

Targeting of Christians

Repression of Christians increased throughout the highlands as a result of the protests. On February 8, the party secretary in Dak Lak, Y Luyen, reportedly convened a meeting at the People's Committee office in Cu Jut district in which he announced that Christian believers in the Central Highlands would be severely punished. Church services were subsequently closed down in many parts of the province, including Buon Ea Mhdar (Buon Don District), and Buon Jung Vi, Buon Pok (Krong Pac District), and in Ea H'leo and Ea Sup districts.[306] Protestant churches in Ban Don district in Dak Lak were also closed, with authorities preventing all assembly for worship in many villages since that time.[307] Villagers in Ea Sup district of Dak Lak described interrogation sessions with the police that started on February 8:

> They asked us questions about *Tin Lanh Dega* (Dega Protestantism), why we had gone to the demonstration, why we wanted to make an independent state, and so on. They told us not to hold any more demonstrations, and said that it was prohibited to follow our religion. They said "Dega Protestantism" was not a real religion but something started by the "FULRO-Dega" group.[308]

---

[305] Human Rights Watch interviews with Jarai man from Buon Ea Sup, Dak Lak, October 20, 2001.
[306] Vietnam Observer, "April 2001 Update on Western Highlands Situation—Vietnam."
[307] U.S. Department of State, Bureau of Democracy, Human Rights, and Labor, *Vietnam: International Religious Freedom Report*, October 2001.
[308] Human Rights Watch interviews with residents of Buon Ea Sup, Dak Lak, October 20, 2001.

Similar pressure was brought to bear on minority Christians in Kontum, Lam Dong and Gia Lai after the demonstrations. In Lam Dong, Christians were not permitted to gather at the church in Phi Lieng commune, Lam Ha district, and authorities confiscated all the furniture in the chapel.[309] In Ayun Pa district, Gia Lai, local authorities closed down a church in Ea To commune, which had been open for approximately five years, and banned house church meetings.[310] A Bible teacher in Chu Se district, Gia Lai, described the situation:

> In the past they had mistreated Christians, but after the protests in February 2001 the situation changed, and they made it much more difficult for us to practice our religion. When we tried to pray, the police were always close by, watching and listening. They were trying to find the leaders of the demonstrations, always coming around and questioning people.[311]

Even highlanders who did not attend the February demonstrations described being regarded as subversives by local authorities because Christianity—particularly "Dega Protestantism"—was regarded as the underlying source of the February unrest. Suppression of minority Christians was to continue and intensify during the year following the protests.

---

[309] "Central Highlands Christian Workers' Situation Reports, December 2001 through February 2002," written by Protestant church leaders who asked to remain anonymous. English translation of Vietnamese language document on file at Human Rights Watch.

[310] Religious gatherings were still banned in that village as of February 2002. Human Rights Watch interviews, Jarai families from Ayun Pa district, Gia Lai, February 20, 2002.

[311] Human Rights Watch interview with a Jarai man from Chu Se district, Gia Lai, June 28, 2001.

XI. INCREASING THE PRESSURE

Every time my arms got tired and I tried to lower them, the policeman would say, "Okay—you want to be beaten up? I haven't heard you tell me who the true Jesus is."
—Jarai man from Kontum, October 2001

Beginning in March 2001, Vietnamese authorities launched a second wave of arrests and increased the pressure on suspected sympathizers of the movement. Their actions were based on information gathered from police interrogation sessions conducted in February, as well as photographs and video footage of the demonstrations. On March 10, police arrested more than twenty ethnic Jarai in Chu Se district, Gia Lai after a confrontation between villagers and security forces at Plei Lao.[312] On March 26, the state newspaper *Lao Dong* (Labor) reported that provincial authorities in Kontum had uncovered an underground separatist network, consisting of a "string of clandestine bases each several people strong." Some forty ethnic minority "troublemakers" had surrendered to local authorities, the paper said, and documents confiscated from the group had enabled local authorities to compile a "blacklist" of the leaders of the underground network.[313]

Police were deployed in many villages, often posted in individual homes, and additional military reinforcements were posted at local commune headquarters throughout the next twelve months. In addition to "public works" projects—helping families plant gardens and assisting in village cleanup programs—the main role of the security forces was to monitor suspected leaders of the demonstrations, thwart escapes to Cambodia, and guard against any other outbursts of unrest. In mid-March, party authorities sent more than 500 troops to Kontum and convened a two-day "awareness" seminar for border guards in Kontum.[314]

In April 2001, the *Quan Doi Nhan Dan* (People's Army Daily) announced that thirteen military regiments—expected to be on alert should a "bad situation occur"—were to be settled in an "economic defense zone" in Dak Lak and

---

[312] See Case Study XV, "The Church Burning and Killing by Security Forces in Plei Lao," p. 150.
[313] Agence France-Presse, "Vietnam says it has dismantled separatist network," March 26, 2001.
[314] Agence France-Presse, "Vietnam arranges meeting to build 'awareness' among minorities," March 29, 2001.

neighboring Binh Phuoc province, which has a sizable population of Mnong and Stieng Christians.[315]

In July 2001, Vietnam's public security minister announced plans to send additional police to Kontum in order to address "problems at grassroots level" and prevent "sudden situations and hot spots in rural areas."[316]

Travel Restrictions and Increased Surveillance

After the demonstrations and refugee exodus to Cambodia, the government began to tightly restrict freedom of movement throughout the Central Highlands. Montagnards arriving at the UNHCR sites in Cambodia reported that strict travel bans had been instituted throughout the highlands with police posted on the roads to stop movement of people and in the hamlets to prevent travel and communication between villages.[317] Highlanders interviewed by Human Rights Watch reported stricter implementation of household registry regulations. In the wake of the protests, authorities required highlanders to register with the police several days in advance of leaving their homes to work in their fields or to visit another village or district.[318] In many areas, only women were allowed to freely leave the villages.

Christian pastors and evangelists were barred from traveling in many localities, making it impossible for them to perform baptisms, marriages, and funerals as they had in the past.[319] Police wrote up charges and often imposed fines on pastors who were caught performing such ceremonies.

Areas from which large numbers of people had attempted to flee to Cambodia faced particularly heavy surveillance and extra travel restrictions.

---

[315] The plan called for the resettlement of close to 100,000 soldiers, militia and their families, who would clear up to 230,000 hectares of land to plant rubber, cashews, cotton, coffee and pepper. Cited in Agence France Presse, "Vietnam settling soldiers, militiamen in restive Central Highlands," April 27, 2001.

[316] Reuters, "Vietnam to Send Extra Police to Troubled Highlands," July 17, 2001.

[317] Seth Meixner, "Montagnard Numbers Rise In Mondolkiri," *Cambodia Daily*, May 22, 2001.

[318] In Vietnam, inscription on a household registry document (*ho khau*) is essential not only to legally reside in one's home, but to legally hold a job, collect grain rations, attend public school, receive public health care (which includes all forms of hospitalization), travel, vote, or formally challenge administrative abuses.

[319] "Report on the Situation of Christian Believers in Dak Lak Province," July 2001, written by a Protestant church leader in the Central Highlands who asked to remain anonymous. English translation of Vietnamese language document on file at Human Rights Watch.

Increasing the Pressure

These included Ea Sup, Ea H'leo, and Ban Don districts of Dak Lak, as well as some districts in Gia Lai, such as Ia Grai and Mang Yang.[320]

An Ede woman from Ban Don district, Dak Lak said that police threatened her with arrest after her husband fled to Cambodia:

> They questioned me several times and then took me to the district on March 10. They asked me what my problem was and why I had gone to the demonstration. They said, 'We don't see your husband any more—we're going to put you on jail.' As soon as I could, I escaped to Cambodia.[321]

"My family is watched and followed everywhere," said a Jarai who fled from Ia Grai district, Gia Lai in February. "They are not allowed to travel outside the village. Letters to my family are opened and read."[322]

In one hamlet in Ban Don district of Dak Lak, Human Rights Watch received reports that security police recruited some villagers to report on anyone who attended Christian meetings and even those who conducted family prayers in their own homes. Advance permission was required in order for people to leave the village to work in their fields. Highlander children in that hamlet were reportedly prohibited from attending school unless their families denounced Christianity.[323]

In Ea Sup district of Dak Lak, party cadres and police continued to reside in individual homes for months after the demonstrations. In June 2001 most of the security forces moved out of the villagers' houses but remained camped nearby. They continued to enter peoples' homes without notice, especially those of families with members who were in prison or who had fled to Cambodia. Guests in these homes were monitored and family members wanting to leave the village to go to their fields were required to report their exact hours of departure and return. If they were late coming home they were questioned at length and not permitted to leave the village.[324]

Pressure was exerted on suspected MFI supporters in Lam Dong province as well. In April 2001 authorities tried to force one of the leaders of the land

---

[320] "Report on the Protestants' Situation in Dak Lak Province," September 3, 2001, written by a Protestant church leader in the Central Highlands who asked to remain anonymous.
[321] Human Rights Watch interview with Ede woman from Dak Lak, July 13, 2001.
[322] Human Rights Watch interview with Jarai man from Ia Grai, Gia Lai, August 8, 2001.
[323] "Report on the Situation of Christian Believers in Dak Lak Province," July 2001, written by a Protestant church leader in the Central Highlands who asked to remain anonymous. Translation of Vietnamese-language document on file at Human Rights Watch.
[324] Ibid.

rights movement in Lam Dong to make a public pledge to abandon the movement:

> The police pressured me to make a public pronouncement but I refused. Instead in front of my whole village, I said I would continue my work. A high-ranking police official from the province then entered my house. He tried to offer me money and his hand. I refused to take either. I said I would not abandon the movement—I want freedom for the ethnic minorities, the same as for the Vietnamese. The police saw that I wasn't going to stop the work and sent many police to monitor me. Some were armed. If I didn't agree to stop, they said they would kill me secretly. In May I escaped for my life.[325]

Restrictions on Diplomatic and Media Access

During and after the demonstrations, foreign journalists were denied access to the Central Highlands, other than a tightly-controlled press tour in mid-March 2001 and another timed to coincide with the first repatriation of refugees in February 2002.

Diplomatic access was also restricted, although representatives of the Danish Embassy flew to Dak Lak in early February 2001 as part of a pre-arranged trip to visit aid projects there. Other European diplomats based in Hanoi were able to briefly visit Gia Lai as part of a four-day tour to five provinces and Ho Chi Minh City conducted at the end of May 2001. However a request by the U.S. ambassador in March to visit the highlands was not granted until July 2001.[326]

In the first days after the protests, police instructed hotels in the region not to accept tourists for at least two weeks following the demonstrations, and the region's main tourist attraction, Yok Don National Park, was temporarily closed.

International aid agencies working in the Central Highlands, such as the British volunteer organization, Voluntary Services Overseas (VSO), the Danish Red Cross, and Germany's development organization Deutsche Gesellschaft für Technische Zusammenarbeit (GTZ), continued their work as usual, although they reported that local authorities had told them not to venture out to the districts at night.[327]

---

[325] Human Rights Watch interview with Montagnard from Lam Dong, October 30, 2001.
[326] Associated Press, "U.S. Urges Vietnam to Grant Access to Central Highlands," March 24, 2001. VNA, Diplomats Make Fact-finding Tour of Viet Nam," May 31, 2001. Reuters, "U.S. ambassador to visit troubled Vietnam highlands," July 3, 2001. Reuters, "U.S. Envoy says obstructed in Vietnam highland tour," July 11, 2001.
[327] Deutsche Presse-Agentur, "Expats stay put in Vietnam's highlands despite unrest," February 12, 2001.

Increasing the Pressure 109

There was no mention in the state-controlled media about the unrest for several days following the protests. One February 7, the lead story on state television was a piece praising economic development policies in the Central Highlands. It featured footage of beaming minorities working in coffee plantations in Gia Lai.[328] Such coverage was to continue for months.

The first official mention in the Vietnamese press about the demonstrations ran on February 8. A report by the Vietnam News Agency, which was carried in *Quan Doi Nhan Dan* (The People's Army Daily), the English-language *Vietnam News*, and on national television, acknowledged that protests had occurred in Pleiku and Buon Ma Thuot. The reports attributed the unrest to the work of "bad elements" and "extremists," but said the situation had been brought under control.[329] The same day a Foreign Ministry Spokeswoman told foreign journalists in a press conference that twenty people had been arrested in Gia Lai for "provocative acts." She attributed the Buon Ma Thuot demonstrations to local people receiving "bad information" about the events in Pleiku.[330]

On March 15, *Quan Doi Nhan Dan* ran a long piece featuring biographies and interviews with several Kok Ksor supporters, including Bom Jana, whom the newspaper described as "appearing in an exhausted condition and with a monotonous and regretful voice."[331] Jana was quoted as saying:

> Please allow me to apologize to the State of Socialist Republic of Vietnam and please give me leniency so that I can soon be back to my family. I call on my 'brothers' who had listened to me to join this organization. Please come to surrender to the administration and enjoy the leniency of the government.[332]

Also interviewed was Ksor Kroih, who had been arrested on February 6:

> The more I think about it, the more I see that what Ksor Kok told us was just distorted propaganda. Before the liberation, we ethnic minority communities lived in poverty: no schools, backward social life, and no medicine when we fell sick. Since the country was liberated, the government built roads, schools and markets.

---

[328] Agence France-Presse, "Vietnam closes off strife-torn highlands as it sends in the army," February 8, 2001.
[329] Reuters, "Vietnam media acknowledges widespread unrest," February 8, 2001.
[330] Agence France-Presse, "Vietnam Admits to More Unrest Among Minorities in Highlands," *New York Times*, February 9, 2001.
[331] *Quan Doi Nhan Dan*, Hanoi (People's Army Daily), March 15, 2001, translated by BBC Worldwide Monitoring, March 23, 2001.
[332] Ibid.

> The government has policies to eradicate hunger and alleviate poverty and to encourage the community activity. Our children can go to school without having to pay school fees. Our people do not have to pay for hospitals when they get sick. Our livelihoods have been on the rise. In February, I participated in enticing the people to join demonstrations and threw rocks. Mr. Kok promised that if we were arrested, he would arrange our release. Now I regret for what I have done. I beg the administration to consider with leniency for my wrongdoing.[333]

On March 16, 2001, after several delays, the Hanoi-based foreign press corps was taken on a four-day guided tour of Dak Lak and Gia Lai. Reporters were not granted promised interviews with highlanders who had participated in the demonstrations but instead were taken to a coffee factory, a highlander cultural show, Yak Don National Park, and an ethnic Lao village where no one had participated in the protests.[334] In Pleiku the journalists were brought to a large stadium to witness a Vietnamese military parade in commemoration of the twenty-sixth anniversary of Pleiku's liberation, a ceremony that is not usually observed in Pleiku.[335]

In Pleiku, Provincial People's Committee chairman Nguyen Vy Ha told the journalists that the demonstrations were caused by misinformation and agitation by outside "reactionaries."

"Religion had no connection with what happened, but a group has abused religion to agitate people," he said. Ha said that minority people had heard rumors that they would receive land, houses and money if they marched on the provincial capital.[336]

It was not until late March 2001 that the first video footage of the demonstrations appeared on Vietnam Television (VTV), the state-controlled national television network. A two-part series on March 27-28 showed large crowds standing in front of the Provincial People's Committee buildings in Pleiku and Buon Ma Thuot, with fleeting glimpses of young men using

---

[333] Ibid.
[334] Human Rights Watch telephone interviews with Hanoi-based western journalists, June 2001. David Brunnstrom, "Officials differ over religion in Vietnam unrest," Reuters, March 16, 2001.
[335] David Brunnstrom, "Media access limited in troubled Vietnam highlands," Reuters, March 16, 2001. Agence France-Presse, "Official whitewash cannot hide depth of crisis in Vietnam highlands," March 17, 2001.
[336] David Brunnstrom, "Officials differ over religion in Vietnam unrest," Reuters, March 16, 2001.

slingshots in Buon Ma Thuot. The fifteen-minute program featured interviews with four protesters and Kok Ksor's brother, all expressing contrition for their involvement with Kok Ksor, and an interview in a Buon Ma Thuot church with one of the minority pastors who had addressed the crowd in Buon Ma Thuot at the government's request. The VTV narrator said: "Life has returned to normal in the Central Highlands, but the situation remains complicated…It's necessary to expose the wicked schemes of hostile forces in exile headed by Kok Ksor, aimed at sowing divisions in national unity."[337]

Intensified Repression of Christians

Those suspected of being "Dega Christians" faced ongoing persecution. Special ceremonies were conducted to extract loyalty oaths from people who had attended the demonstrations (See Case Study XVI, "The Goat's Blood Oath Ceremonies in Ea H'leo," p. 163.)

In addition, officials convened public meetings, which were videotaped and photographed, at which church elders were publicly harangued in front of banners reading: "The party punishes the gang which committed the grievous crime of being Dega Christians."[338] Places in Dak Lak where such religious denunciation sessions took place included Buon Nieng, Buon Cuor Knia, Buon Ko Dung, Buon Tong Yu, and Buon Dha Prong.[339]

In some cases the penalties imposed on Christians who refused to denounce their religion were an attempt to humiliate. In one incident in March 2001, police in Kontum forced a Jarai Christian to stand with his hands raised above his head for an entire morning. They had summoned him to the police station for several days in a row to press him to sign a pledge renouncing Christianity. When he continued to refuse to sign, the police made him stand with his hands raised from 8:15 a.m. until noon. He was ordered to stand looking into the eyes of a picture of Ho Chi Minh in order to "see the real Jesus." Afterwards the man was allowed to go home, despite not signing the pledge. He described the sessions:

---

[337] Videotape and English-language translation of VTV program on file at Human Rights Watch. See also Tini Tran, "Vietnam airs first footage of Central Highlands protests," March 28, 2001.
[338] "Report on the Protestants' Situation in Dak Lak Province," September 3, 2001, written by a Protestant church leader in the Central Highlands who asked to remain anonymous. Vietnamese language document and English translation on file at Human Rights Watch.
[339] Ibid.

Every time my arms got tired and I tried to lower them, the policeman would say, 'Okay—you want to be beaten up? I haven't heard you tell me who the true Jesus is.'[340]

Other actions taken by Vietnamese authorities to break up religious gatherings or close Protestant churches included the following:

- An official citation prepared in Dak Lak on March 18, 2001 recorded the "illegal meeting to engage in Protestant religious activities," when a group of fifty-six people from two hamlets gathered to pray at a private home.[341] A similar citation prepared by commune police in Dak Lak documented an illegal, "large meeting" on April 15, when fifteen people gathered at a private home. The citation referred to Vietnam's 1999 Religion Decree and Vietnam's Constitution and warned the homeowner that if he continued to hold illegal meetings he would be punished in accordance with the law. It stated that advance government permission was required in order to conduct any meetings.[342]
- On April 6, 2001, a village chief in Dak Lak signed a memorandum documenting "the discovery of 115 people, eight small Bibles, and two large Bibles" at an "illegal" religious gathering. According to the official citation, the meeting was shut down, the Bibles confiscated, and the church leader ordered to report for questioning at the Village People's Committee at a later date: "We advised [name withheld] that he could not hold meetings to propagate religion at that time since local authorities have not given permission....The report was completed on the same day and read aloud to [name withheld] and the entire group [of worshippers] present that day."[343]

---

[340] Interview with Jarai man from Kontum, October 31, 2001.
[341] "Proces Verbal (writ), Concerning illegal religious activities," signed and witnessed by the leader of the religious gathering, two government officials, and two policemen, March 18, 2001. Vietnamese language document and English translation on file at Human Rights Watch.
[342] "Proces Verbal," signed by Commune Police Chief and Deputy Chief and [name withheld] head of household, April 25, 2001. Vietnamese language document and English translation on file at Human Rights Watch.
[343] "Proces Verbal," April 6, 2001, signed by "perpetrator" [name withheld], Commune Chief and policeman. Vietnamese language document and English translation on file at Human Rights Watch.

- In late April 2001, district authorities in Dak Lak forced the closure of a communal Christian meeting place used by a number of villages in Cu Mgar district. [344]
- In August 2001, policemen in Sa Thay district, Kontum detained and interrogated a Montagnard church leader at gunpoint. They turned him over to provincial police, who tortured him with electric shocks during interrogation.[345]
- Minority Protestants told Western reporters in February 2002 that there were only two officially recognized Christian pastors for all of Gia Lai province, the building of new churches was forbidden, and that church services outside of the home—and particularly the practice of "Dega Protestantism"—were forbidden.[346]

Reports were received of interrogation and threats of church leaders in Buon Drie, Buon Ea Mohar, Buon Ko Dung, and Buon Nieng in Dak Lak. After a number of church elders from Buon Mohar filed a complaint to the Provincial Bureau of Religious Affairs and the Provincial Security Police, the pressure on them lightened somewhat.[347]

In July 2001, police began summoning one church leader in Buon Don district on a daily basis for weeks in order to conduct intensive interrogations. He was asked who the leaders of the local church were, why he was teaching religion when he was not a pastor, and why he traveled to other hamlets. In fact, he did so to perform funerals and other religious ceremonies. He was forced to sign a document stating that he was guilty of eight crimes, including not having an advanced degree, not having studied in any Bible classes, lacking official permission from local government to carry out religious activities, and

---

[344] "Report on the Situation of Christian Believers in Dak Lak Province," July 2001, written by a Protestant church leader in the Central Highlands who asked to remain anonymous. English translation of Vietnamese language document on file at Human Rights Watch.
[345] "Central Highlands Christian Workers' Situation Reports, December 2001 through February 2002," written by Protestant church leaders who asked to remain anonymous. English translation of Vietnamese language document on file at Human Rights Watch.
[346] David Brunnstrom, "Pastors say some curbs eased in Vietnam highlands," Reuters, February 18, 2002; Clare Arthurs, "First Vietnamese refugees return home," BBC News Online, February 19, 2002; David Brunnstrom, "Tearful minority women defy Vietnamese officials," Reuters, February 9, 2002.
[347] "Report on the Situation of Christian Believers in Dak Lak Province," July 2001, written by a Protestant church leader in the Central Highlands who asked to remain anonymous. English translation of Vietnamese language document on file at Human Rights Watch.

conducting religious activities in his home and not in the church. The man who was interrogated submitted a complaint to local authorities in which he stated:

> [The police chief] was ready to beat me, but he didn't do it. He told me he would smash my mouth, cut open my head. He said he would keep me coming back for questioning for six months, and [asked me] who would work my fields during that time. He said he'd put me in jail, because my eight crimes really merited execution.[348]

Official police records and citizen complaint petitions obtained by Human Rights Watch document other instances of official pressure on whole villages or large groups of people to renounce Christianity. On August 24, 2001, police and village officials disrupted a church service in Buon Don district, photographing the church and the people inside. The officials organized a meeting to order the community to renounce Protestantism. They placed the entire village under surveillance and searched the homes of suspected Christians. A citizen complaint about the incident stated:

> They pressure us to renounce our religion and sent irregular forces to search the homes of believers one by one. They follow us everywhere we go. They know the places where we pray and report them to their superiors. The authorities arrested five believers and forced them to do self criticisms; they accuse that we are believers of the crime of illegal proselytization.[349]

In August 2001, twenty households comprising eighty-nine people in two villages in Dak Lak were forced to sign a pledge to the village People's Committee that they would cease being Protestants or face legal action. A written police decision dated August 27, signed by the village police chief, ordered all households to turn in all Protestant religious materials in the two villages.[350]

---

[348] "Signed Citizen Report," Addressed to General Assembly of the Vietnam Protestant Church, Bureau of Religious Affairs, Dak Lak Province, Governing Body of the Vietnam Protestant Church in Dak Lak, dated July 29, 2001. English translation of Vietnamese language document on file at Human Rights Watch.

[349] See Appendix D, page 182, for entire petition, "Written Complaint to Dak Lak Bureau of Religious Affairs sent by villagers in Buon Don District, Dak Lak," August 2001. Vietnamese-language document and translation on file at Human Rights Watch.

[350] Written Decision signed by Commune Police Chief [name withheld], dated August 27, 2001. "Record of Pledge to Abandon Protestantism," August 7, 2001. Vietnamese-language document and translation on file at Human Rights Watch.

In some areas minority Christians reported increased use of economic pressure against them after the protests, for example, by being excluded from government food distribution programs. This occurred reportedly not only in Gia Lai, but also in Christian minority areas in neighboring Quang Nai and Phu Yen provinces.[351] Minority Christians in Minh Long district in Quang Nai and in Son Hinh and Son Nga districts in Phu Yen reported being systematically excluded from government distribution of relief funds, rice, oil and salt.[352]

In August 2001 in Phu Yen province, minority church members filed a petition with the provincial Bureau of Religious Affairs to protest discriminatory treatment of minority Christians. A drought and failed harvest had caused eleven Christian families to face particular hardship but they were all rejected for government assistance that had been provided to non-Christians in the same village. The petitioners wrote:

> The officials in [name of commune withheld] say: these Protestants are the most stubborn people of all and that Protestantism is an American religion that opposes the programs of the country. In truth, we have done nothing to oppose the government, and we are not stubborn either. The real reason [we were refused drought relief] is that the village authorities do everything they can to make us renounce our religion, and when we refuse, they say all sorts of bad things about us.[353]

The Trials

Soon after the February protests, it was clear that harsh penalties would be imposed against those found to have organized the demonstrations. An indicator came in March 2001 in the VCP daily, *Nhan Dan* (The People), which published sections of the penal code dealing with inciting riots and endangering national security and stated that the law called for strict criminal penalties.[354]

In April, the government's *Tin Tuc* news agency announced that eleven "troublemakers" would be prosecuted in Dak Lak province. Provincial VCP

---

[351] See, for example: "Plea for Help" to Bureau of Religious Affairs, Phu Yen Province, from resident of Song Hinh District, July 25, 2001; Complaint to Religious Affairs Bureau, Phu Yen Province, from Members of the Church of [name withheld] village, Song Hinh District, Phu Yen Province, August 22, 2001. Vietnamese-language document and translation on file at Human Rights Watch.
[352] "Massive Crackdown Against Vietnam's Highland Christians," Vietnam Observer, April 30, 2001.
[353] "Complaint to Religious Affairs Bureau, Phu Yen Province," (Commune name withheld), August 22, 2001. English translation of Vietnamese language document on file at Human Rights Watch.
[354] Reuters, "After unrest, Vietnam paper publishes riot code," March 29, 2001.

official Y Luyen Niec Dan was quoted as saying that strong measures needed to be taken against people exploiting Protestantism to "bend the truth and sabotage the revolution." "We have to unmask the local and international reactionaries who have created this bad situation...and at the same time practice clemency towards all those who have strayed and repented," he said.[355]

In June 2001, the official government legal newspaper, *Phap Luat* (The Law) stated that forty-one people would be tried in Gia Lai province. Seven people had been charged with "damaging national security," twenty with "opposing public officials," and fourteen with "disturbing public order." A court official interviewed by the Associated Press said that defendants had been involved in two rounds of unrest—in Pleiku on February 2 and in Chu Se district on March 10. The official said that the defendants had admitted to receiving instructions from "overseas counterrevolutionary elements" to incite unrest.[356]

Between September 2001 and January 2002, at least thirty-five highlanders were sentenced in a number of trials quietly conducted in Dak Lak and Gia Lai provinces.

- On September 26, 2001, the People's Courts in Dak Lak and Gia Lai sentenced fourteen highlanders to prison sentences ranging from six to twelve years on charges of undermining public security (most likely under article 89 of the Penal Code.)[357] According to the official state press, the men were accused of forming a "reactionary organization" in order to establish an independent state and a separate religion in the Central Highlands. One defendant was also charged with illegal possession of military weapons. State media said that Nay D'Ruk (Y Drut Nie) and Y Phen Ksor from Ea H'leo had raided local government offices and destroyed public property.[358] In addition, Bom Jena—identified as the "mastermind" of the unrest—was found to have

---

[355] Cited in BBC News Online, "Vietnam 'troublemakers' face prosecution," April 18, 2001.
[356] Agence France-Presse, "Vietnam to hold mass trial of 41 people over highlands unrest," June 16, 2001. Associated Press, "Vietnam to place 41 people on trial for highlands unrest," June 18, 2001.
[357] Viet Nam News Service, "Gia Lai provocateurs dealt hefty prison terms for crimes," Viet Nam News, September 28, 2001. VNS, "Stiff jail terms mandated for saboteurs of public security," September 28, 2001.
[358] VNS, "Stiff jail terms mandated for saboteurs of public security," September 28, 2001.

chaired a founding ceremony of an "illegal organization" at co-defendant Ksor Kroih's house in September 2000.[359]
- On October 18, 2001, six highlanders were convicted in courts in Ea H'leo, Ea Sup and Krong Pak districts of Dak Lak, on charges of distributing propaganda and inciting social unrest in Buon Ma Thuot in February 2001. They were given from three years suspended sentences to five years of imprisonment.[360]
- Also in October, four highlanders were sentenced in Ayun Pa district court in Gia Lai to sentences ranging from five to eight years imprisonment. A district official told the Associated Press that the four had detained and beaten the deputy police chief and his nephew on February 4, after the latter barred villagers from attending the demonstrations in Pleiku on February 2.[361]
- Two highlanders from Ia Grai district of Gia Lai were reportedly tried in October, sentenced to prison terms of four and five years respectively.[362]
- On November 19, 2001, five highlanders from Ea Sup district of Dak Lak were reportedly tried and sentenced to between five and seven years of imprisonment.
- On January 25, 2002, four highlanders in Chu Se district, Gia Lai, were sentenced to prison terms of up to six and a half years for "organizing illegal migrations." The official Vietnamese News Agency reported that Cambodian officials arrested and deported the four men in April and May 2001, along with groups of highlanders who had fled to Cambodia.[363]

None of the trial dates were announced in advance, and no diplomats or foreign correspondents were allowed to attend. It is doubtful that the defendants were allowed access to any legal representation, which is in contravention of

---

[359] Vietnam News Agency, "Seven Sentences for Security Destablizers in Central Highlands Province," September 26, 2001. Vietnam News Agency, "Central Highlands Unrest Mastermind Sentenced to 12 Years in Prison," September 27, 2001.
[360] "Dac Lac court concludes trial of six ethnic minority dissidents," October 19, 2001, translation of Vietnamese media by BBC Monitoring Service.
[361] Associated Press, "Vietnamese court sentences five more people in Central Highlands unrest," November 7, 2001.
[362] Human Rights Watch interview with Jarai people from Ia Grai District, November 6, 2001.
[363] *Nhan Dan* (The People), Four receive jail terms for organizing illegal migrations," January 28, 2002. Associated Press, "Four sentenced in Vietnam for organizing border crossings into Cambodia," January 28, 2002.

article 132 of the Vietnamese constitution.[364] The only official press coverage, if any, was the announcements of the verdicts after the trials were over. After the September 26 trial in Dak Lak, the government radio station stated that all the people present at the trial and in Dak Lak province supported the sentences: "The trial has not only punished the criminals but also educated the entire society."[365]

Vietnam's Penal Code, as amended in 1999, lists numerous "crimes against national security," some of which contain provisions, which are contrary to international law or are so vaguely worded that they invite abusive application.[366] For example, article 88, "Conducting propaganda against the Socialist Republic of Vietnam," criminalizes the mere act of expressing a disfavored political opinion, or possessing or circulating material that does the same. It carries sentences of between three and twenty years of imprisonment. Article 87, "Undermining the unity policy," criminalizes "sowing divisions" between the people and the government or the military, between religious and non-religious people, and between religious followers and the government. Offenders are to be sentenced to between two and fifteen years of imprisonment.

One national security offense that is regularly lodged against peaceful critics of the party and government is article 79, "Carrying out activities aimed at overthrowing the people's administration;" punishment for this offense can include the death penalty. Among the actions that have triggered prosecutions under this provision are issuing manifestos or newsletters promoting peaceful political reforms and respect for human rights.[367]

In addition, as the U.N. Working Group on Arbitrary Detention noted in its 1995 report on Vietnam, the Penal Code's characterizations of national security crimes does not distinguish between the use or nonuse of violence or of

---

[364] Reuters, "No defense lawyers for most Vietnam trials, "December 27, 2001.
[365] Voice of Vietnam, Hanoi, in Vietnamese, 26 September 2001, BBC Monitoring.
[366] Penal Code of the Socialist Republic of Vietnam, cited in *A Selection of Fundamental Laws of Vietnam*, the Gioi Publishers, Hanoi, 2001.
[367] Human Rights Watch/Asia, "Vietnam: Human Rights in a Season of Transition: Law and Dissent in the Socialist Republic of Vietnam," *A Human Rights Watch Report*, vol. 7, no. 12, August 1995.

incitement or nonincitement to violence. This means that penalties can be imposed on persons who have merely exercised peacefully their legitimate rights to freedom of opinion or expression.[368]

---

[368] Commission on Human Rights, *Question of the Human Rights of All Persons Subjected to Any Form of Detention or Imprisonment, Working Group on Arbitrary Detention, Visit to Vietnam*, E/CN.4/1995/31/Add.4, January 18, 1995.

XII. INTERPRETING THE UNREST

Their strategy consists of taking advantage of the concepts of freedom and democracy and exaggerating a number of our difficulties and shortcomings during the cultural and economic development process, which aims at the unity of the people and the party. They have made the people lose their confidence in the party and the authorities.
—Confidential VCP advisory issued to cadre in the Central Highlands, June 2001

In the year following the turmoil in the highlands, the Vietnamese government made numerous attempts to placate the highlanders, at least on the surface. These public efforts ranged from pledges of assistance by the Vietnamese Red Cross in February 2001 for disadvantaged minority families, to provision of free medical check-ups for 6,000 highlanders in April, to expansion of additional minority language radio broadcasts in May.[369] On the one hand, such efforts appeared to acknowledge that genuine grievances existed. On the other, as leaked party documents make clear, the government's official interpretation of the unrest was that it was caused by enemies of the party who used religion as their instrument. With the first anniversary of the demonstrations, government surveillance of highlander villages increased, security measures tightened, and repression of minority Christians intensified.

Acknowledgment of Grievances

Internal party documents as well as public statements by Politburo members indicated an awareness that the leadership was out of touch with rural minority communities in the Central Highlands. On February 22, 2001, the state media reported that 10 percent of Gia Lai's administrative officials would be stationed in minority hamlets to resolve conflicts.[370] In addition the government established "working teams" composed of government officials in Dak Lak to address public disputes, in particular those related to land and forestry.[371]

---

[369] Viet Nam News Agency (VNA), "Red Cross Association grants aid to disadvantaged people," February 8, 2001. *Nhan Dan* (The People), "Free treatment for Dak Lak ethnic people," April 16, 2001. Agence France-Presse, "Vietnam to boost minority language broadcasts in face of ethnic unrest," May 1, 2001.
[370] Reuters, "Vietnam to hear complaints in protest-hit highlands," February 22, 2001. Agence France-Presse, "Vietnam authorities to pour in more cadres to calm restive highlands," February 22, 2001.
[371] The teams were to focus on the districts of Krong Buc, Ea H'leo, Cu M'gar, Ea Kar, Krong Pach, and Krong Bong in Buon Ma Thuot city. Voice of Vietnam Radio, Hanoi, "Dac Lac province sets up extra teams to settle complaints," February 22, 2001, translated by BBC Monitoring Asia Pacific-Political, February 23, 2001.

Additional party cadres were dispatched to minority villages in Dak Lak from March 15 to December 15 to "develop production and consolidate social order and security."[372]

Many of the public pronouncements and pledges from Hanoi, however, did not filter down to administrators at the provincial and district levels, where repression and rights violations continued into the year 2002.

After the February 2001 protests, a succession of high-ranking officials toured the Central Highlands. Deputy Prime Minister Nguyen Tan Dung visited on February 9, followed by Politburo member Pham The Duyet in March, and Prime Minister Phan Van Khai and National Police Chief Le Minh Huong in July.

During his March visit, Prime Minister Phan Van Khai attended a three-day conference on socioeconomic development in Buon Ma Thuot, where plans were unveiled for new electricity projects, an agricultural university, and a modern regional hospital. The Prime Minister called on government authorities to address the land problem by allocating unused land to ethnic minority families, and solicit input from grassroots officials to work out new and more effective approaches to the region's development.[373]

In other pledges by officials to address the land problem, Dak Lak province in August 2001 reportedly set aside some 13,800 hectares of land for ethnic minority families who had less than the average 0.73 hectare; the land was reportedly obtained from state farms and forest enterprises or purchased from private plantations.[374] In addition, in October 2001 provincial officials in Dak Lak and Lam Dong announced they would reallocate unused state farm land to minority farmers: 165,000 hectares in Dak Lak and 66,000 hectares in Lam Dong.[375]

In September 2001, VCP General Secretary Nông Dúc Manh, himself a member of an ethnic minority, made a visit to the region. He urged minority elders and commune chiefs to be vigilant against the efforts of "hostile forces" that he said were seeking to take advantage of the region's temporary socioeconomic difficulties in order to undermine national unity or incite people

---

[372] *Nhan Dan* (The People), March 13, 2001, cited in a report by the UNHCR Centre for Documentation and Research, "Vietnam: Indigenous Minority Groups in the Central Highlands," Writenet Paper No. 05/2001, January 2002.
[373] Vietnam News Agency, "PM Khai Pledges to Raise Central Highlands' Living Standards to National Average," July 14, 2001.
[374] *Nhan Dan* (The People), August 13, 2001, cited in a report by the UNHCR Centre for Documentation and Research, "Vietnam: Indigenous Minority Groups in the Central Highlands," Writenet Paper No. 05/2001, January 2002.
[375] Associated Press, "Vietnam Gives Unused Land to Central Highlands Minorities," October 26, 2001.

to flee abroad. In Kontum, Manh urged soldiers to build a "fighting position in the people's hearts" in the Central Highlands.[376]

Hearts and Minds

As part of a stepped-up propaganda campaign in the highlands, beginning in February 2001 the government increased its minority-language radio and television broadcasts and in March the government allocated 300 million dong (U.S. $20,700) to each province in the Central Highlands to cover the printing and distribution of pictures of Ho Chi Minh as well as books and audiotapes extolling the party and its policies toward ethnic minorities.[377] In Lam Dong village chiefs received radios in order to be able to receive and disseminate "accurate information" about party guidelines and policies.[378] In April, the government distributed one million pamphlets and 1,800 audiotapes in Jarai and Bahnar languages to fifty-seven villages in Gia Lai. The materials included information about the penal code, land law, the decree on religious activities, and the constitution.[379]

By the end of June 2001, the government had expanded minority-language television broadcasts from one language (Ede) to five (adding Jarai, Koho, Mnong and Sedang). New television transmitters were constructed in Dak Lak and Kontum, and Gia Lai launched the publication of a trilingual magazine (Jarai, Bahnar and Vietnamese).[380]

Pledges were made to enhance educational opportunities for minorities in the Central Highlands, including the planned expansion of Tay Nguyen University in Buon Ma Thuot, announced in May. In August, Gia Lai authorities donated 30,000 dong (U.S. $2) per student per month and "ethnic costumes" to 2,000 ethnic minority boarding school students, on top of previous monthly allowances of 120,000 dong (U.S. $9). Similar assistance was provided in Dak Lak.[381] Plans were also announced in August for a pilot bilingual education

---

[376] Vietnam News, "Ethnic chiefs have key role for unity: Party leader," September 13, 2001. Reuters, "Vietnam party chief visits troubled highlands," September 15, 2001.
[377] Associated Press, "Vietnam launches major law-awareness campaign in restive Central Highlands," April 17, 2001. Associated Press, "Top Vietnamese ideology officials discuss how to win support from minority groups in Central Highlands," September 7, 2001.
[378] UNHCR Centre for Documentation and Research, "Vietnam: Indigenous Minority Groups in the Central Highlands," Writenet Paper No. 05/2001, January 2002.
[379] Associated Press, "Vietnam launches major law-awareness campaign in restive Central Highlands," April 17, 2001.
[380] Agence France-Presse, "Vietnam to boost minority language broadcasts in face of ethnic unrest," May 1, 2001.
[381] Voice of Vietnam, "Efforts made to enroll more ethnic students in school," August 31, 2001. Vietnam News Service, "Parents Dig Deep for the School Year," August 2001.

program in Ede for third graders in forty-five schools in Dak Lak during the 2001-02 school years.[382]

Throughout 2001 the party convened a number of meetings in the highlands for provincial administrators, party cadres and leaders of the mass organizations, such as for youth and women. The aim was to discuss economic development in the highlands, national security, and political education, and to instruct cadres, including minority cadres, in the party line. As the first anniversary of the protests neared in January 2002, the government convened a three-day meeting in Buon Ma Thuot to implement a Politburo Resolution linking socioeconomic development with national defence and maintenance of security in the Central Highlands.[383]

The June 2001 Party Advisory

In June 2001, the Vietnamese Communist Party issued an internal advisory, specifically directing party cadre how to interpret the ethnic unrest in the Central Highlands. The twenty-two page document, a copy of which was obtained by Human Rights Watch, carries the official seal of the VCP and is entitled "Mobilization to Strengthen the Masses and the Traditional Life, the Revolution, and the Solidarity among all Ethnic Peoples and Oppose the Forces who are Active in Order to Destroy the Progressive Forces and the Protection of our Fatherland, the Socialist Republic of Vietnam."

The document analyzes the 2001 uprising and its purported relationship to the Protestant movement:

> Recently, illegal religious activities of a complex nature have been taking place, in certain places with a clearly political character, especially those involving reactionaries who are taking advantage of Protestants, inspiring divisions among the various nationalities, concentrated among the mountain tribes, especially in the Central Highlands. For this reason our province has not yet permitted Protestants to practice their religion in a normal way.[384]

---

[382] Viet Nam News Agency (VNA), "Ede Minority Group Language to be Taught in Dac Lac Central Highlands Province," August 21, 2001.
[383] *Nhan Dan* (The People), "Central Highlands development, unity, security discussed," January 24, 2002.
[384] Confidential VCP Advisory, "Mobilization to Strengthen the Masses and the Traditional Life, the Revolution, and the Solidarity among all Ethnic Peoples and Oppose the Forces who are Active in Order to Destroy the Progressive Forces and the Protection of our Fatherland, the Socialist Republic of Vietnam," June 2001. Vietnamese-language document and translation on file at Human Rights Watch.

The advisory mentions the government's recognition in February 2001 of the Evangelical Church of the South but states that full participation of Protestant churches in the highlands will have to be a step-by-step process, especially given the political instability in the region and the intentions of "bad elements" who were exploiting religion to oppose the revolution:

> In our area we will by gradual steps allow the various Protestant churches to operate normally when the political situation is stable. …Thus the reason we do not allow the Protestant religion to operate normally is because reactionaries are using religion to promote counter-revolutionary activities.[385]

The June 2001 advisory shows that the party links the highlanders' escalating demands for land rights, religious freedom, and even independence with the growing popularity of evangelical Protestantism. Illustrating the extent to which the government is concerned about its loss of control, the document asserts that the "enemy" had taken advantage of ethnicity and religion in order to create fissures in national unity.[386] These subversive groups, it contends, are misusing religion to cause the masses to lose faith in the party and the government in order to "overthrow the legal government":

> They have gathered a number of bad elements and dragged them into illegal religious activities. They have encouraged them to demand land, to build churches and places of worship and [conduct] other illegal religious gatherings. They have propagated that our local authorities do not pay due attention to the freedom of religious belief.[387]

Tin Lanh Dega, or "Dega Protestantism," is described as targeting minority Protestants to isolate them from mainstream society and lure them into political activities in order to demand an independent state. "Artificial" demands for land and the right to freedom of religion are said to be part of an overall strategy to destabilize society and carry out uprisings against the revolution:

---

[385] Confidential VCP Advisory, "Mobilization to Strengthen the Masses…," June 2001.
[386] Accusations that unauthorized religious groups—such as the banned Unified Church of Vietnam—misuse religion to oppose the government have been a common refrain from the VCP for years.
[387] Confidential VCP Advisory, "Mobilization to Strengthen the Masses…," June 2001.

Interpreting the Unrest 125

> The main purpose of the enemy is to take advantage of ethnicity and religion to launch activities aimed at the minorities in the Central Highlands and combine politics and psychological warfare in order to overthrow the legal government. The purpose is to establish the independent state of Dega, which is also supported from outside, in order to invade our country.[388]

It is clear that the emergence of political activism in the highlands calling not only for independence, but also for land and religious rights, touched a sensitive nerve. The advisory charges that the party's enemies are working to "encourage and spread discontent among our minorities to act illegally to demand land" and to oppose state policies in regard to family planning, migration, and the building of socialist culture. These "hostile forces" are held to be challenging government policies that encourage the development of New Economic Zones and migration by other population groups to more equally distribute the population:

> They have taken advantage of our difficulties and shortcomings during the process of [the government] solving the land issue in order to stir up the people to demand land, create difficulties during the implementation of our development policies in the New Economic Zones with the purpose to develop the economy and the society in the Central Highlands. They have created opposition against migration during a time that the authorities aimed at an equal sharing [of land and resources] between Vietnamese and the [indigenous] minorities and other minorities migrating into the area from the northern provinces.[389]

The June 2001 advisory charges that both FULRO and the United States—which is identified as the main culprit in bringing Christianity to the highlands—have created much of the problem in the Central Highlands, by "forming a human resource to oppose the Socialist government" and inciting the people to rebel.

The advisory alleges that enemies of the party had targeted the Central Highlands, taking advantage of "the concepts of freedom and democracy," as

---
[388] Ibid.
[389] Ibid.

well as the low educational level of the minority groups, in order to highlight social and economic difficulties in the region. The advisory concludes frankly, "They have made the people lose their confidence in the party and the authorities."[390]

---

[390] Ibid.

XIII. REFUGEE FLIGHT TO CAMBODIA

In my heart I didn't want to run to Cambodia and abandon my family. I was in the forest before with FULRO in 1990 and know how difficult it is. All I want is a place that's safe. If the Vietnamese catch me, they will chop me up like chopped fish. Our group needs to stay together; live together and die together. If the U.N. wants to meet me to ask about our problem I will meet them. But I will not abandon my group.
—Jarai man who fled to Cambodia in February 2001

Within days of the government crackdown in the Central Highlands in February 2001, small numbers of highlanders from Dak Lak and Gia Lai had fled from their villages and began to cross the border to Cambodia, where they hid in the forests of Ratanakiri and Mondolkiri provinces. In March 2001, provincial officials in Mondolkiri arrested twenty-four ethnic Ede, who were escorted on March 24 in military helicopters to Phnom Penh, where they were detained at the national Gendarmerie headquarters.

Under considerable pressure from Vietnam, Cambodian officials initially announced that they planned to deport the highlanders as illegal immigrants and barred access to the group by officials from UNHCR.[391] Then in an unusual reversal, Prime Minister Hun Sen defied his long-time allies on March 31, when he agreed to allow UNHCR to interview the group. In a move that infuriated Vietnam, the group of twenty-four were identified as refugees in need of protection and were resettled to the United States in early April, along with fourteen ethnic Jarai, who had managed to make contact with UNHCR as well.[392]

The Vietnamese government charged that the U.S. was interfering in Vietnam's internal affairs and its bilateral relations with Cambodia, as well as encouraging illegal departures of Vietnamese people. In a statement defending his decision, Cambodian Prime Minister Hun Sen said: "I think that what the U.S. is doing on this issue is not an intervention in anybody's internal affairs,

---

[391] Article 37 of Cambodia's Law on Immigration states that any alien who enters Cambodia illegally shall be expelled. However, Article 31 of the 1951 Refugee Convention, to which Cambodia is a signatory, provides that refugees or asylum seekers not be penalized for having entered a country without the legal immigration requirements, which they may not have been able to meet because of their flight. UNHCR, *Handbook for Emergencies*, p. 13, June 2000.
[392] Agence France-Presse, "Vietnam Critical of U.S. Asylum Offer to Fleeing Minorities," April 3, 2001.

but they are fulfilling a humanitarian obligation ... Vietnam should examine its humanitarian obligations too."[393]

Prior to the highlanders' departure from Phnom Penh, the Vietnamese government went to great lengths to press Cambodia to turn over custody of the refugees.[394] On April 9, the Vietnamese Red Cross requested that the Cambodian Red Cross intervene and immediately repatriate the highlanders, an appeal that Cambodian Red Cross President Bun Rany (Hun Sen's wife) rejected.[395] A delegation that included the deputy chief of mission from the Vietnamese Embassy in Phnom Penh, Vietnamese Red Cross representatives, and Vietnamese intelligence agents met the refugees when they were in detention in Phnom Penh.[396] The Vietnamese Red Cross attempted to show the refugees videotapes of their families in Vietnam, pleading for them to return.[397] One of the refugees described the situation:

> We were questioned several times by Vietnamese people when we were in Phnom Penh. Vietnamese people also took videotapes of us there. The Vietnamese Red Cross person tried to force us to take letters and watch a videotape. He argued in English with an American man about this. We all stuck our fingers in our ears and lowered our heads when they put on the video. We refused to take the letters.[398]

Another refugee recognized one of the Vietnamese men who questioned the group when they were in Phnom Penh:

> I had seen him before—at the demonstration in Buon Ma Thuot. He was watching us and talking to the police, but dressed in civilian

---

[393] Agence France-Presse, "Vietnam Rebuffs Hun Sen, Stands Firm on Repatriation of Fugitives from Cambodia," April 5, 2001.
[394] Agencies, "Cambodia lets ethnic refugees go to U.S.; First group flown out as Phnom Penh ignores pressure from Hanoi for repatriation of hill tribespeople," *South China Morning Post*, April 14, 2001.
[395] Voice of Vietnam Radio, Hanoi, "Vietnam Red Cross Society requests return of 24 detainees from Cambodia," April 9, 2001. BBC Monitoring Asia Pacific - Political; Supplied by BBC Worldwide Monitoring, April 10, 2001. *Nhan Dan* (The People), "Vietnam Red Cross asks for return of 24 from Cambodia," April 10, 2001.
[396] Human Rights Watch interview with Western diplomat based in Phnom Penh, April 13, 2001. He reported that Vietnamese intelligence agents not only visited the refugees when they were in detention at the municipal Gendarmerie, but were also present in Pochentong Airport in Phnom Penh when the group departed for the United States.
[397] Associated Press, "Ten hilltribe refugees from Vietnam depart for United States," April 12, 2001.
[398] Human Rights Watch interview with Ede refugee from Dak Lak, April 24, 2001.

clothes. He was staring at me during the demonstration and asked me to stop demonstrating.

When he met me in Phnom Penh, he asked me if I would go back to Vietnam. I said not until we get land for our people. He asked where I lived. I told him it wasn't his business. He told me my family was waiting for me. I said fine, but we need land. He tried to scare me.

There were three Vietnamese there and one Cambodian guard. I'm pretty sure two were from Hanoi. They had a camera and took photographs of us. I asked them where they were from and they said Phnom Penh. I said I guess that you're from Hanoi. They got angry and said how did I know. [They spoke the northern accent]. They looked like strangers, talked very angrily with me, blamed me for causing others to leave Vietnam. They said these people look to you. If those people go back, they will go with you. I said I don't want to see your face.

The next day the Vietnamese called me again for questioning. They asked us to return to Vietnam. I said not until we have land for our people. They asked if we'd done the paperwork [to get land title.] I said we tried hundreds of times; your heart is hard. They said if I returned to Vietnam, there will be no problem but if you go far away there will be big problems.

In April 2001, the increasingly repressive environment in the highlands caused more highlanders to flee to Cambodia, where approximately 150 Ede and Mnong hid in the forests of Mondolkiri for weeks. A local villager who supplied them with food and rice told the *Cambodia Daily* that he advised the group to remain in hiding after hearing that Vietnamese agents were offering bounties for returned refugees, as well as reports that nineteen ethnic Jarai had been arrested and forcibly repatriated in Mondolkiri:

I told them they should not come [out of hiding], as they will be arrested. I talked with them for one hour and I gave them twenty kilos of rice…They cried and I cried. They blamed me, saying that they came here and I can't help them. They said that if they go back they will be killed, and they can't stay in the forest.[399]

---

[399] Thet Sambath and Kevin Doyle, "Mondolkiri Minorities Ask for More Protection," *Cambodia Daily*, April 23, 2001.

From March until May 2001, prior to the establishment of UNHCR refugee camps in Cambodia's border provinces, Cambodian authorities forcibly repatriated more than one hundred refugees back to Vietnam.[400] A Cambodian district official in Mondolkiri stated that Cambodian police were escorting Vietnamese police in Mondolkiri in order to search for refugees, and there were reports that bounties had been offered for each Montagnard refugee deported to Vietnam.[401] (See section on deportations, below.)

On May 11, 2001, after a family of seven Mnong under U.N. protection was forcibly returned to Vietnam, UNHCR staff escorted approximately 150 ethnic minority refugees (thirty families) from several hiding places in the forest in Mondolkiri to an encampment in the provincial capital of Sen Monorum.[402]

The forced repatriation of two large groups of highlanders by Cambodian provincial authorities on May 15 was put in motion the same day that UNHCR Regional Representative Jahanshah Assadi met with Hok Lundy, director general of the Cambodian National Police. At that meeting Hok Lundy assured Assadi that Vietnamese refugees would be protected. That night Cambodian police officials in Ratanakiri transported sixty-three ethnic Jarai in two groups to the Vietnam border, from where they were forcibly returned to Vietnam.[403]

On May 17, UNHCR finally secured Cambodian government approval to establish two camps for refugees, one in Mondolkiri and one in Ratanakiri—which sheltered close to 400 highlanders by the end of May.[404]

Several human rights group issued statements condemning the forced repatriations as a violation of the fundamental principle of non-refoulement—Cambodia's obligation under the Refugee Convention not to return any person to a country where his or her life or freedom may be

---

[400] Thet Sambath and Kevin Doyle, "Mondolkiri Minorities Ask for More Protection," *Cambodia Daily*, April 23, 2001. Human Rights Watch, "Deportation of Montagnard Refugees to Vietnam," May 20, 2001.

[401] Deutsche Presse-Agentur, "Authorities locate 160 ethnic Vietnamese minorities fleeing political unrest," May 4, 2001. Reuters, "Refugees moved after bounty report," *South China Morning Post*, May 13, 2001.

[402] Kevin Doyle and Seth Meixner, "Montagnards Leave Jungle Under U.N. Care," *Cambodia Daily*, May 12, 2001.

[403] The Ratanakiri provincial police commissioner told rights workers that in facilitating the deportations, he was carrying out an order received several years earlier from the director general of the National Police and the Ministry of Interior instructing police to deport any individuals who enter the country illegally. Human Rights Watch, "Deportation of Montagnard Refugees to Vietnam," May 20, 2001.

[404] Matt Reed and Lor Chandara, "Temporary Asylum Granted to Montagnards," *Cambodia Daily*, May 18, 2001.

threatened.[405] On May 22, UNHCR issued a statement expressing concern about the fact that more than one hundred highlanders may have been deported from Cambodia, including "individuals who claimed to be fleeing for political reasons," and called for a proper review of asylum claims before people were forced back to their country of origin.[406]

Most of the first wave of highlanders to flee from Vietnam, from March through May 2001, fled because of fear of arrest or other reprisals because of their participation in the February demonstrations. A Jarai man who was a leader in the land rights movement in his district, described why he fled to Cambodia:

> I fled from my village after I saw forty police ransack my neighbor's house and take him away to jail. I escaped to Cambodia but in my heart I didn't want to come here. I felt I was abandoning the people in Vietnam—not only my wife and children, but also the movement. I didn't come here in order to resettle elsewhere but to get information to our leader so that he could find a way to solve the problem.
>
> Once I got here I realized that I couldn't return to Vietnam or I'd be arrested. The situation hiding in the forest was also very difficult. Police were hunting for us on both sides of the border. We ran out of food, we had no shelter from the rain, and some of us fell ill from malaria. Soon we realized we couldn't stay in Cambodia and we couldn't go back to Vietnam. We asked the U.N. to help us; otherwise we would have been arrested. Now all I wonder is, what about my wife and children in Vietnam—I've had no news about what happened to them after I left.[407]

Beginning in June 2001, some highlanders who had not attended the demonstrations or even heard about them before they took place, began to cross the border. In interviews with Human Rights Watch, members of this group stated they fled to Cambodia because of longstanding grievances about land, religious repression, or political pressure as former FULRO members. For many in this second wave, the government's crackdown was the impetus to flee Vietnam, whether or not they had been active with MFI or joined the protests.

---

[405] Amnesty International Urgent Action, "Fear of forcible repatriation," May 10, 2001. Human Rights Watch, "Deportation of Montagnard Refugees to Vietnam," May 20, 2001. Cambodian Human Rights Action Committee Statement, May 22, 2001.
[406] Reuters, "U.N. urges Cambodia not to deport Vietnamese," May 22, 2001.
[407] Human Rights Watch interview with Jarai man from Gia Lai, March 2001.

Once they heard that the U.N. had set up secure sites for refugees in Cambodia, where they might obtain help and protection, dozens began to cross the border.

A Jarai man who did not attend the demonstrations said he fled after the protests because there were so many police and military in his village, and also because he had been arrested and threatened three times by local authorities in 2000 and 2001 because of his role as a church leader. "After the demonstrations there was no peace or freedom in my village," he said. "When I woke up one morning, the place was full of soldiers, who'd come at night. There were many police and more than twenty soldiers, who entered each house."[408]

Others who fled to Cambodia had heard from family members or MFI organizers abroad that the U.N. would help the highlanders establish an independent state. Representative of this group was an Ede man, who was tortured and imprisoned for several months in Buon Ma Thuot prison after the protests. After release from prison, he escaped to Cambodia as soon as he was strong enough to travel. His aim in fleeing was to obtain an independent state:

> I fled to Cambodia to meet the upper levels—the international community and the U.N.—to solve the problem of land. I don't ever want to see Vietnamese [people] again, until this problem is solved. I abandoned my wife, my house, my children. I fled to Cambodia to show the U.N. about our struggle for the land of Dega. I want the U.N. to [delineate] clearly the map: which is the area of the ethnic minorities, and which is the area of the Vietnamese. I want the international community to understand clearly that I didn't come here to get rich or to resettle abroad. We just want our land. When we have our land, we can support our families and live freely. We want the world to know that we want justice. We want our own country. [409]

Initially, most of the highlanders fleeing to Cambodia expressed little interest in resettlement abroad; instead, they said they had fled in search of a secure place, or in hopes that the U.N. would offer political support for the independence movement. Beginning in June 2001, groups of highlanders fled to Cambodia in hopes of resettlement abroad. Some of the earlier arrivals in the camps eventually began to consider resettlement as well, particularly once they learned from UNHCR staff that the U.N. would not be assisting them in establishing an independent state. Most of those who arrived during the month of July—more than one hundred total—had not attended the demonstrations, but

---

[408] Human Rights Watch interview with Jarai man from Gia Lai, June 26, 2001.
[409] Human Rights Watch interview with Ede man from Dak Lak, July 17, 2001.

had numerous longstanding complaints about conditions in the highlands and hopes for an independent state or resettlement abroad.

A third wave of highlanders fled to Cambodia in late August and during September, with more than one hundred arriving the last week in August alone.[410] Large groups of Jarai from Ea Sup and Ea H'leo districts of Dak Lak fled at that time in order to avoid repressive tactics such as forced oath-swearing procedures such as the "goat's blood ceremonies"[411] and other repressive tactics by the authorities. Dozens of others from Gia Lai arrived around the same time, reporting that they had been in hiding in Vietnam since just after the protests—either in the forest or in pits under people's houses in the villages—until they were able to escape. At the end of September, a first group of refugees from Kontum was able to make it across to refugee camps in Ratanakiri. Others, who were in prison from February through May escaped as soon as they were strong enough to make the journey to Cambodia.

Highlanders who fled from Dak Lak at the end of November 2001 reported that the travel restrictions and increased presence of security forces—intended to hamper political or religious activities and refugee flows—was also interfering with normal economic activities such as farming or selling goods. By the end of the year, some highlanders were fleeing Vietnam not only because of fear of arrest or religious and political repression, but also because it was becoming increasingly difficult for many to make a living.

At the end of 2001, groups of highlanders arrived in Cambodia with reports that repression of Christians had worsened further. In December 2001, dozens of Montagnard Christians were rounded up and detained while trying to organize Christmas ceremonies and prayer services. Additional arrests of church leaders were reported in Gia Lai and Dak Lak in January and February 2002, prompting more villagers to flee to Cambodia.

In late 2001 and early 2002, the UNHCR sites began to see a new (albeit small) flow of highlanders. These fled because of reprisals or threats of arrest from Vietnamese authorities because they had served as guides for others attempting to flee to Cambodia or they had helped people hiding in the forest in Vietnam by giving them food or medicine.

As the one-year anniversary of the unrest in the highlands neared, the heavy-handed approach of the Vietnamese authorities in the Central Highlands appeared to be having the opposite effect to that intended. The more closely villagers were monitored to prevent their leaving Vietnam, the greater the impetus to escape an increasingly unbearable situation. Tightening controls at

---

[410] John Gravois, "116 More Montagnards at U.N. Camps," *Cambodia Daily*, September 3, 2001.
[411] See Case Study XVI, "The Goat's Blood Oath Ceremonies in Ea H'leo," p. 163.

the village level backfired in many instances; it was just this sort of repression that the highlanders had been protesting since February 2001. Nonetheless, by February 2002 the refugee flow came to a virtual standstill when Cambodia implemented a new policy of deporting all new refugees.

The Tripartite Talks

The resettlement of the thirty-eight highlanders to the U.S. in April 2001 infuriated the Vietnamese government, which in turn put immense pressure on UNHCR in a meeting in Hanoi later that same month. After a meeting with the diplomatic community in Phnom Penh on April 24, 2001, UNHCR Regional Representative Jahanshah Assadi announced that protection of first asylum rights and voluntary repatriation would take precedence over third-country resettlement for the time being.[412] On May 17, after discussions between Assadi and Cambodian Deputy Prime Minister Sarkheng in Phnom Penh, UNHCR secured official Cambodian approval to grant temporary asylum to Montagnard refugees currently in Cambodia.[413]

On July 26, 2001, talks opened between Vietnam, Cambodia, and UNHCR in Hanoi, Vietnam, to discuss the fate of more than 300 Montagnard refugees who were then under U.N. protection at the two sites in Cambodia. A primary subject of the talks was the potential for a voluntary repatriation program for the highlanders. The talks broke down after Vietnam refused to allow the U.N. to have unrestricted access to the Central Highlands to monitor the repatriation. The Vietnamese delegation also questioned the need for any repatriation program to be voluntary, charging instead that the Montagnard refugees were illegal immigrants in Cambodia.

However, after a second round of talks in Phnom Penh on January 21, 2002, Cambodia, Vietnam and UNHCR reached a tripartite agreement on repatriation. The agreement made no mention of the fact that, under international law, any return of refugees to Vietnam must be voluntary and that the right of individuals to continue to seek asylum in Cambodia must be respected.[414] In addition, the agreement contained few specifications about post-

---

[412] Kevin Doyle and Seth Meixner, "Diplomats Meet on V.N. Refugee Issue," *Cambodia Daily*, April 26, 2001.
[413] Chhay Sophal, "Cambodia grants temporary asylum to Vietnamese," Reuters, May 17, 2001.
[414] According to UNHCR's *Handbook for Emergencies*, the necessary conditions for a voluntary repatriation must include safeguards as to the voluntary nature of the return; safeguards as to treatment upon return; and continued asylum for those who do not repatriate and remain refugees. Ensuring the voluntary nature of the return includes guaranteeing that the decision to repatriate is made freely; the refugees are making an informed decision based on an accurate country profile; and the decision is made

return monitoring and required UNHCR to obtain permission from Vietnamese authorities before each visit to the Central Highlands. Most importantly, while Vietnamese authorities made numerous public assurances that refugees repatriated to Vietnam would not be punished for having left the country, the agreement carried no protections for Evangelical Christians, and in particular, for leaders of the "Tin Lanh Dega" religion or the movement for land rights and independence.

Within days of signing the agreement, Vietnam announced that it had tried and convicted four highlanders who had been sent back from Cambodia in the late April and mid-May 2001 deportations. In addition, Vietnamese state media reported that Cambodian authorities had forcibly returned eighty-one highlanders from Cambodia to Vietnam. The Vietnamese government made it clear in dozens of press statements that it did not perceive the highlanders in Cambodia as legitimate asylum seekers or refugees, and instead used the word "illegal migrants" or even "illegal escapees" to refer to them.[415] Gia Lai provincial governor Nguyen Van Ha told reporters in February 2002: "They are not asylum seekers or refugees, because we did not do anything to force them to flee…All of them…illegally crossed the border into Cambodia."[416]

A statement issued by the Vietnamese Embassy in Washington, D.C. on February 8, 2002 summed up the stance of the Vietnamese government:

> Without a clear future, these Vietnamese citizens who were deceived and enticed to make their illegal border crossing are under miserable living conditions in tents temporarily set up by UNHCR inside Cambodia, experiencing shortages, diseases and sickness. They are not refugees because they have never been suppressed, persecuted or discriminated in Vietnam. Moreover, their families living in Vietnam are longing for their return.[417]

The VCP daily, *Nhan Dan* (The People) offered a description of prison-like conditions in refugee camps in Cambodia. It was based on an interview with a village chief in Dak Mil, who was escorted to the Mondolkiri UNHCR site by Cambodian and Vietnamese police to visit refugees there on January 28, 2002:

---

expressly. UNHCR, *Handbook for Emergencies*, June 2000, and UNHCR, *Handbook, Voluntary Repatriation: International Protection*, 1996.
[415] Voice of Vietnam Radio, "Vietnam criticizes USA's 'brutal interference' in repatriation plan," February 16, 2002, BBC Monitoring Service.
[416] Associated Press, "Vietnam Officials Blame U.S. for Refugee Repatriation Delay," February 18, 2002.
[417] Embassy of the Socialist Republic of Vietnam, "On the return of Vietnamese minority people from CPC [sic]," February 8, 2002.

I saw them live a miserable life. They do not have enough rice to eat. Most of them are suffering from dropsy and malaria. They are kept under surveillance, so many people want to return home but they cannot escape. Some families who went there with all their family members could not escape now because, if only one member of their families escapes, their relatives will be beaten. The people there will die because of hunger or disease if they do not return soon.[418]

After the signing of the tripartite agreement, Vietnam increased its pressure on Cambodia and UNHCR to immediately repatriate all of the Vietnamese highlanders in Cambodia, who numbered well over 1,000 at that time. As UNHCR made preparations for a first group of fifteen refugees to voluntarily return to Vietnam on February 19, 2002 the tripartite agreement began to crumble, with Vietnam demanding an expedited timetable, obstructing UNHCR's pre-return home visits, and insisting that the repatriation program did not need to be voluntary.[419]

On February 21, during a visit to Phnom Penh by the Vietnamese deputy prime minister, Cambodia and Vietnam reached an agreement in which the two countries agreed to bilaterally implement the repatriation agreement—with or without UNHCR involvement—and return all of the highlanders to Vietnam by April 30. The following day, Hok Lundy, the director general of the Cambodian National Police, accompanied the governor of Dak Lak province and the Vietnamese ambassador to Cambodia to the Mondolkiri UNHCR site.

Accompanied by fifty policemen and a fire engine, the delegation entered the camp, which was surrounded on the periphery by armed Cambodian soldiers. Using a bullhorn the police summoned the residents of the camp to meet in a barn usually used for church services. The majority of the camp population—approximately 400 people—attended the meeting. The governor of Dak Lak announced that it was time for everyone to return to Vietnam, telling them that they had no choice. People should not be afraid, he said, because they had been tricked by hostile foreign forces into leaving Vietnam. As he spoke, the camp population began to chant "Lies, lies!" The Governor then asked the group, "Who wants to go back, and who wants to stay?" At that, everyone in the hall rose to their feet and shouted that they wanted to stay. Cambodian police in

---

[418] *Nhan Dan* (The People), "Dac Min district hopes for fled members early return," February 21, 2002.
[419] Kevin Doyle, "Deadline set for return of Vietnam asylum seekers," February 22, 2002; Reuters, "U.S. opposes deadline for return of Vietnam refugees," February 22, 2002.

white helmets descended on the crowd, and one officer began to beat people with an electric truncheon. He had hit five people by the time he was physically removed from the hall by a UNHCR staff person and Cambodian police.[420]

It took twenty minutes to restore order. After several more speeches, in which Hok Lundy made it clear that there would be no third country resettlement of anyone from the camps and that people should start preparing themselves to return to Vietnam, the delegation left the site.

In a subsequent meeting with UNHCR, Hok Lundy reportedly said that there were going to be some changes in the way the tripartite agreement was to be implemented. When questioned as to whether setting a deadline for the return of all Montagnard refugees to Vietnam contravened the spirit of the agreement, the Vietnamese ambassador reportedly said: "Show me the word 'voluntary' in that document."

In a statement on February 23, 2001, UNHCR expressed concerns about the incident at the Mondolkiri site, the fact that its monitoring team in the Central Highlands had been refused permission to visit villages of potential returnees on February 21, and the imposition of a deadline by Cambodia and Vietnam for the return of all highlanders from Cambodia. "The introduction of a deadline clearly undermines the voluntary nature of return," UNHCR stated. "In general, UNHCR opposes visits to refugee camps by officials from the countries they have fled." For all intents and purposes, the repatriation program was suspended, for the time being, as Cambodia's policy shifted from accepting new refugees to forcibly deporting all new arrivals.[421]

On March 2, the tripartite agreement appeared to be further deteriorating, when a group of sixty-one highlanders in UNHCR's Ratanakiri site, who had expressed interest in voluntary repatriation, were escorted back to Vietnam in a bilateral operation conducted by Cambodian and Vietnamese authorities without the involvement of UNHCR.[422]

---

[420] Human Rights Watch interviews with witnesses, UNHCR Mondolkiri site, February 22, 2002. Kevin Doyle, "Cambodian police use batons in U.N. camp—witnesses," Reuters, February 23, 2002. Seth Meixner, "Beatings of Montagnards Condemned," *Cambodia Daily*, February 25, 2001.

[421] UNHCR News, "Tripartite Agreement on Montagnards Under Threat," February 23, 2002. Agence France-Presse, U.N. suspends repatriation of Vietnamese refugees from Cambodia," February 23, 2002.

[422] According to the terms of the tripartite agreement, voluntary repatriation from Cambodia was to occur only after UNHCR had monitored village conditions in the Central Highlands in an "effective and credible" manner. In addition, UNHCR staff members were to accompany returnees back to Vietnam, and conduct follow-up visits on their well-being after repatriation. See "The Report of the Second Tripartite Meeting on Vietnamese 'Montagnards' in Cambodia," Phnom Penh, 21 January 2002.

That same day, Cambodian Deputy Prime Minister Sarkheng defended national-level instructions to Ratanakiri provincial authorities to deport a second group of sixty-three refugees, who had just arrived in Ratanakiri. "We did not violate any agreement with UNHCR," he said. "They are illegal immigrants, we must send them back. Every country in the world sends back illegal immigrants who cross their borders. This country belongs to Cambodia, not to UNHCR."[423]

The final blow to the tripartite agreement came on March 21, 2002. Over the objections of UNHCR field staff, Vietnamese authorities transported a delegation of more than 400 people in twelve tour buses from Vietnam to the Mondolkiri UNHCR site to pressure the refugees to return to Vietnam. While many of the visitors were relatives of the refugees, UNHCR officials estimated that as many as one hundred were Vietnamese officials. Several dozen armed Cambodian policemen accompanied the delegation, which was allowed to seek out individual refugees and make searches of their huts. Cambodian police brought out their guns and electric batons, but did not use them, as delegation members threatened and manhandled UNHCR staffpersons and refugees. In response to the incident, on March 22 UNHCR announced its withdrawal from the tripartite agreement and formally terminated its involvement with the repatriation process.[424]

Flight to Cambodia: Arrest, Mistreatment and Forced Return

More than 500 Montagnard refugees who fled to Cambodia in the year following the February 2001 protests were forcibly returned to Vietnam. Human Rights Watch received reports that some of the returnees—particularly those who led others to flee—were beaten and imprisoned upon return to Vietnam.

Others who were forcibly returned were allowed to return to their homes, but placed under heavy surveillance or house arrest. Some were forced to tell others in their villages not to go to Cambodia and to say that conditions in the UNHCR camps were very poor.[425] The families of those who have fled were placed under intense pressure, as described by a Mnong man from Dak Lak:

> The police are watching our families and constantly asking where we are, pressing our families to get us to return and report on us to the

---

[423] Kevin Doyle, "U.N. concerned over Cambodian deportations," Reuters, March 3, 2002.
[424] Agence France-Presse, "UNHCR withdraws from repatriation accord for hill-tribe people," March 23, 2002. Reuters, "U.N. halts Vietnam hilltribe return from Cambodia," March 23, 2002.
[425] Human Rights Watch interviews with refugees in Ratanakiri and Mondolkiri, October, 2001. See also Associated Press, "Cambodia Begins Returning Some Hill Tribe Members-Vietnam," August 23, 2001.

police. There are many police and soldiers in our villages—they've established a police post in our village.[426]

Refugees arriving in Cambodia in October and November 2001 described being shown a video, allegedly of the UNHCR sites in Cambodia, at public meetings organized by local authorities. The video showed thin, sickly refugees and stated that there was inadequate food, medical care and shelter at the camps.

In many cases, there was evident close cooperation between Cambodian and Vietnamese authorities in deporting and persecuting refugees, with fees paid on occasion to Cambodian civilians or policemen who turned over refugees to Vietnamese authorities. A partial list of forced returns from Cambodia or arrests in Vietnam of highlanders seeking to flee since February 2001 includes the following:

- On March 26, 2001, the first deputy police commissioner of Mondolkiri province, accompanied by the commander of the provincial Gendarmerie, transported nineteen ethnic Jarai men to the Vietnamese border. The Cambodian authorities then signed documents, together with their Vietnamese counterparts, authorizing the transfer. The group was arrested by Vietnamese police, beaten and detained in the provincial police station and then imprisoned in Chi Hoa prison in Ho Chi Minh City for a week before being released to their villages, where they were placed under heavy surveillance.[427]
- On April 25, 2001 twenty-four Ede from Buon Dha Prong in Dak Lak were arrested in Vietnam while trying to flee to Cambodia. Members of the group were beaten, kicked, handcuffed, and jailed for a week at the district police station. Afterwards nine were sent to the provincial prisons in Pleiku and Buon Ma Thuot; the rest were placed under surveillance and prohibited from leaving their villages.[428]
- On April 30, 2001, thirty-two Ede and Jarai from Chu Se district, Gia Lai and Buon Dha Ea Bong, Dak Lak were forcibly returned from Cambodia to Vietnam. Nine members of the group were reportedly imprisoned. In February 2002, two members of the group—Siu Beng

---

[426] Human Rights Watch interviews on October 31, 2001 with ethnic Mnong men who were screened out of the UNHCR site in Mondolkiri in June 2001 and returned to Dak Lak, Vietnam. Some returned to Cambodia again in September 2001.
[427] For documentation and more details see Case Study XVII, "Arrest and Torture of Highlanders Deported from Cambodia," p. 166.
[428] Human Rights Watch interview with Ede men from Buon Dha Prong, October 29, 2001.

and Siu Be—were sentenced to six and a half years and three and a half years of imprisonment respectively, on charges of "organizing illegal migrations." The fact that the group was forced back by Cambodian police, the dates of the return, and the number of returnees was confirmed in a January 2002 article in the Vietnamese government daily, *Nhan Dan* (The People).[429]

- On May 8, Y Lim (also known as Dien Y Lien), his wife Maria Nam Linh and their five children—ethnic Mnong refugees who had received official UNHCR protection documents on April 25—were loaded onto a truck in Mondolkiri by Cambodian police and sent back to Vietnam. On April 26, May 1 and again on May 2, UNHCR met with Mondolkiri provincial authorities to secure assurances that persons seeking asylum would not be forcibly returned. The day before the family of seven was forcibly returned, Director General of the National Police Hok Lundy met with U.S. Ambassador Kent Wiedemann and assured him that no deportations would take place.[430]

- On May 10, 2001, thirty-two highlanders were forced back from Koh Nhek district, Mondolkiri. After being handed over to Vietnamese authorities, the refugees were detained for one night at the border, where they were interrogated intensively about their reasons for trying to leave Vietnam and their involvement with the demonstrations. Some were slapped during the questioning. They were then transported to the prison in Buon Ma Thuot, where they were held for five nights and questioned further. The group was then sent to T-20 prison in Pleiku. Some were released after several days, while others were held up to one month. Three members of the group who were perceived to be most politically active remained in prison as of November, 2001.[431]

- On May 15, 2001, Cambodian district and provincial police in Ratanakiri province accompanied three vehicles carrying sixty-three highlanders to the Vietnamese border, where the group was deported. Vietnamese officials detained them for one night at the border, where they were interrogated and some members of the group were beaten. The entire group was then transported to T-20 prison in Pleiku, where

---

[429] *Nhan Dan* (The People), "Four receive jail terms for organizing illegal migrations," January 28, 2002.
[430] Kevin Doyle and Thet Sambath, "Missing Family Sought Only Safety in Cambodia," *Cambodia Daily*, May 10, 2001; Reuters, "U.N. searches for Vietnamese missing from Cambodia," May 13, 2001; Amnesty International Urgent Action, "Fear of forcible repatriation," 10 May 2001, AI Index: ASA 23/003/2001. Human Rights Watch, "Deportation of Montagnard Refugees to Vietnam," May 20, 2001.
[431] Interviews with Jarai men from Gia Lai, November 2001.

members of the group were held for different lengths of time. In January 2002, two members of the group—Kpa Hling and Hnoch—were tried and convicted of organizing illegal migrations and sentenced to five and a half years of imprisonment.[432]

- On May 31, 2001, a group of seven Jarai were arrested in Vietnam three kilometers from the Ratanakiri border when they became afraid and scattered. Two made it to Cambodia but five were arrested by Vietnamese authorities. As of November 2001 at least one of the five was still in prison; it was expected that he could be held for a long time.[433]
- In June 2001, nineteen highlanders were reportedly imprisoned in Dak Lak after being returned from Cambodia. Their current location is unknown.
- In July 2001, six Ede from Buon Sup, who had fled to Cambodia, were sent back to Dak Lak. At first they were allowed to return to their homes in Dak Lak but later they were apprehended during the night and imprisoned in a "dark place."[434]
- On August 3, 2001, three Ede men from Buon Cuor Knia who tried to escape to Cambodia in July were beaten severely by public security officers. Two of the men subsequently went missing on August 8; their whereabouts as of March 2002 were unknown. The remaining six were reportedly fearful for their lives.[435]
- In late August 2001, fifty people who fled Krong Pac district in Dak Lak were reportedly returned to Vietnam by Cambodian authorities. As

---

[432] Such deportations amount to a possible violation of the fundamental principle of non-refoulement, or the prohibition under the 1951 Refugee Convention on returning refugees to any country where their life or freedom would be threatened or they are likely to face persecution. The fact that the group was deported by Cambodian police, the dates of the deportation, and the number of returnees was confirmed in a January 2002 article in the official Vietnamese government daily. *Nhan Dan* (The People), "Four receive jail terms for organizing illegal migrations," January 28, 2002. See also, Human Rights Watch, "Deportation of Montagnard Refugees to Vietnam," May 20, 2001.

[433] Human Rights Watch interview with a Jarai man whose relative was detained at the time of the incident, October 17, 2001.

[434] Human Rights Watch interview with relative of one of the people imprisoned, July 27, 2001. Such deportations amount to a possible violation of the fundamental principle of non-refoulement, or the prohibition under the 1951 Refugee Convention on returning refugees to any country where their life or freedom would be threatened or they are likely to face persecution.

[435] "Report on the Protestants' Situation in Dak Lak Province," September 3, 2001, written by a Protestant church leader in the Central Highlands who asked to remain anonymous. Vietnamese language document and English translation on file at Human Rights Watch.

of early September, these fifty people were being held incommunicado at an undisclosed location.[436] There was no further information by March 2002.

- On September 24, 2001, a large group of ethnic Jarai who were attempting to flee from Gia Lai and Kontum provinces to Cambodia were intercepted by Cambodian border police in Ratanakiri. The Cambodian police fired over the group's heads. Most of the group managed to escape, but eight were arrested, beaten and handed over to Vietnamese police in exchange for U.S. $300. The eight were then sent back to Vietnam; their whereabouts as of February 2002 were unknown. Ironically, the next morning another group of Cambodian border police escorted the remaining sixty-eight members of the group of refugees to the UNHCR site in Ratanakiri provincial town.[437]

- On December 28, 2001, Cambodian authorities in Mondolkiri province forced back 167 highlanders, who had fled across the border from Vietnam after dozens of Montagnard Christians were rounded up and detained in Vietnam while trying to organize Christmas ceremonies and prayer services.[438] While some of the women in the group forced back to Cambodia subsequently returned to their villages, a number of the men were still missing as of March 2002.

- In March 2002, there were unconfirmed reports that eighty-one highlanders had fled into Cambodia, where they were arrested and forced back to Vietnam. The official Vietnamese army newspaper, *Quan Doi Nhan Dan*, carried an article on February 8 in which the reporter said he had met members of the group of eighty-one highlanders deported from Cambodia, some who had returned voluntarily and others "who had been sent back by Cambodian border guards or been saved by Vietnamese forces."[439]

---

[436] "Report on the Protestants' Situation in Dak Lak Province," September 3, 2001, written by a Protestant church leader in the Central Highlands who asked to remain anonymous. Vietnamese language document and English translation on file at Human Rights Watch.
[437] Thet Sambath, "Montagnards Reportedly Sold to Vietnamese," *The Cambodia Daily*, October 2, 2001.
[438] Human Rights Watch interviews with a Western diplomat in Phnom Penh and UNHCR field staff in Cambodia, who confirmed the report with national-level and provincial authorities, January 2002.
[439] Associated Press, "Report: 81 more Vietnamese minority people flee to Cambodia," February 6, 2002; Steve Kirby, "New exodus of Vietnam hill people clouds U.N. repatriation efforts," Agence France-Presse, February 6, 2002; Agence France-Presse, "Hanoi daily says Cambodia 'sending back' asylum-seekers," February 8, 2002.

- On March 2, 2002 Ratanakiri provincial police stated they were following orders from National Police headquarters when they forced back a group of sixty-three refugees to Vietnam over the objections of UNHCR, which was denied access to the group.[440]
- On March 15, 2002, thirty-five highlanders were deported from Mondolkiri province to Vietnam. The VCP daily, *Nhan Dan* (The People) reported that Mondolkiri provincial authorities returned the group to the Cambodia-Vietnam border, where they were "welcomed at the border gate by Gia Lai provincial authorities before they rejoined their families."[441]

---

[440] Kevin Doyle, "Cambodia deports 63 hilltribe asylum seekers," Reuters, March 2, 2002.
[441] Viet Nam News Agency, "Gia Lai Province Welcomes Another 35 Illegal Migrants," March 15, 2001.

XIV. TIGHTENING CONTROLS

The authorities are suspicious of many people, but mainly of Christian pastors, evangelists and church elders in all villages where there are Christian believers. They accused pastors and church leaders of planning Christmas celebrations in order to organize escapes to Cambodia. Then, since December they have seized many people in an extra-legal manner, coming under cover of darkness, without arrest warrants. Some people, after being beaten are interrogated non-stop for two or three days straight and then sent home.... Others, such as A.T., who was seized on February 6—until now his family has no idea where he is.
—Protestant church leader, Dak Lak, February 23, 2002

Towards the end of 2001, in response to increasing numbers of highlanders fleeing to U.N. refugee camps in Cambodia, the Vietnamese authorities began an organized effort to increase pressure on villagers to swear loyalty to the government and renounce their religion and politics.

Periodic detention or placement of people under house arrest continued to be reported in the highlands from September 2001 through early 2002. This often consisted of the temporary detention of large groups of refugees who had been forcibly deported from Cambodia, with the leaders or guides of the groups singled out for longer prison terms. Many evangelical Protestant leaders and church elders continued to be summoned throughout the year for interrogation or "working sessions" with the police, where they were questioned about their religious and political activities and ordered not to organize gatherings for religious services.

During and after the visit of Party Secretary Nông Dúc Manh to Gia Lai and Dak Lak in September 2001, eight Jarai were reportedly arrested in Chu Se district, Gia Lai. As of March 2002, their whereabouts were unknown.

Human Rights Watch received reports of additional arrests in September in Mang Yang district, Dak Lak, where local authorities arrested fifty-eight highlanders. They sent thirty-four to the district jail and the rest to the commune police headquarters, where they were ordered to perform labor and sign documents pledging to cease all activities with Kok Ksor and renouncing evangelical Christianity. As of March 2002 some of the detainees had not returned to their villages.[442]

---

[442] Human Rights Watch interviews with Mang Yang residents, October 13, 2001 and February 28, 2002.

Another round of arrests was reported in October and November 2001, when ten highlanders were detained in Dak Doa and Chu Se districts of Gia Lai, and in Dak Mil and Krong Pac districts, Dak Lak. Their whereabouts as of March 2002 were unknown.

In late January and early February 2002, Human Rights Watch received reports of numerous arrests. These included the detention of at least seven church leaders in Dak Doa district of Gia Lai and Cu Ebur, Buon Don, Krong Buk, and Cu Mgar districts of Dak Lak. Another eight highlanders were arrested on February 20 in Ea H'leo. As of the end of February, two had returned to their villages but the whereabouts of the rest was unknown.[443]

Human Rights Watch received reports through March 2002 that the Vietnamese authorities were continuing to ban large religious gatherings and pressure Christians to renounce their religion in many places, including Ea H'leo, Cu Mgar, Buon Don, Mdrak and Ea Sup districts of Dak Lak; Ayun Pa, Phu Thien, An Khe districts of Gia Lai; Dak Ha and Sa Thay districts of Kontum; and Lam Ha and Lac Duong districts of Lam Dong.[444]

As more highlanders fled to Cambodia, in September 2001 Vietnamese authorities started a new campaign, forcing the heads of households in many villages to sign documents to guarantee that their family members would not attempt to flee to Cambodia or participate in political organizing.

The Christmas Crackdown

In December 2001, MFI announced that thousands of highlanders would be conducting Christmas prayer vigils on December 24-25. On December 10, twenty minority church leaders from the Central Highlands were summoned to Hanoi, where they were warned against using religion to undermine national unity. The minority pastors were asked to publicly express support for the VCP's policies on religion and call for the maintenance of social order.[445]

---

[443] "Report on the Situation in Dak Lak," February 23, 2002, written by a Protestant church leader who asked to remain anonymous. English language translation of Vietnamese document on file at Human Rights Watch.

[444] "Report on the Protestants' Situation in Dak Lak Province," September 3, 2001, written by a Protestant church leader in the Central Highlands who asked to remain anonymous. "Central Highlands Christian Workers' Situation Reports, December 2001 through February 2002," written by Protestant church leaders who asked to remain anonymous. English translations of Vietnamese language documents on file at Human Rights Watch.

[445] Agence France-Presse, "Communist Vietnam in Christmas warning to minority Protestants," December 12, 2001. Associated Press, "Vietnam Communist Party asks Protestants to help maintain political and social order in restive Central Highlands," December 11, 2001. Voice of Vietnam Radio, "Vietnam radio condemns western media's allegation on 'lack of religious freedom,'" December 23, 2001, BBC Monitoring,

During the third week of December, dozens of local "house church" leaders were rounded up and detained throughout the Central Highlands to prevent them from conducting Christmas services. More than 160 highlanders attempting to flee to Cambodia at that time were arrested and deported back to Vietnam.[446] While many of the women subsequently returned to their villages, the whereabouts of some of the men was still unknown as of late March 2002.

Official efforts to thwart Christmas celebrations included the following:[447]

- On December 22, 2001 in Ea H'leo district of Dak Lak, local authorities summoned Protestant church pastors and elders. They were pressured to sign agreements not to conduct Christmas celebrations and told that gatherings outside their homes were illegal. Security police disbanded, disrupted or monitored Christmas gatherings in Ea Qui, Diai Giang, Ea Drang, and Ea H'leo commune town.
- On December 22 in Ayun Pa district, Gia Lai, commune and village police and a village chief apprehended a minority Christian, beat him, and made him do forced labor at the commune office. On December 24 and 25 the authorities went house by house to warn people not to gather for Christmas ceremonies outside their homes. The authorities in one commune summoned minority church leaders to attend a seminar on Decree No. 26 (concerning religious activities) on December 24.
- On December 23, soldiers and police burst into a church service in Phu Thien district, Gia Lai and accused the congregation of being "Dega Christians." The leader of the service, who was filling in for a church elder who had been arrested, was detained at the commune office for two days and interrogated.
- On December 23, security and traffic police and soldiers surrounded and disbanded a Christmas gathering in An Khe district, Gia Lai. Afterwards, church leaders were summoned by local authorities, who accused them of organizing illegal Christmas services. The church

---

December 24, 2001. Montagnard Foundation, Inc. Media Release, "Hundreds of Thousands of Montagnards to Join Christmas Prayer Vigil," December 2001.
[446] Zenit.org, "Vietnam Cracking Down on Christian Tribes in Mountains," January 28, 2002. Montagnard Foundation, Inc. Report and Media Release, "Torture, Arrests, Kidnappings of Degars [Montagnard] Hilltribe People who Celebrated Christmas in Vietnam in December 2001," January 2002. Human Rights Watch, "No Montagnard Repatriation Without Protection," January 15, 2002.
[447] Information is from: "Central Highlands Christian Workers' Situation Reports, December 2001 through February 2002," written by Protestant church leaders who asked to remain anonymous. English translation of Vietnamese language document on file at Human Rights Watch.

Tightening Controls 147

leaders were told that churches could no longer meet each week for worship.
- On December 23, district security police in Dak Ha district, Kontum, warned local Christians not to observe Christmas in groups. Several church leaders were summoned to sign pledges not to organize ceremonies.
- On December 24 in Kontum provincial town, police and government officials attempted to prevent people from entering a church, and videotaped the service. Three church leaders were summoned over the next two days for videotaped interrogation sessions with the district secretary and the chairman of the VCP Fatherland Front.
- On December 24 in Sa Thay district, Kontum, police entered the home of a church leader. They confiscated his Bible and interrogated and warned him against organizing any religious gatherings.
- On December 25 in Dakbla commune, Kontum, police and local officials detained a Christian who was traveling to the next commune. They confiscated his Bible, hymnbook and motorcycle on charges that he was illegally propagating religion. That evening police searched the homes of several Christians in the adjoining commune.
- On December 22, local officials summoned church elders from three communes in Mdrak district, Dak Lak and told them they were prohibited from organizing groups of people for Christmas ceremonies or church meetings. In one commune, church elders were pressured to sign pledges that they would no longer gather people in groups. On December 24 in the same district, local officials terminated a Christmas service.
- After Christmas 2001, authorities no longer permitted Christians to gather in a church in Krong No commune, Lak district, Dak Lak.
- In Lam Dong, authorities banned services in churches in three communes in Lac Duong district after Christmas, and restricted religious gatherings to no more than ten people. In early February 2002, the authorities issued a citation for a church meeting in the same district and confiscated seven Bibles and hymnbooks. The pastor was summoned for interrogation and church services were terminated from that time.

The One-Year Anniversary

As February 2002 and the first anniversary of the protests approached, extra benefits were given out in the highlands to commemorate Tet, the Vietnamese New Year. Cambodian and Vietnamese officials allowed some highlanders to freely cross the border to visit their relatives in the refugee camps at that time, deliver New Year's gifts, and encourage their relatives to go back to Vietnam.

Despite these gestures, highlanders interviewed by Human Rights Watch and Western reporters in February 2002 reported that the actual situation had not improved. They cited ongoing abuses including harassment of Christians, mistreatment of refugees from Cambodia, and a repressive police presence in the villages.[448]

During a government-organized press tour to the Central Highlands conducted in mid-February 2002, Jarai women wept as they told foreign journalists about ongoing violations and their fears of further reprisals by the government. "They follow us and watch us all the time," a Jarai woman told reporters in Chu Se district, Gia Lai on February 19, 2002. She said she feared that her husband, who fled to Cambodia after the protests, would be arrested if he returned to Vietnam.[449] Another woman told reporters: "We tried to have a Protestant gathering and the government wouldn't allow it. The government doesn't accept our religion."[450]

Members of the first group of refugees who returned to Kontum on February 19 under a UNHCR repatriation program expressed concerns about their safety after their return.[451] Another man told reporters that he was arrested and beaten by Vietnamese border guards and authorities in his village the previous year when he attempted to flee to Cambodia.[452]

A Jarai man and former FULRO supporter attempted to "self-repatriate" from Cambodia to Vietnam on February 14, 2002, together with his wife and four children, acting on his own, not under U.N. auspices. On his return to Vietnam, however, he found such repression in his village in Gia Lai that he immediately turned around and fled back to Cambodia.

---

[448] Human Rights Watch interview with Jarai villagers from Ayun Pa district, Gia Lai, February 19, 2002. Clare Arthurs, "First Vietnamese refugees return home," BBC News Online, February 19, 2002. David Brunnstrom, "Tearful minority women defy Vietnamese officials," Reuters, February 9, 2002. David Thurber, "Relatives worry as U.N. repatriates first group of Vietnamese refugees from Cambodia," Associated Press, February 19, 2002. David Brunnstrom, "Vietnam minorities say they still face hardships," February 19, 2002. Amy Kazmin, "Vietnam denies ethnic persecution," *Financial Times*, February 20, 2002.
[449] David Brunnstrom, "Tearful minority women defy Vietnamese officials," Reuters, February 9, 2002.
[450] "Relatives worry as U.N. repatriates first group of Vietnamese refugees from Cambodia," Associated Press, February 19, 2002.
[451] David Brunnstrom, "Christian refugees fearful after return to Vietnam," Reuters, February 21, 2002.
[452] Clare Arthurs, "First Vietnamese refugees return home," BBC News Online, February 19, 2002.

"There were police and soldiers all over the place, and my relatives told me they had been there the whole past year," he told Human Rights Watch after reaching Cambodia again. The church in his village, which had been used every Sunday since 1995, had been closed. Villagers told him Christians suffered much more repression than before the demonstrations, with many regularly fined or called by police to do forced labor making fences or cutting grass at the commune center. Christians who had held positions in the government had been fired, he was told, and many Christians had been cut out of government rice distribution programs.

"All of these were new developments since the demonstrations," the man said. "My relatives warned me to flee immediately. They said the police had been looking for me ever since I first left."[453]

A Montagnard church leader summed up the atmosphere in a note smuggled out of the Central Highlands at the end of February 2002:

> Now the authorities have sent soldiers to various villages. They forbid Christians to meet for worship, or to read the Bible, or to pray before eating, or sing Christian songs. They forbid anything to do with Christianity. They are sowing confusion, suspicion and fear among the people.[454]

---

[453] The man had escaped to Cambodia with his family before the February 2001 demonstrations because he had been tortured and imprisoned in Vietnam. Human Rights Watch interview with Jarai man from Ayun Pa district, Gia Lai, February 19, 2002.

[454] "Report on the Situation in Dak Lak," February 23, 2002, written by a Protestant church leader who asked to remain anonymous. English language translation of Vietnamese document on file at Human Rights Watch.

XV. CASE STUDY: THE CHURCH BURNING AND KILLING BY SECURITY FORCES IN PLEI LAO

> *First the police ordered some Vietnamese civilians to ransack and destroy the church with axes. They used a cable tied to a vehicle to topple it and the soldiers used their gun butts. Then they forced the ethnic Jarai to burn it. The police made the Jarai pour five liters of gasoline and ten liters of machine oil on the church, but they couldn't get it to burn. So then the police took over and they set fire to it. Everyone was crying—for the dead and wounded, and for the church.*
> —Jarai man from Plei Lao, June 28, 2001

Just weeks after the February 2001 protests in the provincial towns of the Central Highlands, a major confrontation took place between Vietnamese security forces and several hundred ethnic Jarai civilians in Plei Lao village, located about thirty-five kilometers from Pleiku in Gia Lai. On March 10, 2001, hundreds of police and soldiers, who were apparently attempting to break up a peaceful all-night prayer service, that villagers acknowledged included discussions of independence, fired into a crowd of ethnic Jarai, killing at least one villager. The police then burned down the church and arrested dozens of villagers, one of whom—Siu Boc—was subsequently tried and sentenced to eleven years in prison for "disrupting security." His trial was held in Pleiku in September 2001.

The exact circumstances of what happened at Plei Lao remain unclear. Human Rights Watch has obtained eyewitness accounts from villagers whose testimonies suggest excessive use of force by police. It appears that villagers did try to block traffic and interfere with arrests that they believed were unfair. They also acknowledge throwing rocks at a police jeep after security forces arrested one villager. No impartial observers were present to assess whether the police decision to open fire was in any way proportional to the threat they faced from an angry crowd, and the government has allowed no access to the site by independent observers since the incident. The police also then proceeded to burn down a church, an indefensible act under any circumstances.

Provincial and district authorities were clearly extremely apprehensive about the large number of Jarai who began to gather for an extended prayer meeting at the church in Plei Lao, beginning in early March. Villagers told Human Rights Watch they were praying for protection during a time of extreme duress after the February protests, when villages were flooded with police and soldiers. The authorities, for their part, were wary of some of the political content of the church services. Some of the villagers reportedly had organized

Case Study: The Church Burning and Killing by Security Forces in Plei Lao   151

small groups to monitor and observe the police when and if they entered the village, to try to prevent authorities from dispersing religious meetings or carrying out arrests. Photographs of Plei Lao taken on March 10, obtained by Human Rights Watch, show that at least one of the access roads to the village appears to have been partially blocked by a farm cart, most likely dragged into the road by villagers.

In interviews conducted in June and October 2001 by Human Rights Watch with more than a dozen eyewitnesses to the incident at Plei Lao, villagers gave equal weight to the problems of land confiscation and religious repression as underlying causes of the turmoil that erupted not only in the streets of the provincial towns, but in their hamlet of 400 people, in early 2001.

The Church at Plei Lao

In March 2001, Plei Lao stood out among other villages in Nhon Hoa Commune of Chu Se District, Gia Lai. It was the only village in the commune that had a church building—a simple wooden and thatch structure that villagers had built in July 2000. Several hundred Plei Lao residents—more than half the village—gathered there each Sunday. Once a month villagers from a dozen other hamlets in Nhon Hoa commune would gather at Plei Lao for larger church services.

Elders from Plei Lao say that the Jarai there have been Christians since 1974, when a Jarai man brought the religion to the village. "Christianity did not come to Plei Lao from foreigners," a Plei Lao villager told Human Rights Watch. "The Jarai became Christians because we saw that religion could help us have harmony in the family. God could protect us."[455]

Since the mid-1970s, villagers said, local authorities had harassed villagers for practicing Christianity, sometimes detaining and interrogating religious followers. Nonetheless, in July 2000, villagers were able to build a sizable church (12 x 6.5 meters). Local authorities largely turned a blind eye to its construction, although policemen regularly monitored church services.

In February 2001, hundreds of villagers from Nhon Hoa commune—200 from Plei Lao alone—joined the demonstrations in Pleiku, leaving their homes before dawn on the morning of February 2. Most were blocked from reaching the provincial town, turned back by police at barricades. After the demonstrations, policemen were posted in the village and approximately thirty soldiers were dispatched to the commune headquarters.

---

[455] Human Rights Watch interview with a Jarai man from Plei Lao, June 27, 2001.

The Prayer Meetings

In early March, Plei Lao villagers started to hold a prayer meeting at the church, which went on day and night for ten days—until it was broken up by security forces. Villagers from more than a dozen surrounding hamlets joined, swelling the numbers in attendance to more than 500, and possibly as many as 1,000.[456]

"After the demonstrations we were afraid all the time," a villager from Plei Lao told Human Rights Watch. "There were police and soldiers constantly patrolling in our village. We had many prayer meetings—not just on Sundays—to pray and respect God and ask for help and protection."[457]

Another villager explained: "This is our tradition to pray day and night—as a prayer for help and protection—especially during times when we are fearful."[458]

Services started at 9:00 a.m. and went until 3:00 p.m. In the evening services commenced again, from 5:00 until 10:00 p.m., when villagers slept for a while. At 1:00 a.m. villagers would start worshipping again, until dawn.

Villagers said they were not afraid to gather in this manner—despite the crackdown after February. "We weren't afraid because we were just meeting to worship, and not to confront the authorities," said one villager. Nonetheless, after praying, talk often turned to politics, he said. "When we meet like this, part [of the meeting] is religious and part is political; for example talking about the fact that this land is the property of the ethnic minorities and the international community has approved our proposal for independence already."[459]

The Shooting

Beginning at 7:00 p.m. on the evening of March 9, hundreds of soldiers and riot police surrounded Plei Lao. At 4:00 a.m. on March 10, approximately sixty members of the security forces entered the village in three jeeps and several army trucks as villagers were praying in the church. According to eyewitnesses and photographs obtained by Human Rights Watch, the police were wearing white helmets and uniforms with protective padding. They carried plastic shields, batons, electric truncheons, tear gas canisters, and guns—both AK47 assault rifles and revolvers. Some of the soldiers were dressed in camouflage uniforms, rather than the usual olive green.

---

[456] Among the hamlets that joined were Plei Kia, Plei Klu, Plei Bo I, Plei Bo II, Plei Tao, Plei Poi, Plei Luh Yo, Plei Khy Ki, Plei Djrek, and Plei Puoi.
[457] Human Rights Watch interview with a Jarai man from Plei Lao, June 28, 2001.
[458] Human Rights Watch interview with a Jarai man from Plei Lao, June 27, 2001.
[459] Human Rights Watch interview with a Jarai man from a neighboring village who was present during the incident at Plei Lao, June 27, 2001.

Case Study: The Church Burning and Killing by Security Forces in Plei Lao

S, a young Jarai man, was sleeping in a hammock in a coffee plantation on the edge of the village. Awoken by the soldiers, he tried to run to warn the villagers in the church, but the police caught him. He was bound, gagged and put into one of three police jeeps. The rest of the villagers were unaware that anyone had been arrested, because it was still dark.

Many of the men continued praying in the church, but a contingent of women and girls went out to stand or sit across the road from the security forces, silently watching them. Some of the women wept as they saw more police and soldiers arrive. "We wanted to protect the church," said one man. "We sent the women to guard the road because we thought the police wouldn't hit or arrest the women."[460]

During the night more security reinforcements were called in from Pleiku, villagers said, with hundreds of police and soldiers posted on the perimeter of the village by daybreak, but not all entering the hamlet.

With the first light of dawn, some villagers realized that S had been arrested and was handcuffed in the police vehicle. A major confrontation broke out as about sixty villagers crowded around the jeep, trying to pull S out. The police fired tear gas and beat people with their batons. One eyewitness described what happened:

> We worshipped until 4:00 a.m., when the soldiers came, shining their flashlights. We were praying at the time. The people tried to stop the soldiers, and told them we were praying. Some of us got close to the police jeep. When it got light, I saw one person handcuffed and gagged inside. His name is S. I don't know if he'd left the church or if they'd arrested him on the road. We tried to open the door to get him out. When the people hadn't yet gotten S out of the jeep, the police beat his sister until blood came out of her mouth. She was screaming for them to release her brother. She didn't hit the police. The police attacked first. They hit her with an electric baton and with their fists. They hit other people nearby. The people fought back.
>
> After the people got S out of the jeep the police fired into the air. Then more police and soldiers came. They fired tear gas into the crowd and beat some of the people badly. Many people ran. Then the police lowered their guns and fired at people running away. Some

---

[460] Human Rights Watch interview with a Jarai man from a village in Nhon Hoa commune who was present during the incident at Plei Lao, June 27, 2001.

people fought back and attacked the jeep. Some threw rocks and broke the jeep's mirror.[461]

A nineteen-year-old boy who was very close to the police jeep, offered this description of what happened:

> The police and soldiers arrested one guy and gagged him so he could not speak. They handcuffed him and put him in their car. The people were angry and hit the car with rocks, breaking the mirror. The police fired tear gas. People carrying babies on their backs ran. The police used electric batons to shock some of the people. The tear gas was too thick.
>
> I was about five meters from the vehicle. The people surrounded the car and tried the pull S out. The police beat the hands of the people trying to pull him out. The people weren't hitting the police, just trying to drag S out. There were both men and women trying to do this. There was a lot of smoke from the tear gas—it was hard to see. People were choking and gagging and dizzy. Some people were screaming; others carrying children in their arms were crying.
>
> Once the people pulled S out of the car the police fired more tear gas and tried to prevent the people from taking him away. The shooting started when we ran. I don't know if they fired first into the air or not—but I know one person was shot in the leg. The people were able to get S into a house and cut off his handcuffs.[462]

Among those shot was Rmah Blin, thirty-three, from Plei Luh Yo. Police took him to the provincial hospital in Pleiku, where he died at 2:00 p.m. the same day. Seventeen people were injured from being beaten with batons or electric truncheons, and several sustained bullet wounds.

The Church Burning
After the shooting, the police conducted a house-to-house search in Plei Lao and gathered all the villagers near the church. Approximately twenty people from Plei Lao alone were arrested and handcuffed. Some were sent for

---
[461] Human Rights Watch interview with a Jarai man who was present during the March 10 incident, June 27, 2001.
[462] Human Rights Watch interview with a Jarai man who was present during the incident at Plei Lao, June 27, 2001.

Case Study: The Church Burning and Killing by Security Forces in Plei Lao 155

questioning at the commune headquarters for one to three days, while others were sent to T-20 prison in Pleiku.

The dying and wounded were laid out near the church before being sent to hospital. The police then ordered the Jarai to burn down the church. One witness, who was arrested and sent to the commune headquarters afterwards, described the church burning and the condition of a number of the victims:

> When they burned the church I was there, handcuffed. It happened around 12:00 noon. The police gathered everyone near the church, including those who were tied and handcuffed.
>
> First the police ordered some Vietnamese civilians to ransack and destroy the church with axes. They used a cable tied to a vehicle to topple it and the soldiers used their gun butts. Then they forced the ethnic Jarai to burn it. The police made the Jarai pour five liters of gasoline and ten liters of machine oil on the church, but they couldn't get it to burn. So then the police took over and they set fire to it. Everyone was crying—for the dead and wounded, and for the church.
>
> The wounded people were laid out nearby. One person with a bullet in his forehead didn't die. Another with a bullet in his head died later in Pleiku hospital. Another shot in both legs didn't die. After they burned the church the police took the wounded people for treatment, some to the district hospital and some to the provincial hospital.
>
> Afterwards the police put fresh earth over the ashes and smoothed it so outsiders couldn't tell there had ever been a church there.[463]

The Arrests

Villagers said that approximately seventy men were arrested as a result of the March 10 incident. At least eleven men—six people from Plei Lao and five from Plei Kia—were sent for questioning at the commune headquarters. They were kicked and beaten by police officers in the truck along the way to the police station, but not at the police station itself.[464] They were interrogated until around midnight on the night of March 10, and then released.

A young man who was sent to the commune office for interrogation described the arrests:

---

[463] Human Rights Watch interview with a Jarai man from Plei Lao, June 28, 2001.
[464] Human Rights Watch interview with a Jarai man from a village in Nhon Hoa commune who was present during the incident at Plei Lao, June 27, 2001.

I was one of those arrested. I hadn't fought back or hit the police—I was too afraid. I just wanted to protect the church and prevent the police from going there. They were searching the whole village and entered each house. Around 9:00 a.m. they arrested me, near the church. They tied my hands behind my back, put me in the jeep, and kicked and hit me. When they arrested me I had blacked out—I think from the gas, or maybe from being shocked with an electric baton. I only came to when they threw me in the jeep to take me to the commune office. My mother and uncle were crying. The police said they were taking me to hospital but they took me to the commune office, where they took my photograph and interrogated me.

The police beat and kicked some of those arrested until they were covered in blood, calling us Dega. They beat us in the vehicle on the way to the commune office. In the commune office I saw many people who were bloody and wounded.

They asked me about our work, what we were doing, who the political leaders were. I told them we had no leaders, that all of us had woken up at the same time to struggle together. They didn't accept that and forced us to talk. So I told them the names of the two political leaders in my village.

At midnight they let me go, and my sister took me home. It was only then that I realized that the church had been burned down, and my uncle—who had cried when I was taken away that morning—had been arrested. He had not returned to the village as of the time I fled to Cambodia in May. [465]

More than twenty others were sent for questioning and detention at the provincial prison in Pleiku. These included twelve villagers from Plei Lao, of whom four people—Siu Boc, Siu Thuc, Kpa Thop, and Siu Grih—had not returned as of November 2001. Fourteen people from Plei Kia were arrested and sent either to the district or the provincial police stations, but most were reportedly back in the village as of mid-May.

Three people from Plei Bo I were sent to prison in Pleiku and had not returned as of May. Soldiers also reportedly took away a fourth person from Plei

---

[465] Human Rights Watch interview with a Jarai man who was present during the incident at Plei Lao, June 27, 2001.

Case Study: The Church Burning and Killing by Security Forces in Plei Lao 157

Bo I, who had been shot in both legs. "They said they were taking him to hospital, but we think he went to prison," a villager told Human Rights Watch. "He was in the hospital first, but when his family went to see him there the police said he'd been sent to jail."[466]

Those who were arrested and then released a month or two later from prison in Pleiku said that they had been beaten after first arriving in prison, where they were detained in common rooms, not individual cells. Shackles were not used.[467]

The Aftermath

After the March 10 confrontation in Plei Lao, police were dispatched to most of the nearby villages in an attempt to restore order. In at least two villages, Plei Kli and Plei Djrek, police fired into the air and threw tear gas canisters as they entered the villages on the afternoon of March 10, where they carried out arrests.[468] One person who was shot in the leg in Plei Djrek was brought to the hospital. Police later arrested him in the hospital and sent him to prison, where he remained as of September.[469]

In the weeks following March 10, commune and district authorities and local police conducted daily meetings in Plei Lao and the surrounding villages, criticizing Kok Ksor and charging that people were using religious services to conduct political activities.

Soldiers were dispatched to stay in many of the villages in Nhon Hoa commune, with three soldiers assigned to stay in each of the homes of families who were suspected of being church leaders or Kok Ksor supporters. In the surrounding hamlets, the military presence was also increased, but primarily at night, in order to prevent people from trying to escape. Villagers interviewed by Human Rights Watch in June 2001 said that the stepped up military presence continued in Nhon Hoa commune for months.

Villagers did not report any mistreatment from the soldiers, who ate separately from the villagers. But the surveillance was heavy: "If we went to our fields too often, or stayed in the house too much, they would tell us not to do that," said one Plei Lao villager.[470] Those who returned to the village after being detained in Pleiku or the commune office were placed under even more scrutiny. They were not allowed to leave their houses when the police were in the village

---

[466] Human Rights Watch interview with a Jarai man who was present during the March 10 incident, June 27, 2001.
[467] Interviews with Jarai men from Plei Lao and neighboring villages, October 31, 2001.
[468] Human Rights Watch interview with Jarai man from a village near Plei Lao, who was present during the March 10 incident, June 27, 2001.
[469] Interviews with villagers from Plei Lao and neighboring villages, October 31, 2001.
[470] Human Rights Watch interview with a Jarai man from Plei Lao, June 27, 2001.

although some were able to slip off to their fields when the police were not around.

The version of the role of the military offered by the official state media was significantly different. On March 15, 2001, a group of correspondents from the *Quan Doi Nhan Dan* (People's Army Daily) newspaper visited Plei Lao and offered this description of the situation:

> We went to Lao Hamlet, one of the "hot spots" in Gia Lai. The local public roads were quite wide. Coffee and pepper orchards were green and flourishing. Children have since returned to school. The local people's life is back to normal.
>
> Along the roads, troops from the K52 Work Team under the Gia Lai Military Command were working with the local people in rebuilding roads, watering the coffee orchards, and picking pepper… The people's life was so peaceful. No more cheating by the representatives of the so-called "the Autonomous Government of Dega"….
>
> Deputy Hamlet Chief Rmah Kril said: "Our villagers mistakenly listened to the bad people. Now many people are hungry. I visited every house to learn about their situation so that the troops can provide rice and salt. I hope the government will strictly punish those who caused hardship to the people." [471]

Testimony from one villager about military activities in Nhon Hoa commune after the March 10 incident confirmed that soldiers did carry out some public service activities, but with the overall goal of surveillance:

> In Plei Lao the soldiers were helping the people make gardens and fences, clean the houses. Whatever the people did, they did with them. In Plei Lao, for families of the arrested people, they'd stay with that family. The reason was that those were the political struggle people—the soldiers didn't want others to meet them. [472]

---

[471] *Quan Doi Nhan Dan*, Hanoi (People's Army Daily), March 16, 2001, "Vietnam: Army daily cites U.S.' 'active support' of ethnic unrest in highlands," translated by BBC Worldwide Monitoring, March 29, 2001.
[472] Human Rights Watch interview with a Jarai man from a village in Nhon Hoa commune, June 28, 2001.

Case Study: The Church Burning and Killing by Security Forces in Plei Lao   159

Another man told Human Rights Watch that after March 10, police would break up all gatherings of more than four people:

If we had five people sitting together, they'd accuse us of having a political meeting. So we didn't meet each other so much. They would watch each house. If they saw four or five people together in a house they'd arrest and interrogate them. From that time we never dared worship in groups, except in the family.[473]

Church services stopped as well: "After the incident we stopped going to church or gathering for religious services and only prayed individually in our homes," said one man from a village near Plei Lao. "The people were extremely worried."[474]

In June 2001, Vietnamese state media and court officials announced that forty-one people would be tried in Gia Lai, including some in connection with the unrest in Chu Se district on March 10.[475] On September 26, 2001, one Plei Lao villager, Siu Boc, was among seven highlanders brought to trial in Gia Lai provincial court. He was sentenced to eleven years in prison, on charges of "disrupting security" under Article 89 of the penal code.

Although the military presence in Plei Lao persisted for months, a number of residents were eventually able to escape to Cambodia. "I fled because I was afraid," said one person who safely reached Cambodia, after having been beaten and detained at the commune office on March 10. "The soldiers had entered my house four times after the incident. I was worried they were getting ready to arrest me."[476]

At least six people who attended the Plei Lao meeting were among sixty-three refugees deported by Cambodian authorities on the night of May 15-16, 2001. Witnesses reported that several of the highlanders wept as they were handcuffed by Vietnamese police and taken away.

Two of the deported highlanders had been interrogated at the Nhon Hoa commune office on March 10; fellow villagers feared the authorities were preparing to arrest them before their attempted escape to Cambodia.

Asked what he thought would happen to Plei Lao villagers deported from Cambodia back to Vietnam, one young man from Nhon Hoa commune paused,

---

[473] Human Rights Watch interview with Jarai man from a village in Nhon Hoa commune, June 28, 2001.
[474] Human Rights Watch interview with a Jarai man from a village in Nhon Hoa Commune, June 28, 2001.
[475] Agence France-Presse, "Vietnam to hold mass trial of 41 people over highlands unrest," June 16, 2001.
[476] Human Rights Watch interview with a Jarai man from Plei Lao, June 28, 2001.

gulped, and then said: "The second time they're arrested like this I can't guess—but maybe they won't release them again. Instead, they may detain them a long long time. If they don't kill them outright they might beat them to death, and let them die at home."[477]

A note handwritten in Jarai by villagers in Nhon Hoa commune, dated March 20 and obtained by Human Rights Watch, stated:

> Now they've killed and arrested many of us. Since March 10 the people are very afraid. Some have fled to the forest, others are in hiding elsewhere, afraid to return to the village to work. The government doesn't allow us to follow our religion. If we don't follow the government and continue to conduct our worship meetings, the authorities said they will arrest us and put us in jail or even shoot and kill like before. Please let the U.N. and the international organizations know about this immediately, to protect the people.[478]

The Government's Response

Statements in the Vietnamese state media suggest that local government officials were seriously concerned about the large gathering of highlanders at the church in Plei Lao in early March. The official version of events at Plei Lao, as recounted in *Quan Doi Nhan Dan* (People's Army Daily) on March 16, was that local authorities had tried to stop villagers from conducting meetings to discuss ways to "oppose the authorities at Kok Ksor's instigation."[479] According to these state press accounts, local "gang leaders" such as Siu Thuc, Siu Boc, and Siu Grih threatened the local officials and forced the people to join the February protest:

> These reactionaries called on the people "to sell all their land, buffaloes, and cows and to donate the money to the Dega government and the government will then return everything to the people. Children will not have to go to school. No more family planning, and so on."

> Many families sold their buffaloes and cows in support of them. When these reactionaries ran out of money, they confiscated the last

---

[477] Human Rights Watch interview with a Jarai man from a village in Nhon Hoa commune who was present at the March 10 incident, June 28, 2001.
[478] Jarai-language document and translation on file at Human Rights Watch.
[479] *Quan Doi Nhan Dan*, Hanoi (People's Army Daily), March 16, 2001, "Vietnam: Army daily cites U.S.' 'active support' of ethnic unrest in highlands," translated by BBC Worldwide Monitoring, March 29, 2001.

Case Study: The Church Burning and Killing by Security Forces in Plei Lao 161

can of rice and last *dong* from the people. Many families fell into starvation because of them.[480]

The tensions in Plei Lao may have been a factor in the rescheduling of a government-sponsored press tour planned for Western journalists to the Central Highlands. On March 9, the Vietnamese Foreign Ministry abruptly postponed the tour, originally planned to start on March 12.[481] The Foreign Ministry gave little explanation for the delay, saying only that local officials were not yet prepared to receive visitors. It is conceivable, however, that the brewing tensions in Plei Lao were a factor: on the evening of March 9—the day the tour was cancelled— troops were being moved into position to surround the hamlet.

Western wire service reporters were not able to visit Plei Lao during the tour. The first Western wire service reports were published on March 27, 2001. Largely based on official sources and government media accounts, these reports said that the government had identified three people as leaders of the disturbances at Plei Lao: Siu Puoh (Boc), Siu Thuc and Kpa Thap. Together with other "stubborn elements," they had been arrested after trying to stop police from destroying a church. A district official stated that the three men had forced villagers to donate funds to build the church.[482] On March 27, the *Lao Dong* (Labor) state newspaper said that "troublemakers" had incited villagers to stop working in their fields, causing food shortages in the district.

In another wire service account, government sources alleged that hundreds of youth had set up a "no-go zone" in the Central Highlands as early as October 2000, with villagers in Chu Se district forced to act as a "human shield" as part of the campaign to "declare a breakaway state of Dega." Agence France-Presse cited *Lao Dong* in reporting the following:

> Fugitive separatist leaders from among the region's mainly Christian indigenous minorities had mobilized the youngsters to mount patrols "blocking off access by outsiders," the trade union daily *Lao Dong* (Labor) said…The local authorities had finally moved in to arrest the "troublemakers" in the village of Plei Lao on March 10 after they "incited villagers to provoke extremely serious disturbances." [483]

---

[480] Ibid.
[481] Deutsche Presse-Agentur, "Vietnam postpones journalists' visit to troubled Central Highlands," March 9, 2001.
[482] Tini Tran, "Vietnamese villagers clash with Cops," Associated Press, March 27, 2001.
[483] Steve Kirby, "Vietnam admits to large-scale rural unrest in highlands," Agence France Press, March 27, 2001.

"Underground churches" in Chu Se district were singled out in the report by *Lao Dong* as being used as a "gathering place where the troublemakers persistently met to discuss measures aimed at sparking fresh disturbances through the use of sticks, knives, stones....."[484]

Human Rights Watch questioned eyewitnesses to the incident at Plei Lao about the "human shield" report. One Plei Lao resident of Plei Lao stated that villagers in Plei Lao organized themselves after the February demonstrations to make sure that no one was arrested:

> Before March 2001, no one was arrested in the village. The people didn't let them [carry out arrests.] We protected ourselves. We had some youth—when the police came to investigate or interrogate someone, the youth would surround them—standing off to the side a bit—to see if they were going to arrest the person. The youth would say, we demand our rights to our land, religious freedom, and so on. They wouldn't yell anything, but simply ask the police why they were here—we're not making a war or fighting with you. The youth told the police that we don't use violence in our demands, only our voices. There were many youths who protected in this way. They didn't carry anything in their hands, but would just gather near the house of the person being interrogated. This made the police angry because the youth wouldn't let them carry out arrests. The police didn't argue with the youth. But if the police had tried to arrest us, the youth would have taken us back. No one from Pleiku or outside the village helped organize this—we organized it ourselves. I don't know if other villages did anything similar.[485]

Other Nhon Hoa residents interviewed by Human Rights Watch said they did not know anything about villagers organizing a "human shield" or gathering to protect villagers from arrest by police. As one villager put it, "No, the neighbors would *not* gather around when the police entered someone's house to interrogate them. We were afraid, and kept away when the police came by."[486]

---

[484] Ibid.
[485] Human Rights Watch interview with a Jarai man from Plei Lao, June 28, 2001.
[486] Human Rights Watch interview with a Jarai man from Plei Lao, June 28, 2001.

XVI. CASE STUDY: THE GOAT'S BLOOD OATH CEREMONIES IN EA H'LEO

We were afraid [the wine] had poison in it and that they wanted to kill off all of the demonstrators. We remembered about the Bible saying not to drink blood, and we were afraid that we had violated God.
— Jarai man from Ea H'leo, October 30, 2001

As in many other parts of the Central Highland, immediately after the February 2001 unrest police carried out a number of arrests in Ea H'leo district, a primarily ethnic Jarai area in Dak Lak near the Gia Lai border. In March and April 2001, police stepped up the pressure, regularly summoning dozens of villagers to police stations for weekly "working sessions" in which they were intensively interrogated and warned against future religious or political organizing. When it seemed that the government's message was not getting through, the authorities instituted even harsher measures to bear down on political organizing and religious freedom: the "goat's blood ceremonies," which were conducted in dozens of villages in Dak Lak beginning in May.

The origins of the ceremonies, which were perhaps provincial officials' crude approximation of "animist" rituals followed by non-Christian highlanders, are unknown.[487]

Crude—and Cruel—Rituals

The goat's blood ceremonies were conducted in dozens of villages in Ea H'leo district of Dak Lak, starting in May 2001. The ceremony was also reported to have taken place in villages in Gia Lai during the latter half of 2001, but to a lesser extent. Ea H'leo and neighboring Ea Sup districts of Dak Lak were perhaps targeted because of the high level of political activism there, combined with the districts' relative remoteness from the provincial towns.

During the ceremonies, people who had participated in the February 2001 demonstrations were forced to stand up in front of their entire village and provincial authorities to admit their wrongdoing, pledge to cease any contacts with outside groups, and renounce their religion. Formal procedures were staged

---

[487] Ethnic Jarai from the Central Highlands told Human Rights Watch that they had never heard of such ceremonies being conducted in the past, although some reported the practice of "biting a knife" to consecrate a pledge. It should be noted that non-Christian Jarai living just across the border in Cambodia, who follow a holistic spiritual system that could be called animist, are not known to drink goat's blood mixed with wine. Human Rights Watch interviews with Jarai from Vietnam and from Cambodia, October 2001.

in dozens of villages, all following a similar script. Any villager known to have participated in the February demonstrations would be issued an order ("*Giay Trieu Tap*") to attend a "working session" with the local People's Committee on a certain date. The entire village would assemble on the appointed day, together with high-ranking government officials and military and police commanders from the province, district, commune and village. A blue banner would be erected, reading in some areas: "Judgment Ceremony of the People who Opposed the Government and Joined the Demonstrations," and in other areas, "The Ceremony to Repent from Following Dega Christianity."[488]

Soldiers would surround the village so that no one could elude the ceremony. Known demonstrators would be required to stand in front of the banner to read a document prepared by the authorities, in which the person confessed his wrongdoings, urged others not to follow his mistakes, agreed to follow the laws of the state or face prosecution, and renounced Christianity. A slightly different version of the document, an official pledge (*Ban Cam Ket*) signed by the district chief (See Appendix G, p. 190), was given to each participant afterwards. Then, to seal the pledge, the individual repentant would be forced to drink rice wine mixed with goat's blood while other villagers were enlisted to beat ceremonial brass gongs.

Humiliation

While a number of highlanders interviewed by Human Rights Watch said that they had signed various pledges under duress, they generally said what they wrote or said did not reflect their true feelings. Much more disturbing—and humiliating—was the forced drinking of goat's blood. Some said that as Christians, they believed it was a sin to receive or give away blood that was not the blood of Jesus.[489]

One man, who was able to escape before being forced to participate in the ceremony, commented: "The police told me that drinking blood with wine would cleanse my sins and wrongdoings. If we didn't drink, they would charge that we still opposed the government and that we were not their people."

Another young man who succumbed to the pressure looked dazed and afraid as he recounted in a monotone what had happened: "They asked us to drink goat's blood, but we never saw any goat. We wondered where the blood was from. If we didn't drink it, they would beat us. We didn't know if it was

---

[488] Human Rights Watch interviews with Ea H'leo residents, March 12, 2001. See also: "Report on the Protestants' Situation in Dak Lak Province," September 3, 2001, written by a Protestant church leader in the Central Highlands who asked to remain anonymous.
[489] Human Rights Watch interviews with Ea H'leo residents, October 30, 2001.

Case Study: The Goat's Blood Oath Ceremonies in Ea H'leo

from a chicken or a dog or what. I am afraid I will have health problems in the future."[490]

Others were clearly traumatized by the pressure. One man said that police visited him at home several times after his release from prison in May. They threatened to throw him back into prison if he didn't agree to the goat's blood ceremony. "I wanted to kill myself, slit my own throat because of the pressure," he said. "Sometimes when the police would come, I'd say kill me, I don't care. Finally I was able to escape to Cambodia."[491]

From May until mid-August, when many participants fled to Cambodia, goat's blood ceremonies were conducted in at least two dozen villages in Ea H'leo district alone.[492] The ceremonies were reported to have taken place in Ea Sup district as well as in several districts in Gia Lai.[493]

---

[490] Human Rights Watch interview with Ea H'leo resident, October 30, 2001.
[491] Human Rights Watch interview with Ede man from a village in Dak Lak, October 11, 2001.
[492] Villages where the ceremonies were conducted in Ea H'leo included: Buon Dang, Buon Treng, Buon Sam A, Buon Sam B, Buon Tung, Buon Areng, Buon Le, Buon Blec, Buon Dung, Buon Breng, Buon Druh, Buon Tri A, Buon Tri B, Buon Sec, Buon Kha, Buon Cuah, Buon Drai, Buon Hyao, Buon Bir, Buon Hvuai, Buon Hving, Buon Co, and Buon Ta Li.
[493] "Report on the Protestants' Situation in Dak Lak Province," September 3, 2001, written by a Protestant church leader in the Central Highlands who asked to remain anonymous.

XVII. CASE STUDY: ARREST AND TORTURE OF HIGHLANDERS DEPORTED FROM CAMBODIA

They beat us over our whole body, including our heads. They beat our fingers, hands, arms, and necks—everywhere. There was no blood because they used a rubber truncheon. After beating us they took our photographs again.
—Buon Ea Sup resident, October 20, 2001

During the last week in March 2001, Cambodian provincial authorities arrested two groups of highlanders who had fled from Dak Lak to Mondolkiri. One group of twenty-four ethnic Ede was transported by helicopter on March 24 to Phnom Penh, where they were eventually screened by UNHCR and resettled in the United States.[494]

A second group of nineteen Jarai men was deported on the night of March 25-26 to Vietnam, where they were subsequently arrested, imprisoned, and tortured.

On March 24, during the time both groups were seeking asylum in Cambodia, Sao Sokha, commander of the Royal Gendarmerie, conducted a meeting at the Mondolkiri Police Commissariat to address the issue of "illegal immigrants." According to one person in attendance at that meeting Sokha—who was in Mondolkiri to coordinate the transfer of the twenty-four Ede to Phnom Penh—reportedly ordered provincial authorities to immediately deport any Vietnamese nationals entering Cambodia: there was no need to consult with immigration or other central authorities first.[495]

The difference between the fates of the two groups lay largely in the fact that foreign diplomats and Cambodian and international press quickly learned of the existence of the first group. The second group, from Buon Ea Sup, was silently and secretly deported back to Vietnam. This was in violation of the fundamental principle of non-refoulement—the obligation of states such as Cambodia, which are party to the 1951 Refugee Convention, not to return any person to a country where his or her life or freedom may be threatened.[496]

---

[494] Srei Neat, "Hun Sen Orders sending arrested Vietnamese rebels to Phnom Penh," *Rasmei Kampuchea* (Light of Cambodia) newspaper, March 26-27, 2001.
[495] Interview with a participant in the March 24 meeting with Sao Sokha, April 7, 2001.
[496] Convention Relating to the Status of Refugees, art. 33(1), adopted July 28, 1951. G.A. Res. 429(V). 189 U.N.T.S. 137 (entered into force April 22, 1954 and accessioned by Cambodia on October 15, 1992).

Case Study: Arrest and Torture of Highlanders Deported from Cambodia 167

Buon Ea Sup: Why People Fled

Buon Ea Sup is a village of some 900 ethnic Jarai located eighty kilometers north of Buon Ma Thuot in Dak Lak. Residents of Buon Ea Sup joined the February 3 demonstrations for similar reasons to villagers from dozens of other ethnic minority hamlets in the highlands. The government's response in Buon Sup duplicated the response in scores of other hamlets. It was not long before the first group of villagers prepared to flee.

The trigger came in early March, when Ea Sup villagers heard that arrests were to be carried out on March 18. Several villagers had already fled to their farm fields or the forest to evade the police sessions. Over a period of days others slipped out of the village. By the third week in March, nineteen men had gathered at one spot near the border, where they crossed over to Cambodia on March 21. After only a few days in Koh Nhek district in northern Mondolkiri, local Cambodian police spotted the group. They were sent to the commune headquarters for a night and then escorted on foot by thirteen Cambodian police and soldiers to Koh Nhek district town. The police confiscated the men's watches, money and other belongings and then handcuffed each man and put them in a dilapidated pickup truck.

Documents obtained by Human Rights Watch show that on March 25, the First Deputy Police Commissioner of Mondolkiri province, accompanied by the commander of the provincial gendarmerie, transported the nineteen men from Koh Nhek district to the Bou Praing border crossing, where the group was sent back to Vietnam in the early morning hours of March 26. The third deputy governor of Mondolkiri province signed a document authorizing the transfer, which was also signed by Vietnamese authorities as the "receivers." The Mondolkiri Police Commissioner subsequently issued an official report to Hok Lundy, the Director General of the Cambodian National Police, dated March 29, on the "transfer and delivery of nineteen Vietnamese illegal immigrants" into the hands of the provincial governor, military commander, and police chief of neighboring Dak Lak province in Vietnam.[497]

At the Post 10 border checkpoint, Vietnamese police took photographs of the group and interrogated and beat them. "They asked us why we were so hard headed and stubborn," one of the nineteen Jarai said later. "They said we had lied to the authorities and opposed the government. 'You've signed the pledges already,' they told us, 'but your attitude is the same.'"[498]

---

[497] See Appendices H and I, pages 200-202: "Report on the Transfer and Delivery of 19 Illegal Vietnamese Immigrants," sent from the Police Commissioner of Mondolkiri Province to the Director General of the Cambodian National Police, March 28, 2001, and "Minutes of the Transfer of Illegal Immigrants," signed by Cambodian and Vietnamese provincial officials, March 27, 2001.
[498] Human Rights Watch interview with a resident of Buon Ea Sup, October 20, 2001.

Torture and Detention

At the Vietnam border the group was transferred to a windowless police van and transported to Buon Ma Thuot in Dak Lak. "There wasn't any water at all in the van," said one of the group. "We couldn't tell if it was day or night." In Buon Ma Thuot the group was videotaped and photographed again, each holding a card with an identification number. In Buon Ma Thuot the group was beaten even more severely than at the border post:

> They used a rubber truncheon to beat us over our whole body, including our heads. They pried open our eyes and pinched and twisted our eyelids and ears. They asked different people different questions. They accused me of being stubborn and hard headed and of being the leader of the group; the one who prepared the escape plan.[499]

The beating went on for three or four hours, until 4:00 p.m. when the detainees were handcuffed, put into a police van, and transported to Ho Chi Minh City, a journey that must have taken at least seven hours.

> We had never seen Ho Chi Minh City and did not know where we were. We were not sure what place we had been taken to but later we learned it was called "Bo An Ninh" and that it was a secret place.[500] They stuck us in dark cells there; two people each in tiny cement rooms. There were no windows, only a small slot for air near the ceiling. There were many mosquitoes. We spent seven days there. They didn't let us out during that time other than for interrogation. All water [for drinking, bathing] was inside the cell, as was the bucket for our excrement.[501]

During their time in prison, the men were interrogated four or five times. Some were not beaten during the questioning while others were slapped or hit; overall, however, the beatings were not as harsh as in Buon Ma Thuot.

---

[499] Ibid.
[500] "Bo An Ninh" means "Ministry of Security" in Vietnamese and is used to refer to prisons. Undoubtedly the group had been sent to Chi Hoa, the main prison in Ho Chi Minh City.
[501] Human Rights Watch interviews with residents of Buon Ea Sup, October 20, 2001.

In the sessions they pressured us to agree to abandon politics and religion. We agreed verbally, but not in our hearts. We agreed because we were afraid of being killed. The Vietnamese police wrote up a report about our agreement, which they asked us to read into a tape recorder. The ideas were from the Vietnamese police, not us. They forced us to read it. The report said that Kok Ksor had no ability to help the ethnic minorities, that we accepted our wrongdoings and didn't want others to repeat our mistakes. Ethnic minorities should be one together with the Vietnamese and should not oppose the government. Finally, it said we should abandon politics and religion.[502]

After seven days in prison in Ho Chi Minh City, the police handcuffed the group and sent them by bus to Dak Lak, where they spent two nights in the provincial prison. Again, police interrogated the group and forced them to sign confessions: "They wrote it up and forced us with two hands to sign it," said one of the Jarai.

Afterwards, all but four of the nineteen Jarai were released, on condition that their families vouch for them in writing. Once back in the village, members of the group were not allowed to leave the village to work in their fields without advance permission, and they were prohibited from gathering in groups of more than three people. Religious repression increased throughout the village, with authorities confiscating guitars and electric organs used in church services as well as Bibles and hymnals.

The police presence in the village continued strong. In early August the police issued official "letters of invitation" to the forty villagers who had participated in the demonstrations to attend a mandatory "goat's blood ceremony" on August 18. At the time, provincial authorities were already conducting such ceremonies not only in Ea Sup district but also in neighboring Ea H'leo district.

To evade further repression, small groups of men from both Ea Sup and Ea H'leo districts began to slip out of the villages again. On August 24, seventy-eight men from both districts gathered at a spot near the Cambodian border, where they hid in the forest for more than a week without food. On September 1, the group was finally able to cross the border and reach the UNHCR facility in

---

[502] Human Rights Watch interviews with residents of Buon Ea Sup, October 20, 2001.

Mondolkiri. They were exhausted, frightened, and close to starvation. But at least they were safe for the time being.

SELECTED BIBLIOGRAPHY

Rambo, A.T., Robert R. Reed, Le Trong Cuc, and Michael R. DiGregorio, eds., "The Challenges of Highland Development in Vietnam," East West Center, Center for Natural Resources and Environmental Studies, Center for Southeast Asia Studies, October 1995.

Booth, G., "RRA Report of Two Communes in the Se San Watershed," Regional Environmental Technical Assistance 5771—Poverty Reduction & Environmental Management in Remote Greater Mekong Subregion Watersheds Project (Phase I), Helsinki, 1999.

Buttinger, J., *Vietnam: A Dragon Embattled*, New York: Frederick A. Praeger, Inc., 1967.

Colm, S., "Land Rights: The Challenge for Ratanakiri's Indigenous Communities," *Watershed: People's Forum on Ecology*, Vol. 3, No. 1, Bangkok: Terra, July 1997.

Colm, S., "Sacred Balance: Conserving the Ancestral Lands of Cambodia's Indigenous Communities," *Indigenous Affairs*, International Working Group on Indigenous Affairs, No. 4, October-December 2000.

Commission on Human Rights, *Civil and Political Rights, Including the Question of Religious Intolerance; Addendum: Visit to Vietnam*, Report submitted by Abdelfattah Amor, December 12, 1998.

Commission on Human Rights, *Question of the Human Rights of All Persons Subjected to Any Form of Detention or Imprisonment, Working Group on Arbitrary Detention, Visit to Vietnam*, E/CN.4/1995/31/Add.4, January 18, 1995.

Condominas, G., *We Have Eaten the Forest: The Story of a Montagnard Village in the Central Highlands of Vietnam*, New York: Kodansga International, 1994.

Dennis, J., "A Review of National Social Policies, Viet Nam," Poverty Reduction & Environmental Management in Remote Greater Mekong Subregion (GMS) Watersheds Project (Phase I), 2000

Do, V.H., "Resettlement in Vietnam: its Effects on Population and Production," *International Seminar on Internal Migration: Implications for Migration Policy in Vietnam*, Population Council, Vietnam, May 1998.

Evans, G, "Internal Colonialism in the Central Highlands of Vietnam," Sojourn, volume 7, Number 2, Singapore, 1992.

Freedom House, Center for Religious Freedom, "Correct Thinking in Vietnam: New Official Vietnam Documents Revealing Policy to Repress Tribal Christians," July 2001.

Gebert, R., "Gender Issues in the MRC—GTZ Sustainable management of Resources in the Lower Mekong River Basin Project, Dak Lak Province, Vietnam," Deutsche Gesellschaft für Technische Zusammenarbeit (GTZ) GmbH and Mekong River Commission Secretariat, Hanoi, 1997.

Hickey, G.C., *Free in the Forest: Ethnohistory of the Vietnamese Central Highlands, 1954-1976*. New Haven: Yale University Press, 1982.

Hickey, G.C., *Shattered World: Adaptation and Survival among Vietnam's Highland People's during the Vietnam War*, Philadelphia: University of Pennsylvania Press, 1993.

Hoang, D., "Rural-rural Migration and Redistribution of Labor and Population in Accordance with Planning for Socio-Economic Development in Vietnam," in *International Seminar on Internal Migration: Implications for Migration Policy in Vietnam*, Population Council, Vietnam, May 1998.

Hoang, N., "The Vietnamese Homeland in the Vietnamese Nation," published in Vietnam News Agency, "Vietnam Image of the Community of 54 Ethnic Groups," The Ethnic Cultures Publishing House, Hanoi, 1996.

Huynh, T.X., Vice-Chairwoman, Dak Lak Provincial People's Committee, "The Impact of Rural-Rural Migration to Resettlement Areas in Dak Lak Province," in *International Seminar on Internal Migration: Implications for Migration Policy in Vietnam*, Population Council, Vietnam, May 1998.

Jamieson, N., Le Trong Cuc and A. Terry Rambo, "The Development Crisis in Vietnam's Mountains," East-West Center Special Reports No. 6, 1998.

Jamieson, N., "Ethnic Minorities in Vietnam: A Country Profile," Winrock, International, Hanoi, Vietnam, March 1996.

Nguyen, M.Q., "Evangelism," *Religious Problems in Vietnam*, The Gioi Publishers, 2001.

Salemink, O., "Customary Law, Land Rights and Internal Migration," *Vietnam Social Sciences*, February, 2000.

Salemink, O., "Mois and Maquis: The Invention and Appropriation of Vietnam's Montagnards from Sabatier to the CIA," in George W. Stocking, Jr. (ed.), *Colonial Situations: Essays in Ethnographic Contextualization* (History of Anthropology, Vol. 7), Madison: University of Wisconsin Press, 1991.

Salemink, O., "The King of Fire and Vietnamese Ethnic Policy in the Central Highlands," in Don McCaskill and K. Kampe, eds., *Development or Domestication? Indigenous Peoples of Southeast Asia*, Chiang Mai: Silkworm Books, 1997.

Selected Bibliography

Sikor, T., "Decree 327 and the Restoration of Barren Land in the Vietnamese Highlands," in A. Terry Rambo et al, eds., "The Challenges of Highland Development in Vietnam," East West Center, Center for Natural Resources and Environmental Studies, Center for Southeast Asia Studies, October 1995.

Socialist Republic of Viet Nam, Committee for Ethnic Minorities and Mountainous Areas, UNDP, "Framework for External Assistance to Ethnic Minority Development," Hanoi, November 1995.

Thayer, N., "Montagnard Army Seeks U.N. Help," *Phnom Penh Post*, Sept. 12, 1992.

Tran, N., "A Study of the Rural Poverty in Dak Lak Province—Vietnam; Constraints and Opportunities for Alleviation," Dissertation submitted in partial fulfillment of the requirements for the MSc in Rural Resources and Environmental Policy, Wye College, University of London, 1999.

Tuyet Hoa Nie Kdam, Pham Van Hien, Nay Ky Hiep, "An Assessment of Households' Economic Conditions Participating in Pilot Project of FLA in Ea Sol Commune, Ea H'leo District," MRC/GTZ, October 1999.

UNHCR Centre for Documentation and Research, "Vietnam: Indigenous Minority Groups in the Central Highlands," Writenet Paper No. 05/2001, January 2002.

APPENDIX A: THE LAND CONFLICT IN D VILLAGE: FIRST COMPLAINT, 1995 [503]

* * * * * * *

Socialist Republic of Vietnam
Independence – Freedom – Happiness

Resolution of the People of D Hamlet

TO: CENTRAL COMMITTEE ON NATIONALITIES OF THE NATIONAL ASSEMBLY

Of the Socialist Republic of Vietnam

cc: Ministry of the Interior, Hanoi

Re: Loss of land needed to make a living
Peoples Committee of [name withheld] Commune, Buon Ma Thuot City, Dak Lak Province

Dear Committee:

We are the entire population of D Hamlet, [name withheld] Commune, Buon Ma Thuot City, Dak Lak Province.

We respectfully request the committee and the central government to resolve the problem we all have in making a living as a result of the following events:

The population of our hamlet is comprised of farmers of the Ede minority, totaling 113 households with 615 people. We obeyed the decisions of the local government in 1985 to move our village and established a new village on both sides of the road leading to the [name withheld] reservoir. At that time we had sufficient land on which to make a living since the illegal occupation of land had not yet begun.

However beginning in 1985 the land belonging to our village was divided. Villages 2 and 3 and the [name withheld] reservoir were distributed to ethnic Vietnamese. In addition, a [nursery], currently called the Science Committee, was established.

In 1990 this area was divided in two, with the western part going to the nursery and the eastern part to the Science Committee. Since then, the amount of land left to the village, after these land seizures, only amounts to ten hectares, which is not enough for 113 households, not to mention future generations.

---

[503] Original Vietnamese language document, obtained by Human Rights Watch in September 2001, is on file at Human Rights Watch.

Appendix A: The Land Conflict in D Village: First Complaint, 1995

In the process of taking the land of our village, in the month of April 1995 the forestry service even used armed units.

As far as the [nursery] goes, we agree with the economic plan of the state as it was set out in the beginning. But at present, the [nursery] is not operating according to plan; to the contrary, the trees are being cut down and the land has been leased out and rent collected on it. In the meantime we villagers are not allowed to work the land. We resolved to collectively plant trees on the land but the forestry service would not allow us to. Therefore we are sending this petition to you and ask you to investigate the situation and find a resolution that satisfies the hopes of our people.

At present, the forestry service isn't using the land for its intended purpose but rather has sold the land taken from the local people to people from other regions to plant coffee and sugar cane.

As for us, the local population, we lack land because the land was taken away from us by the forestry service. The service won't allow us to work the land, and instead will only pay for our labor in plowing the land at the rate of 100,000 dong for one tenth of a hectare.

As a result of this situation the people of the hamlet of D are in desperate straits, and before long deaths are going to result either as a result of starvation or struggles to make a living.

We plead with the committee and the central government to review this matter urgently so that we can make a normal living.

Thank you.

Cc: Peoples Committee of Dak Lak Province
     Peoples Committee of Buon Ma Thuot City
     Peoples Committee of [name withheld] Commune

Dated: April 27, 1995

Representing the entire people of D Hamlet

[signature]
[name withheld]

APPENDIX B: THE LAND CONFLICT IN D VILLAGE
Second Complaint, 2000[504]

* * * * * * *

Socialist Republic of Vietnam
Independence – Freedom – Happiness

Supplemented Petition

(regarding the wrongful exploitation of land of the hamlet of D, Buon Ma Thuot City, Dak Lak Province)

We are 644 individuals, in excess of 113 households, constituting all of the Ede people of the hamlet of D, Buon Ma Thuot City, Dak Lak Province. We make the following supplemental resolution:

Since long before liberation in 1975, we have lived and worked on the land of D village. In 1985, in accordance with the decisions of the City of Buon Ma Thuot on relocation, we moved to a new settlement. At that time Comrade [name withheld], the first secretary of the Communist Party in D Village, personally was in charge and he promised us that the land on which the village was formerly located was still ours to cultivate.

In 1986, [name of cadre withheld] was reassigned to work in the city [of Buon Ma Thuot]. That same year, the Province decided to take all of the land of the old village, consisting of 480 hectares, to establish a provincial forestry service. [Name withheld], the first secretary of the provincial Party, himself mobilized the people of D hamlet to turn the land over to the province to establish the forestry service and on many occasions promised the villagers that we would become members of or be hired by this new entity. But the people directly responsible for the forestry service completely ignored the promises made by their superiors to the villagers.

In 1990, the land of the forestry service was divided into two separate zones: the western part was the Science Committee, and the eastern part was the nursery. We asked the forestry service to contract with the villagers to plant trees on this area to provide at least a minimal livelihood for the 644 people, old and young, of our village. But the forestry service did not agree. We continued

---

[504] Original Vietnamese language document, obtained by Human Rights Watch in September 2001, is on file at Human Rights Watch.

to hold our position, and waited, but they just strung us along and never made a decision.

Then in 1992, goaded by money, the forestry service signed a contract with Mr. Y, a Vietnamese from Ha Bac Province who had just moved to Dak Lak, allowing him to exploit 40 hectares of land. In addition to planting trees on the hills, Mr. Y arrogantly planted cashew trees on land belonging to our village.

By 1995 the people of our village understood very clearly that what the forestry service, and more directly Mr. Y, was doing was neither contributing anything to the state nor helping the people of our village make a living. The land taken from our village was not being used at all for the intended purpose of growing trees, but rather was taken by people in authority, from parts of a hectare to a few hectares each, to plant coffee or sold or otherwise used for personal purposes. And under the disguise of developing agriculture and forestry, the Forestry Service entered into contracts dividing the land into parcels from less than a hectare to several hectares with family members and friends from other provinces to plant coffee, cashews, sugar cane, and vegetables and then selling the land to others after making a lot of money (list attached). Thus we were not able to work the land that we had cultivated for a long, long time.

There were altercations between the two sides, and the Forestry Service and Mr. Y hired armed forces, about ten people, to guard the recreation area (the former Science Committee area) and set up a sentry box. They even fired military-issue weapons to threaten us during one of these struggles, which terrified our people, so much that they could not work.

The very lives of our 644 people were being directly threatened. We lost our livelihood when we lost our land. Faced with this disastrous situation, on July 27, 1995, the entire population of our village signed a petition which we sent to all of the authorities concerned asking them to resolve the problem. But since then, five full years have gone by, and we have received no reply. Our difficult economic situation has become even worse. Indeed, we have gotten to the point where we may die of starvation. We are losing all of our confidence.

For these reasons we are writing this supplemental petition. We implore you as a matter of urgency to respond. If this land is indeed not being used for community purposes, which is the case, we ask that it be returned to the people of the village to use. In principal the land was released in 1996 to D village to manage, but in name only. We completely disagree with what the Forestry Service has been doing, letting a few individuals use the land for personal ends. We ask you to tell us: who agreed to sign contracts with these individuals? Who is using this land while we villagers have been brutally thrown out?

Once more we ask you to save the livelihoods of the villagers of D village, for which the entire population of the village will thank you.
   Attached are the signatures of the villagers.

D village, October 24, 2000
For the Self-Governing Committee, [signature]

APPENDIX C: THE INTERROGATION OF A PROTESTANT CHURCH LEADER, DAK LAK, JULY 2001 [505]

* * * * * * *

Socialist Republic of Vietnam
Independence – Freedom – Happiness

REPORT

To: General Assembly of the Vietnam Protestant Church
Religion Committee of Dak Lak Province
Governing Body of the Vietnam Protestant Church in Dak Lak Province

My name is N, born 1967 in [village and commune withheld], Buon Don District, Dak Lak Province. I wish to report the following events:

At 6:30 in the morning on July 18, 2001 I received a summons from the office of the District Police of Buon Don, signed by the chief of the district police force, Mr. P. The topic was the practice of religion in [village and commune names withheld]. I began my visits to the police station on July 18, 2001. I was questioned by Mr. H. He first stated to me: I have summoned you here for questioning and there is no time limit on this work; it can last from two to three months and only when I'm finished will it be over. I have been to the police station eight days already, leaving home in the morning and returning in the afternoon, using a liter of gasoline each day. Those were on the 18th, 19th, 20th, 23rd, 24th, 26th, 27th, and 28th. I must continue going, and was told I had to buy a pen with my own funds.

1. At my first meeting with H, he told me to write a full report on (1) when the church governing body in [commune name withheld] was established, (2) who was the chairman, (3) who was the deputy chairman, (4) who was secretary, (5) who was the treasurer, and who were the other members and their positions. I told him that we hadn't elected a governing body because the government had not yet permitted it. Mr. H then asked me, your name is on the governing board, who chose you for this position? I told him that Ama T had selected me to assist him in the church on occasions such as weddings and funerals etc.

2. H asked me, why are you teaching religion when you're not a pastor? I responded, in our commune, Ama T is the teacher, but if he is sick or busy with other work, he has me read the Bible and lead prayers and then end the service.

---

[505] Original Vietnamese language document, obtained by Human Rights Watch in September 2001, is on file at Human Rights Watch. Names have been withheld to protect the security of the petitioner.

3. H asked me, Why do you go to [name withheld commune]? I responded that I only went there to bury the dead and to celebrate Tet, because that hamlet has a recreation area.

4. H asked again about my reading the Bible at Ama T's home—you aren't a pastor, why are you teaching religion? Do you admit that you are in the wrong? I didn't respond. He continued, "You write down these illegal actions on your part":

You are not a pastor or missionary;
You have no degree/diploma;
You haven't studied in any Bible classes;
You call yourself a preacher, because you do what Ama T tells you to do;
You don't have any authority or official position;
You haven't asked permission from the local government;
You carry on activities in your home and not in the church;
You carry on activities in Ama T's house;

When he finished speaking he told me to write down my crimes. When I had finished writing he summarized: "You are guilty of eight crimes in total." I responded that I wasn't guilty of eight crimes. He pressured me to admit to eight crimes, and when I had admitted to them, he said that now I had to accept my punishment for each of the crimes. I first wrote that I would accept the punishment imposed on me by the police, but he didn't accept this. Then I wrote that I should be obligated to engage in self-criticism in front of all the people, but he didn't accept this either. He told me that the crimes of which I was guilty warranted imprisonment or even capital punishment. Then I wrote that I deserved to be killed because I was a criminal; I would be executed in front of the people.

5. Mr. H cursed me, and said I was stupid: "So you believe in God? Have you ever seen him? What has God given you? Has he given you money? Have you borrowed money from the bank? God hasn't given you anything at all, but the state lets you borrow money, the state builds roads, the state gives you electricity!"

6. He was ready to beat me, but he didn't do it, he told me he would smash my mouth, cut open my head. He said he would keep me coming back for six months, and asked who would work the fields during this time. He said he'd put me in jail, and that my eight crimes really merited execution. I said I hadn't committed eight crimes, that the eight crimes were really only one and involved religious activities, and I hadn't done anything bad. If I have done anything wrong I will correct it and learn from it. He didn't listen to anything I said—he just had me return to the police station for more questioning.

Appendix C: The Interrogation of a Protestant Church Leader, Dak Lak

This is my report which I send to you for consideration. The district police refuse to give me the chance to correct the mistakes I have made in the past and learn from them but have determined that I must: (1) be reeducated, (2) be jailed, (3) be executed.

I ask you to help me so that I don't have to be going continually to the district police station. Since I have been going there, no one in the family has been available to work the fields, and my whole family is suffering.

Thank you very much.

July 29, 2001

[signature]

N

APPENDIX D: COMPLAINT FROM BUON DON DISTRICT VILLAGERS TO BUREAU OF RELIGIOUS AFFAIRS [506]

* * * * * *

COMPLAINT

To: Bureau of Religious Affairs of Dak Lak Province

We wish to report the following:

On August 24, 2001, the police of Buon Don District together with village officials took photographs of the church and believers inside the church to send to the regional authorities. They stated that these people are followers of the Dega Protestant religion.

They pressure us to renounce our religion and sent irregular forces to search the homes of believers one by one. They follow us everywhere we go. They know the places where we pray and report them to their superiors. The authorities arrested five believers and forced them to do self-criticisms; they accuse we believers of the crime of illegal proselytization.

They organized a meeting for the following:
- Begin a campaign to encourage the people to renounce the Protestant religion
- The whole people must fight all kinds of violations of law.

On that day we were severely oppressed. They said that we wanted to overthrow the government through the propagation of the Protestant religion. They prepared sticks to beat us with if we opposed them.

They said in front of all the people that Protestants were thieves, they sowed divisions [among the people], lacked unity…

As a result our ability to pray and bear witness to our religion has become very difficult. We dare not hold meetings of any length to study the Bible, we can only do so for a few minutes.

At present the local authorities are keeping close watch on every activity, everything done by believers and church leaders.

Please pray for us and for God's work in this place.

[Names of Petitioners withheld]

---

[506] Original Vietnamese language document, obtained by Human Rights Watch in September 2001, is on file at Human Rights Watch.

APPENDIX E: EMPLOYMENT DISCRIMINATION AGAINST MINORITY CHRISTIANS [507]

* * * * * * *

Socialist Republic of Vietnam
Independence – Freedom – Happiness

GUARANTEE

To: Peoples Committee of [name withheld] Village, Ea H'Leo, Dak Lak
cc: [Name Withheld] Elementary School

My name is: [Name withheld]
Place of Birth: [Village and Commune withheld], Ea H'Leo
Religion: Protestant

In the immediate past I have been studying at the kindergarten teachers' normal school of Dak Lak Province. I have now graduated and returned home. I am awaiting acceptance by the local authorities and by the school board of the [name withheld] Elementary School.

I solemnly undertake as follows:

I will obey all of the rules and regulations of the school and all laws of the state.
I will complete any and all tasks assigned to me by my superiors.
I will not do anything contrary to the political program of the Party or the laws of the state.

If I fail to comply with any of the foregoing I will accept legal responsibility.

By the person making this undertaking: [signature]

The decision of the Peoples Committee of [name withheld] Village upon receipt of the foregoing guarantee by [name withheld] is that it cannot yet request the school to hire her.

---

[507] Original Vietnamese language document, obtained by Human Rights Watch in September 2001, is on file at Human Rights Watch.

If she undertakes in writing to abandon Protestantism then the Village Committee will permit the school to hire her.

*On behalf of the Peoples Committee,
[seal and signature]*

APPENDIX F: CITIZEN PETITION: "A REPORT ON THE CRUEL ACTION AGAINST THE TRIBAL PEOPLE IN THE HIGHLANDS" [508]

(Note: Translated from Ede, this December 2001 petition was written prior to the outbreak of unrest in the Central Highlands in February 2001. The names of the village and the petitioners have been withheld to protect the security of the sources.)

* * * * * * *

A Report of the Cruel Action against the Tribal People in the Highlands

We represent the Dega people who are living in the collective village of X in Krong Ana district, Dak Lak province. We would like to report all the oppressive policies of the Hanoi government against our people, the Dega, as follows:

I. Summary of the lives of the Dega in X village—under the rule of the South Vietnamese government from the Presidency of Nguyen Van Thieu to the current government of the Vietnamese Communist.

1. Educated persons: The Hanoi regime sees educated Dega people as a real threat to their government so that they always look for an appropriate excuse to destroy them. During the French Indochina Colonial Government, the Vietnamese officials executed several of our educated people. Among of them were Mr. Y and Mr. J. These are the only true leaders we have ever had. But both of them were brutally killed at the hands of ethnic Vietnamese people.

2. After South Vietnam was overthrown by the Hanoi Regime in 1975, the Hanoi Regime established a systematic plan to oppress the Montagnard people in many ways. For example, the Hanoi government put all the Dega intelligentsia in jail, tortured and even killed them secretly in many places. Only a few of these prisoners of war were released. But after returning home, the prisoners of war only lived one or two years, then they all died unexpectedly. Others suffered from paralysis because they had been abused with poisonous injection during their time in the communist prisons.

Those who have worked for the former government of South Vietnam or served in military of the South Vietnamese government or were involved in the

---

[508] Original Ede-language document, obtained by Human Rights Watch in July 2001, is on file at Human Rights Watch.

FULRO movement received especially bad treatment by the Hanoi government. At that time, some of the Dega also were put in jail just because they were suspected of having associated with the FULRO members. Actually, the Vietnamese people just hate our people without any reasons.

In dealing with those Dega who worked for their government, the dictatorship of Hanoi designed a clever plan for early retirement. They encouraged many of the Dega officials who had been actively working for them to receive an early retirement plan. But in reality, the Hanoi regime was only attempting to get rid all of the Dega leaders from their government system because they knew that sooner or later the Dega leaders would discover the inhumane policies the government had towards the Dega. As we have stated, all these Dega retirees were suffering from paralysis diseases. The Hanoi regime has no plan for caring for the health of these retired people.

They feel lonely and go on suffering in their own lives. They really have no future. As a result, all of these retired persons have passed away with pitiful and regrettable lives. Among of these retired persons were Mr. L, Mr. T, and Mr. R. They were the most outstanding teachers we have ever had and they contributed a great deal to the education of the Montagnard people today. But all of them have passed away secretly, including the case of Ama N, who served many years with the local police department.

Others great hero leaders such as Major General B and Major General N were also suffering from the disease of paralysis. And others such as Dr. N and Dr. K, they both have passed away because of suffering from serious ulcers. Today our Dega people have lost all of their most of the admirable and respected leaders. But we have never seen that Vietnamese leaders who has passed away for the same reasons.

3. Concerning the Montagnard students: After graduating from the same college or university with the Vietnamese students, Dega students have not been allowed to apply for any jobs in the government or apply for positions in their fields of study, because most of these Dega students belonged to the Protestant religion. They were also suspected of having associated with the South Vietnamese government or being related to the FULRO movement. So they were denied the rights to participate normally in any activities in the Vietnamese society.

In order to cover the true face of discrimination, the Hanoi government did appoint some of the Dega people, people who had a little schooling, to work for them. They trained these Dega workers just to give them just enough background of understanding so that they can easily handle and control them. They were not equipped with the real skills that they needed. It was possible to say that the Hanoi government verbally dominated and publicly eliminated our culture from the Vietnamese educational systems. The Dega students who were over the usual school age, were not allowed to enroll in the school even though they had a good relationship with their local government. As a result, there were more than 80 per cent of the Dega students who could not go to the school. This policy brought deep despair to the Dega students because they had no other place to go. The Hanoi government kept watching over the Dega students all the time.

4. Child birth issues: The Hanoi government has used false propaganda in talking about birth control with the Dega. They strongly encouraged our people to participate in birth control plans so that they can destroy the life of the baby and also to exterminate the whole of the Dega population. By doing this, they hope that they can have more land to occupy. As a result, those who participated in birth control programs, they have suffered too much pain and dizziness. Their bodies no longer functioned as they used to function, and the government did not pay any attention at all to their health.

5. Concerning the resettlement issues: Recently the Hanoi government resettled tens of thousands of the Vietnamese from the North. They occupied all of our land throughout the areas. There was nothing left for our people to live on. Therefore, the Hanoi government attempted to cover up this matter by introducing many projects.

First, they built a vocational school, a school of education for levels II and III, and colleges and universities everywhere in our land. Then they recruited just as many of the Vietnamese students as needed, but no Dega students.

Secondly they opened as many farm camps and the schools of forestry with the hope that they can:

a. occupy all the fertile land.

b. settle as many of the Viet people from the North as possible.

In 1985, the Hanoi government has opened as many farm camps and recruited as many of the Dega Montagnard workers, because most of these lands were owned by the Dega people. Therefore, during the seasons of planting and growing, the Hanoi government provided very little fertilizer to care for the crop and also provided only a few old tools to cultivate of the land. As a result, they could not receive good fruits from their labors. The coffee trees and the plants could not develop properly as expected. Therefore, the government decided that the Montagnard workers did not know how to take care of the crops.

Eventually, the government took all the lands back from the Montagnard workers and gave it to the Viet workers. Moreover, the government collected very high property taxes on the Montagnard landowners too. As a result, the Montagnard workers/owners felt like they could not afford to own the land any more.

In order to secure of all the land area, the government forced the Montagnard people to sign a release contract with the government by saying, "I will not take the land back and if I break my promise, I will be charged as a criminal for violating the laws of the land." Since that day, the government freely cultivated all the land as needed. As in the case of Y Village, more than ten of thousand Viet people from the North came to occupy the land around the area of that village. This new influx produced dozens of new villages. Under the policies of the resettlement in 1983 and 1984, the Hanoi government promised to establish a new area for the Montagnards of Village Y, but when this was completed they allowed the Viet people only to move in this new area, not the tribal people.

In the year 2000, the Hanoi government opened many new villages in the areas of Dak Mil and Dak Nong. The conflict over the land between the Viet people and the tribal people became more intense than ever. The tribal people have sent complaint letters to the local government officials but they were simply ignored. Instead of solving these problems, they sent these letters back to the Viet people. As a result, the Viet people from Nam Ngai came to settle in the land of Y and Z villages and the government also took all the land at Village D to build the School of Forestry Products. Then the government also confiscated a large cemetery of ours so that they can make up a lake in order to provide water to the coffee and rubber plantation areas.

On December 27, 1982, Mrs. Q wrote a letter complaining about her land of 3.45 hectares that had been taken over by the local government. Again, the government continued to ignore the complaint. The government built a camp at T, and put more Viet workers in this camp. These new settlers exploited all of the forest products in the area. They did not care whether or not the land already had the owner. These abuses resulted in fighting between the Viet and the tribal people of Village Y.

6. Concerning the Protestant religion: The Protestant faith is the only religion that is not allowed to be practiced by the tribal people. The Hanoi government is strongly opposed to the idea of worshiping God. No Protestant churches were allowed to be built. From 1975 until now, the Dega believers suffered far too much from persecution at the hands of the Hanoi government because of their deep belief in God. The church has been completely closed and has not been allowed to evangelize and spread the Word of God to the Dega people. They only allowed us to worship our God in our own heart, but not conduct meetings within the form of a church. As a result, when we got caught by the local government, we had to pay a penalty of one cow of for each individual believer at the meeting. Therefore, we had to hold secret meetings in our own houses.

Appendix F: Citizen Petition

As we reported, there were several times our believers were caught and punished by sending them to a hard labor camp. After completing the hard labor sentence in a camp, the government refused to issue us a release paper because they were afraid that we would show the letter to foreigners. They also called our pastors and church leaders to their offices regularly for interrogation.

They also brought us to stand in front of our people and forced us to make a public commitment that we would not continue to practice our religion any more. And if we did continue we would be expelled from the village. So, we attempted to ask the question as to why the government was so angry with us. But they only answered us that it was the laws and also the order from the central government.

In the case of Mr. H, when he listened to the preaching of the Word of God from the Bible broadcast from Manila, Philippines, the government took away his radio and did not return it. That really made it difficult to understand why the Vietnamese government was so strongly opposed to our religion and us. We did not do any thing wrong. People preach the word of God to us to give us new hope in our life, and they teach us not to provoke people and kill each other.

So we hope you will help us find out if there are any special laws provided to the Vietnamese people, that give them the right to continuously oppose our Dega Christianity. Please help us in this matter.

Written in Village X on December 15, 2000

Prepared by:
[Signatures and names of eight villagers follow]

APPENDIX G: "OFFICIAL PLEDGE" READ DURING THE GOAT'S BLOOD CEREMONIES [509]
****

Socialist Republic of Vietnam
Independence – Freedom – Happiness

OFFICIAL PLEDGE

To: Ea H'leo Commune People's Committee

Name: [Withheld]   Birthdate: 1960
Village: [Village Name Withheld], Ea H'leo Commune Ea H'leo, Dak Lak
Regarding Political Activities, February 5, 2001 in Ea H'leo.

After having recognized my mistakes, reconsidered and listened to the opinion of the entire population in my hamlet, listened to the law and the progress being made in [our community], I truly recognize my mistakes and honestly swear by signing this pledge to officially promise to the local authorities regarding the following:

1. Honestly and with all my effort I will try to correct myself and never violate any laws.

2. I will not listen to the perpetrators / bad group, never follow their advice or orders but instead, report the efforts of those who are trying to make use of the good progress our revolution has brought for the unity of the entire population. I promise to protect and maintain the security and public order of my entire community.

3. With all my strength I will confidently participate in the production effort [i.e. work hard] to create good opportunities for my family and the entire society.

4. I will build a new way of life with new cultural values for the family and reject all kinds of superstition [meaning religion].

5. I will completely follow all advice, instructions, and laws provided by the party and the state.

---

[509] Original Vietnamese language document, obtained by Human Rights Watch in October 2001, is on file at Human Rights Watch.

Appendix G: "Official Pledge" Read during the Goat's Blood Ceremonies   191

If I violate the above points I have signed I will face complete responsibility under the laws of our country.

(Official Signature and seal)	Ea H'leo, 26 May 2001
Ea H'leo Commune People's Committee	Pledger's Name
Chairman, R Chum Y Rok	

APPENDIX H: MARCH 26, 2001 DEPORTATIONS DOCUMENT 1[510]

* * * * * * *

KINGDOM OF CAMBODIA

Nation   Religion   King
Ministry of Interior

General Department of National Police
Provincial Police Commissariat
Mondolkiri province, Sen Monorum   Date: 29 March 2001
No. 128 r.b.k (ror bor kor)

Police Commissioner of Mondolkiri Province
Respectfully to:
His Excellency, the Director General of National Police

Report on the Transfer and Delivery of 19 Illegal Vietnamese Immigrants

On 25 March 2001, the Provincial Police Commissioner received an order from Mr. Nha Raing Chan, Third Deputy Governor of Mondolkiri province, and in cooperation with the commander of Provincial Gendarmerie, transferred nineteen male illegal immigrants of Vietnamese nationality, who entered Cambodia through Koh Nhek district, to Vietnam at Bou Praing border checkpoint. Officers present from the Vietnamese side were:
-Dak Lak Provincial Governor
-Dak Lak Provincial Military Commander
-Dak Lak Provincial Police Chief
Attached are the minutes of the transfer and delivery notes and the list of the names of the nineteen illegal immigrants.

---

[510] Original Cambodian language document, obtained by Human Rights Watch in April 2001, is on file at Human Rights Watch.

Appendix H: March 26, 2001, Deportations, Document 1

Therefore, we respectfully request that Your Excellency, the Director General of National Police please be informed of the above-mentioned report.

                                Signature/Seal
                                Lt. Col. Nhem Vanny

cc: -General Department of National Police
      -Cabinet office of Provincial Governor's Office

APPENDIX I: MARCH 26, 2001 DEPORTATIONS
DOCUMENT 2 [511]
****
KINGDOM OF CAMBODIA
Nation　　　Religion　　　King

Ministry of Interior
Mondolkiri Provincial Office
Post Dak Dam, 27 March 2001

Minutes on the Transfer of Illegal Immigrants

-I am, Nha Raing Chan, Third Deputy Governor of Mondolkiri province. Participants in the transfer of the immigrants were:
- Colonel Duang Choam, commander of Provincial Gendarmerie
- Lt. Col. Nhem Vanny, First Deputy Police Commissioner
- Lt. Col. Chey Saphon, Deputy Police Commissioner, in charge of transportation means.

We carried out the transfer of nineteen illegal immigrants of Vietnamese nationals, who crossed the border on 25 March 2001, [back] to Vietnam at Bou Praing border checkpoint.

Participants from the Vietnamese side in receiving the nineteen men were
- Dak Lak Provincial Governor
- Dak Lak Chief of Border Military
- Dak Lak Provincial Police Chief

Signature of receiver　　　　　Signature of transferring person
Vietnam side　　　　　　　　　Cambodian Side
(Signatures)　　　　　　　　　(Signature)
-Tr'eeg　　　　　　　　　　　-Nha Raing Chan
-Dang' Ru Yin
-Nay T-rRly

(Names of nineteen Jarai men from Buon Ea Sup, attached.)

---

[511] Original Cambodian language document, obtained by Human Rights Watch in April 2001, is on file at Human Rights Watch.